PETERBOROUGH
ROYAL FOXHOUND
SHOW

Queen Elizabeth the Queen Mother with Earl Fitzwilliam, Chairman, during her visit to Peterborough Royal Foxhound show in 1976.

PETERBOROUGH
ROYAL FOXHOUND
SHOW

A HISTORY

MICHAEL CLAYTON

Quiller Press

First published in the UK in 2006
by Quiller Press, an imprint of Quiller Publishing Ltd

British Library Cataloguing-in-Publication Data
A catalogue record for this book
is available from the British Library

ISBN 1 904057 88 8
    978 1 904057 88 8

Printed in China

Quiller Press

An imprint of Quiller Publishing Ltd
Wykey House, Wykey, Shrewsbury, SY4 1JA
Tel: 01939 261616 Fax: 01939 261606
E-mail: info@quillerbooks.com
Website: www.countrybooksdirect.com

CONTENTS

Portman Latimer ('51), right, Peterborough champion doghound 1953, and Portman Playfair ('51), reserve champion 1952, depicted by Peter Biegel, and presented to the breeder, Lt. Col. Sir Peter Farquhar, Master and huntsman of the Portman.

I was fortunate to attend Peterborough Royal Foxhound Show as President in 1978, its centenary year. I was following in the footsteps of my great-great grandfather, King Edward VII, who, one hundred years earlier, as Prince of Wales, had visited the first show. I remarked in a presidential message in the catalogue that "having heard so much about the Foxhound Show, and the passions it arouses among the enthusiastic competitors, I look forward to seeing the whole thing for myself".

The show entirely lived up to my expectations, justifying its reputation for maintaining the remarkably high standard of Foxhound breeding in this country. It was an enormously enjoyable visit and it was clear that underlying the traditional formality of Peterborough there is indeed a passion for the excellence of this great breed of working hound, carefully selected and cherished for centuries.

Peterborough's major role in assisting the evolution of the modern Foxhound as a beautiful, athletic type, is well-worth recording. Michael Clayton, with his usual insight and panache, has produced a detailed history of the Show which is not only informative, but entertaining, and which reveals some of the humour which can occur in the judging process. I can only imagine that this splendid book will be greatly appreciated by everyone who values the achievements of the Royal Foxhound Show and appreciates the very special place that it holds in this country's sporting calendar.

ACKNOWLEDGEMENTS

This book would not have been possible without the assistance of Sir Philip Naylor-Leyland, chairman of Peterborough Royal Foxhound Society, the dedicated and hard working retiring Secretary for forty years, Mr Roy Bird, and the incoming Secretary, Mr Andrew Mercer, Chief Executive of the East of England Agricultural Society.

I am grateful to Mr Joe Odam, who represented the East of England Show on the Foxhound Society committee, and Mr William Craven, Senior Assistant Agent for the Milton Estates, Peterborough, for their advice, information, and practical help; and Mr George Pearson, of Pearson Publishing, Cambridge, for allowing me to peruse early back numbers of *Baily's Hunting Directory*.

This history is greatly indebted to Mark Hedges, Editor-in-Chief, for allowing me to consult and quote from late nineteenth century reports in *The Field* and *Horse and Hound* on the first and some subsequent shows, and from later reports in *Horse and Hound* which has supported Peterborough financially and with trophies for over thirty years.

Mrs Judy Hart, trustee for the late Daphne Moore, kindly made available Daphne's meticulously annotated Peterborough catalogues since early post-war years. I hope this history gives further, much deserved, recognition to Daphne's contribution to Foxhound breeding records, including her standard work, *The Book of the Foxhound* published by J.A. Allen in 1964.

Mr Martin Scott not only contributed the authoritative Chapter 10 on hound pedigrees, but read the manuscript and provided invaluable information and advice. I am also greatly indebted to Mr Simon Clarke and Mr Edmund Vestey who read the manuscript, and contributed to Chapter 11; plus the following contributors, Lord Kimball, Captain Brian Fanshawe, Mr Alastair Jackson, Mr Nigel Peel, Mr Tim Unwin, and Mr Dermot Kelly.

I was fortunate and grateful to obtain invaluable interviews with two distinguished ex-huntsmen, Bill Lander, and Albert Buckle, who retired after fifty years as an assistant steward in 2005, at the age of ninety. Warm thanks are due to Hugh J. Robards MFH for permission to quote an amusing excerpt from his *Foxhunting in England, Ireland and North America – A Life in Hunt Service* (The Derrydale Press).

Mrs Jenny Dancey, Curator of the Melton Carnegie Museum, Melton, Mowbray, kindly enabled me, as a Trustee of the Museum of Hunting Trust, to consult books in their hunting library, and crucially arranged for provision of photographs in Chapter 1 of Peterborough 2005, and photographic copies of pictures in the Melton House collections; special thanks are due to photographer Roger Rixon for these pictures. Mrs Dancey organised the superb Hunting Museum exhibit at the 2005 Festival of Hunting.

Sir Philip Naylor-Leyland and Mr William Craven kindly enabled access to pictures of Fitzwilliam hounds, and early Fitzwilliam connections with the show, in the Milton collection which help to illustrate early chapters. I learned anew of the excellent works of the late Cuthbert Bradley, who wrote such splendid hunting books and articles in the late nineteenth and early twentieth centuries, and illustrated them, some examples appearing here.

Mr John King, the distinguished contemporary hunting artist, kindly made available his lovely 2005 studies of hounds from the Duke of Beaufort's kennel.

For Peterborough photographs since 1946 the History is immensely indebted to the invaluable contribution from the doyen of hunting photographers, Mr Jim Meads, who in 2006 is due to attend the show as contributor for his sixtieth consecutive year, a unique record much appreciated by the hunting world. The book would not have been possible in this format without Jim's involvement. Mr Robin Smith Ryland made two vintage Warwickshire doghound photographs available from his collection. The Marquis of Huntly kindly assisted with information on the 11th Marquis, and gave permission to publish his photograhs.

I am grateful to Andrew Johnston and his team at Quiller for their usual level of expertise, and my special thanks are due to my wife, Marilyn, for her practical and moral support in yet another literary endeavour.

AUTHOR'S PREFACE

Having enjoyed and reported the show for many years, I accepted with pleasure, but with some trepidation, when I was invited by the Chairman, Sir Philip Naylor-Leyland Bt, to write a history of Peterborough Royal Foxhound Show.

It has been a fascinating task, but the need for research was even greater than I had anticipated, and feared. The book is larger, and of much greater detail than I had expected, but I could not resist extending its scope. Picture research has been especially interesting, and I have just scratched the surface of the possibilities for illustration.

Despite the length of this history, I apologise if not everyone's favourite hound, or judge, or official gets a mention, or justice. However, I have done my best to keep the narrative flowing, and I have tried to ensure that Peterborough's array of remarkable human personalities is given rein, but does not over-ride the book's essential focus: the noble, beautiful, brave, tireless English Foxhound.

The Royal Foxhound Show Society's progress since 1878 is an aspect of social history. Part of the show's appeal is its apparently timeless quality, but the core of its existence, the Foxhound, has undergone great changes in conformation and type.

The huge controversy, over the use of Welsh outcrosses in English hounds, which reverberated throughout the early twentieth century, and the protracted post-war rivalry between the green-coat packs, Duke of Beaufort's and Heythrop, are reflected here. I trust there is, as well, enough attention given to the many other strands which have made Peterborough a national institution.

There is humour and fun in Peterborough's history which I hope will entertain my far more knowledgeable friends who sit at the ring-side every year. I hope it may tempt others, some who call themselves foxhunters, to attend this wonderful annual event for the first time. It may even inspire them to take more interest in the breeding of the beautiful animals which have made possible the 'golden thread' of hunting in British rural life.

The show owes its survival to the Royal Foxhound Show Society's officers and committees, and they deserve warm tribute for their staunch adherence to traditionalism at its best, whilst adapting to change when necessary. There will be future changes in the twenty-first century, perhaps even lady MFHs will regularly be among judges in the hallowed ring, but the key issue is that the hounds on show will continue to be bred for work, and not merely for showing.

Peterborough's formality and politeness has always cloaked strong passions of enthusiasm, and ambition. The greatest passion is for the survival of the sport of Foxhunting, and the new Festival of Hunting at Peterborough gave great hope that there is enough resolve in the hunting community to ensure that the iniquitous Bill to ban hunting with hounds, enacted in February 2005, will be repealed or substantially amended to ensure the future of our unique, incomparable heritage, the Foxhound.

Huntsmen showing doghounds at the 2005 show.

1. GLORY – AND DEFIANCE

I t was a breathtaking spectacle. For the hound lover it was pure delight. Huntsmen's scarlet coats, and two green ones, filled all sides and corners of the show ring amid a sea of waving sterns in the two-couples bitch class. At times the judges and steward were almost lost to sight.

Forty-one packs competed in the 117th Peterborough Royal Foxhound Show on 20 July 2005, an all time record, and nearly twice as many as the previous year.

Britain's most prestigious Foxhound show was part of a remarkable Festival of Hunting on the East of England Showground at Alwalton. On the lawns outside the Foxhound arena were displays of Britain's superb range of hounds which have worked for centuries in our island.

For the first time, Peterborough's Harriers and Beagles Show was held on the showground on the same day. Altogether, over 1500 hounds were on show from nearly eighty packs. For Foxhound enthusiasts the most significant 'first' was the separate ring in which Old English type hounds were judged in their own classes within the main show category. It was a historic occasion because throughout the first half of the previous century a controversy raged among Masters of Foxhounds who bred and hunted hounds, as to whether Welsh outcrosses should be added to Old English blood-lines. The innovators won the day, and most modern packs have elements of Welsh breeding, and some have Fell or American outcrosses.

The Belvoir, fount of traditional English breeding in the nineteenth and early twentieth centuries and still adhering to Old English hounds, was competing at Peterborough for the first time in 2005. The Dukes of Rutland, owners of this famous Shires pack kennelled at Belvoir Castle, had a non-showing policy. Later in the twentieth century the few remaining packs still adhering strictly to Old English breeding lapsed from regular hound showing because their type became difficult to judge against the so-called modern hound.

There was so much at the 2005 show on which the East of England Show executive, and Peterborough's chairman for twenty years, Sir Philip Naylor-Leyland, and his team could be warmly congratulated. The array of hounds was a huge success, but there was a darker background. The triumph was a response to the disaster so long threatened, but never accepted as an inevitability: a government Bill banning hunting with hounds.

Captain Brian Fanshawe, President of the 2005 show, in his foreword to the show catalogue, summed up the hunting world's resolution to keep its Hunts and packs of hounds intact: 'All of us here owe it our hounds and to our antecedents that the pernicious Hunting Act 2004 is repealed, or amended, so hunting can resume its proper role in our countryside and Peterborough Royal Foxhound Show can remain a very major feature of the hunting calendar for at least another 117 years.'

Sir Philip Naylor-Leyland Bt., Chairman, makes a presentation at the 2005 show to Roy Bird, retiring after 40 years as Secretary of Peterborough Royal Foxhound Show Society.

Every hunting person present at Peterborough 2005 knew that Labour's iniquitous Hunting Act, which imposed the ban from 18 February that year, posed a threat to the future of working hounds on which Britons have devoted the utmost care in breeding and selection for many centuries. Hunting with hounds was believed to be a natural heritage of people living in a 'free country'. The battle to achieve the restoration of the sport of hunting in Britain is equally a battle for the future of the Foxhound and all other working hounds and dogs.

Milton, the great manor house of Peterborough, has been in the Fitzwilliam family since 1502, and there has always been a pack of hounds within the property. As we shall see, the family has been crucial to the establishment, development and survival of the great Foxhound Show at Peterborough, and remains so to-day. It is a classic demonstration of the value of continuity. The commitment of country people to the survival of their packs of hounds, is proof of the huge contribution which hunting has always made to English country life in sheer pleasure, and in binding together all areas of the rural community.

Thus, there was at Peterborough 2005 a poignant background of huge concern about the working future of the beautiful hounds on show. The huge level of support for the show at the same time reinforced optimism and resolution that somehow the future of the Foxhound would be preserved as a heritage for future generations in the twenty-first century and beyond. Hunting, and its great annual Foxhound show, survived the immense disruption of two world wars. There was reason to hope the sport, and its hounds, could still survive the ban imposed for political rather than animal welfare reasons.

Full members of the Society, Vice Presidents, book seats, and tend to sit every year in the same favourite ringside position. They look around the ring and see friends in their customary seats, note some regrettable absences, and can make mental notes not only on the quality of the hounds on show, but on the standard of this year's hats worn by the ladies

Bowler hats and dark blue suits for men, summer dresses and hats for the ladies remain *de rigeur* for Peterborough. Ronnie Wallace, as chairman of the Masters of Foxhounds Association for twenty-two years (1970-92), was keen to preserve the traditions of Peterborough, and was heard on occasions to remonstrate with the very few Masters who had dared to enter the Peterborough enclosure wearing headgear other than bowlers. 'This is *not* the show for Panama hats', he would tell offenders in the Peterborough Enclosure, no doubt one of the reasons it has been often referred to as the 'Holy of Holies'.

Brian Fanshawe recalled in his 2005 Presidential message: 'I first went to Peterborough Royal Foxhound Show in 1953 when the Show was held in the middle of the town. I was proudly attired in my first trilby hat until I received an imperial rocket for not wearing a bowler! I am glad to say Peterborough standards are still upheld.'

Panamas as well as bowlers in 2005.

Formality survives when judges and stewards meet...

Politeness with formality...

ABOVE:
*Affability
with
formality…*

LEFT:
*Before the
show at the
kennels…
2005
President
Brian
Fanshawe
and (LEFT) C.
Martin Wood
III, Joint
Master, Live
Oak, USA.*

Judging is an 'opinion sport', and like all other forms of animal shows, Peterborough has had its share of controversies, sometimes causing acute disappointment, but mostly evoking some amusement. Hound judging is less rigorously controlled than most horse classes; judges are allowed to consult catalogues while they judge, and they are well aware of the ownership and breeding of every hound. Unlike most other livestock shows, in the modern Peterborough there is no commercial element because the MFHA rigorously forbids Foxhounds registered in its stud-book to be sold within the United Kingdom.

Peterborough Royal Foxhound Show has evolved a classic formula of classes in each of the two sections, for doghounds in the morning, for bitches in the afternoon: first, an unentered restricted class for packs not having won at the show for the previous two years; second, an open unentered couples class; plus a *Horse and Hound* cup for the single best unentered hound; third, a couples class for entered hounds; fourth, a two-couples class; fifth a class either for stallion hounds or brood bitches; and finally, the overall championship for doghound or bitch. (See Appendix VI – conformation of the Foxhound sought by judges.)

In recent decades, most Hunts use mixed packs, or bitch packs, in the hunting field, whereas formerly it was the practice to hunt a bitch pack and a separate doghound pack. This has resulted in a much reduced number of doghounds retained in packs, and the result has been higher quality in the bitch sections at hound shows because of the wider choice of bitches available. Some believe the modern practice will be detrimental to the breed, through reducing the available male gene pool.

Professional huntsmen, or kennel-huntsmen, wear full Hunt livery, minus spurs; they wear arm-bands indicating the names of the Hunts; and rosettes they win are attached to the other arm, indicating by the end of the day those packs which are most successful. Peterborough's rosettes are: first, red; second, blue; third, orange; champion, red and blue; reserve, green.

Hounds are shown on couples, hunting's term for collars and leads, and hounds are un-coupled to show their movement to the judges. This is achieved by the huntsman throwing biscuits across the ring, which the hounds chase. After each hound, or group of hounds, has been shown, all the hounds in the class are assembled in the ring on couples, and the judges inspect them again, and send out those they wish to eliminate from the judging for the top four placings: first, second, third and reserve. Hounds being considered for the awards are usually un-coupled and run across the ring together, so that the judges may compare their movement.

The hound's role as a working animal makes this element of the judging extremely important. A hound must show itself; 'shy' hounds which will not obey the huntsman are usually discounted in the judging. All hounds must be in the *Foxhound Kennel Stud Book*, which does not make a stipulation as to the height of the hound, but it is generally not more than twenty-six inches to the top of the shoulder.

The skills of professional huntsmen in showing their hounds to best advantage play a large part in the judging process; more of this later.

Signs of success…

Duke of Beaufort's kennel-huntsman Tony Holdsworth shows the art of getting a hound's attention…

…and the Duke of Beaufort's 2005 champion doghound, Gamecock ('04), now stands correctly.

Two bowler-hatted stewards assist the two judges in each section. The stewards are advised by the judges that a hound is to leave the ring; the steward approaches the huntsman and touches his hat, and the huntsman takes his hounds form the ring. Results of each class are announced on a public address system, an innovation shunned by Peterborough until post-war years.

Judges should not make decisions based on the colour of the hound's coat, the colour of its eyes, nor on whether it has a smooth or a woolly coat; the latter is a normal characteristic of Welsh hounds. No knowledgeable Master breeds hounds to achieve a particular colour, but it is true that so-called 'modern' hounds often tend to be white, or lemon and white. In contrast, traditional Old English hounds are mainly tri-coloured: tan, black and white.

The Foxhound world in the show-ring regards as a fault a hound with an excessively curly tail, called its stern. This is the only decision based on fashion; all other judging decisions are strictly utilitarian and assessed on the conformation which the judge thinks will make it a more effective animal to hunt, and to run up to 100 miles per day in a long day in the hunting field. Its hunting characteristics and abilities can only be tested in the hunting field.

The modern Foxhound derives from an animal which for most of its history was bred to hunt deer, wild boar and wolves as well as foxes. Deer hunting was the premier sport in English history until the clearance of many forests in the late eighteenth and early nineteenth centuries. Then it was discovered the fox was an ideal quarry to hunt over the new grass enclosures created by the emergence of modern stock farming. As we shall see, the Foxhound was subject to considerable change in type in the twentieth century, and Peterborough was in the eye of the storm of controversy over this development. Foxhound judging is based entirely on the merits of the hound as an athletic working animal, and much controversy developed over the conformation deemed most desirable for the hound's task in the hunting field.

The results of each class at Peterborough are indicated in numbers on a black and white board, high above the hound entrance, by staff standing on a long narrow platform. Hounds are numbered in the catalogue, as well as listed under the name of their Hunts, and their sires and dams are given, plus the sire of each dam. In unentered classes the catalogue shows the date of the hound's birth; in entered classes the hound's name is accompanied by the date that it is entered, that is the date on which it starts hunting.

Hounds are whelped in Hunt kennels and then sent out to 'walk', the old term used for Hunt supporters, known as puppy walkers, rearing young hounds at private homes and farms, before they are returned to the pack in their first year of adult life for 'entering' to the pack in the hunting field. Their training is in the hands of their huntsman, but much of it is conveyed naturally by older, experienced hounds in the pack. Puppy walkers are among the keenest of spectators at Peterborough, and there are special trophies for those who walk the unentered champions.

Currently, the overall doghound champion exhibitor is awarded a perpetual challenge cup awarded by the late 10th Duke of Beaufort, who – as we shall see – was the most outstanding exhibitor in the twentieth century. The Master of the

Peterborough's traditional hand operated results board.

Capt. Simon Clarke (LEFT) presents the cup awarded by the 10th Duke of Beaufort to Capt. Ian Farquhar, Joint Master of the Duke of Beaufort's, for winning the 2003 doghound championship with Palmer ('02).

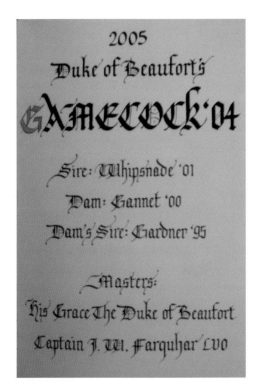

2005

Duke of Beaufort's

GAMECOCK '04

Sire: Whipsnade '01

Dam: Gannet '00

Dam's Sire: Gardner '95

Masters:

His Grace The Duke of Beaufort

Captain J. W. Farquhar LVO

Elegant record of success – every champion has a certificate in fine script, maintained in a magnificently bound book.

pack showing the champion dog-hound is presented with the Captain Charlie Barclay Memorial Memento, in memory of the late Captain C.G. Barclay, Master of the Puckeridge 1947-2002. The bitch champion receives a perpetual challenge cup presented by the late 10th Earl Fitzwilliam, chairman of the show for thirty-six years, who was crucial to the post-war development of the Royal Foxhound Show and the East of England Show.

The huntsman showing the champion doghound is awarded a salver, presented by the East of England Agricultural Society. The huntsman showing the champion bitch receives a salver presented by Mr John Dawes in memory of his former business partner, Joseph Stephenson, who was Secretary of the Foxhound Society for a remarkable fifty-two years, from 1913-65 (see also, Chapter 8). The Master of the pack showing the champion bitch receives a memento in memory of the late Lt. Colonel Sir Peter Farquhar who was one of the leading breeders of the modern Foxhound.

Presentations of trophies are made at the side of the ring or in the ring, by the Show President, an honorary appointment for one year only. The President sits in a separate viewing box at one side of the ring. Guests are invited into the box throughout the day, and have often included members of the royal family who have supported the show since its inception. The Mayor and Mayoress of Peterborough are often among the guests.

Two professional huntsmen act as assistant stewards, organising hounds in the collecting ring and entrance to the showring. Hounds are kennelled in cage-like enclosures across a lawn at the back of the Hound Enclosure, each pack having its name on its kennel. Visitors stroll about the lawns, talk to huntsmen and inspect the hounds, before showing commences. There is a lunch break of an hour to ninety minutes, and during the judging, tea and other refreshments are served. At the end of the day the bars and tea tents are filled with hunting people, gossiping about the day's judging.

Hunt staff have a separate dining tent and bar, and it has always been a Peterborough tradition that in the Hound Enclosure, at the end where hounds enter, there are tiered seats for current and retired Hunt staff and their wives.

Seats have always been reserved for Hunt staff and families.

Peterborough's formality assists the serious side of the judging; concentration has to be intense in every class, never more so than deciding winners in crowded couples and two-couples classes.

Judges are themselves judged not only for their wisdom, but on their speed of decision. It is depressing and frustrating for the experienced afficianado at the ring-side if the judges show painful indecision, and even forget their previous awards by clearly overlooking winning hounds when they appear later in another class.

Judging at Peterborough can be especially un-nerving. Daphne Moore, doyen of Peterborough correspondents for *Horse and Hound* for over forty years, wrote: 'There is a certain atmosphere, almost ecclesiastical, which pervades the ring at Peterborough, which might well be called The Temple of the Foxhound.'*

In the late twentieth and early twenty-first centuries, cheering has sometimes been heard after championship victories, especially when the winners are packs which have not won this prize for many years. Mainly, Peterborough victories are greeted only by polite hand-clapping, and a smile may be seen below the bowler hat, or floral headgear, of a winning MFH. It is a refreshing contrast to hysterical

***The Book of the Foxhound*, Daphne Moore, 1st edition 1964.*

exhibitions of joy over victory in many other sports in modern Britain, although latterly the volume of enthusiastic cheering at Peterborough has increased when there is a championship win, and that is no bad thing.

Even when there has been a day of exceptionally controversial decision making by the judges, the atmosphere in the Peterborough bar afterwards is jocular, if a trace tetchy at times among the few most deeply disappointed Masters. The show is a great meeting place for the inner fraternity of hunting people who care most about hounds and their breeding, the essential core of their sport.

The breeding of working animals is a dynamic process. Peterborough's influence and contribution to the Foxhound's evolution as the world's greatest working breed of pack hound takes pride of place in this history.

Tom Parrington, founder of hound shows, in this sketch by Cuthbert Bradley, is judging fourth from left, at Peterborough in the 1880s. Others l. to r. : Tom Whitemore, Oakley huntsman; Will Goodall, Pytchley huntsman; Merthyr Guest MFH, Blackmore Vale; Mr C.B.E. Wright; and George Carter, Fitzwilliam huntsman.

2. YORKSHIRE RELISH

he credit for inventing the modern Foxhound show must go to Yorkshire – but it was preserved by Peterborough.

Mr Thomas Parrington, a life-long Yorkshire hunting man, is credited with organising the first open Foxhound show on 9 September 1859. He was not a member of foxhunting's Establishment, but he was a true foxhunter who loved the sport passionately, and had considerable experience as a Master, huntsman and hound breeder in North Yorkshire.

Parrington was employed as agent to Lord Feversham, the title of the Duncombe family long established in the Sinnington country. As a young man, Parrington was a popular amateur huntsman of the Hurworth whose country is in North Yorkshire, Durham and Cleveland. One of the Masters was Thomas R. Wilkinson, son of one of three Wilkinson brothers of Neasham Abbey who founded the Hunt in the late eighteenth century.

Later Parrington was to be Master of the Sinnington in North Yorkshire for five seasons (1879-84) when it was still a trencher fed pack. The Sinnington was one of the packs hunting hounds deriving from the 2nd Duke of Buckingham's pack in the late seventeenth century, and remained a trencher fed pack – hounds kept at supporters' homes between hunting days – for about 160 years until 1891.

Parrington was appointed Secretary of Cleveland Agricultural Society, held at Redcar, and largely devoted to cattle and sheep classes. He persuaded his committee to add classes for Foxhounds from 1859, and the innovation of a public, open show was immediately successful. The secretary gave tangible backing by donating the first champion cup. The Foxhound show proved to be the right venture at the right time.

Communication by rail as well as road was improving in rural England in the mid nineteenth century. Foxhunters could more easily visit packs far outside their home countries. They could compare performances of hounds and huntsmen, aided and encouraged by the growth of sporting journalism.

'Nimrod' (Charles James Apperley) and Robert Smith Surtees, hunting correspondent as well as great comic novelist, earlier in the century had created readerships for a proliferation of foxhunting journalism. Continuing enclosure of land, with the advent of modern stock farming, encouraged a major growth in foxhunting's popularity, and new money began to arrive from the industrial revolution to help finance it.

Masters breeding their packs of Foxhounds needed to see hounds shown on 'the flags' – flagstones used rather than grass to reveal the condition of hounds' feet – to help make better decisions about using stallion hounds for out-crosses in their own kennels. Visiting other Hunt kennels, and their puppy shows, had long served this purpose. A few Masters in the eighteenth century

The Rev. Cecil Legard (LEFT), the pedigrees pundit, in customary Regency style, judging a Belvoir puppy show in 1911, with Quorn huntsman George Leaf. Legard was the only non-MFH to judge at Peterborough in his time.

matched their hounds for speed against hounds of other packs, on racecourses. In 1768 ten couple of the Fitzwilliam pack were matched in this way against those of Hugo Meynell, Master of the Quorn for the second half of the eighteenth century, and 'Father of Foxhunting'. Milton hounds, Darter and Druid, were outright winners.

Although hounds are bred for work, the value of a show for comparing conformation was soon recognised by enough MFHs to make it successful. It was quickly established too as an enjoyable meeting place for the hunting fraternity, largely male, during the summer desert of non-hunting days.

Not every Master agreed with risking the reputation of their hounds to judges for the purpose of winning cups and rosettes. A minority have remained firmly resistant to showing their hounds publicly until the present day. Arguments for and against hound shows were occasionally to enliven the columns of the sporting press in the twentieth century, (see Chapter 4). Even the value of Peterborough was to be hotly debated at times.

Thomas Parrington's hound show was all the more remarkable because the *Foxhound Kennel Stud Book* was not purchased by the Masters of Foxhounds Association until 1886, five years after the Association was formed under the chairmanship of the 8th Duke of Beaufort, setting out rules of conducting sport for Masters throughout Britain. The first edition of the stud book was published in 1864 by Mr Cornelius Tongue, who wrote under the pseudonym 'Cecil'. He researched and published it at his own cost. It was edited from 1884 by the Rev. Cecil Legard, one of foxhunting's pundits, who judged at Peterborough although he had not been an MFH, and who strongly favoured traditional English breeding.

When the Cleveland show began, foxhunting was still very loosely administered by the Foxhunting Committee formed in 1856 at Boodles Club in London, forerunner of the MFHA, formed in 1881.

THE FITZWILLIAM LINK

At the first show organised at Redcar in 1859 by Mr Parrington, the Fitzwilliam (Milton) pack were exhibitors – and a couple of their hounds, Hardwick and Friendly won their class*. Their huntsman Tom Sebright took them all the way up to Redcar from Peterborough, probably by train. Sebright was the Fitzwilliam's huntsman for forty years, and is credited with breeding the pack to their peak. He served under the 4th and 5th Earls and the Hon. George Fitzwilliam, later the 6th Earl.

The Fitzwilliam had good reason to exhibit their hounds. They were already renowned as a source for other kennels seeking stallion hounds, inclu-ding the much sought after Belvoir blood. Mr George Fitzwilliam was the younger brother of the 6th Earl Fitzwilliam, and the Peterborough estates, including Milton, passed to George on the death of their father, the 5th Earl Fitzwilliam in 1857. The new 6th Earl inherited the family seat of Wentworth Woodhouse, near Rotherham, and from

Hunts frequently used trains to transport horses and hounds from Victorian times. Here the Fitzwilliam are unloading for a meet at Ramsey. Packs used trains to compete at Peterborough.

*Foxhunting from Shire to Shire, Cuthbert Bradley, 'Whipster' of The Field, 1912.

1860 established his own private pack there. It was known as the Fitzwilliam (Wentworth) and hunted the Yorkshire country which had previously only been cubhunted by the Milton pack, paying a visit every autumn. The Earl's hounds went out three days a week during his twenty years' Mastership.

At Milton, the Hon. George Fitzwilliam was not only Master, but hunted the family pack with great success for seventeen years from 1857; he was considered one of the finest huntsmen of his time. Tragically, he died in office in 1874 after a bad fall out hunting. His son, George Charles Wentworth Fitzwilliam, to whom the Milton estate and the hounds now passed, was then only eight-years-old. His uncle the Hon.Charles W. Fitzwilliam took charge of the estate and was appointed Master*.

Charles went to live abroad in 1877, and the Mastership was taken over for a brief but crucial term, 1877-80, by the Marquis of Huntly, who lived at the Manor House at Orton, Peterborough.

Mr Parrington's hound show remained with the Cleveland Agricultural Society Show for four years, and took place at Middlesborough as well as Redcar. The show was in abeyance in 1864 when the Society was reported to be in financial difficulty. Parrington became Secretary of Yorkshire Agricultural Society. His Foxhound show was attached to their annual show which was held each year at different venues in the huge county of Yorkshire. This was a difficult undertaking when transport could only be made by rail or horse-drawn vehicle.

There was to be a change of Show Secretary in 1877, and the future of the Foxhound show was in considerable doubt. The Sporting Times reported later: 'When Mr Parrington retired from the secretaryship of the Yorkshire Agricultural in 1877, and there seemed to be every probability that the Foxhound Show would drop through, it was Mr [William] Barford who came to the rescue and the Hound Show has, under his supervision, become one of the leading functions of the year.'

William Barford was Chairman of Peterborough Agricultural show at that time. According to information provided by his grandson, Geoffrey Barford, William was chairman of both the Foxhound and Agricultural Societies up to 1894 when he received presentations and tributes for his great contribution.

William Barford was one of Peterborough's leading businessmen, founder of the engineering firm Barford and Perkins which became part of Aveling-Barford Ltd at Grantham. Perkins diesel engines became one of Peterborough's most successful products.

Barford's prompt action in arranging from the transferring of the Foxhound Show proved to be of inestimable value to both societies.

Although agriculture had its periodic declines, industry and the professions were booming in late Victorian England, and the middle classes were expanding. More people had time and surplus income for leisure pursuits, and new subscription Hunts were formed at this time. It was an excellent opportunity for Peterborough to offer a summer meeting place for hunting people. The Foxhound Show added significant value and prestige to Peterborough Agricultural show, attracting visitors from all over Britain and abroad.

*Foxhunting in Northamptonshire, by Ralph Greaves.

PETERBOROUGH FOXHOUND SHOW BORN

The 6th Earl Fitzwilliam warmly approved Peterborough as the best alternative venue. It was a coup for Peterborough; only two years earlier the Marquis of Huntly and Mr Barford were part of a delegation which sought to ensure the Royal Show visited Peterborough*. To Peterborough's disappointment, the Royal Agricultural Society chose Birmingham instead. The value of Peterborough becoming permanent home to the Foxhound Shows was soon demonstrated when The Prince of Wales readily agreed to be its first patron.

The Marquis of Huntly chaired a meeting at the Angel Hotel, Peterborough in 1878 to found Peterborough Foxhound Show Society, with the 6th Earl Fitzwilliam as the first President. It appears that Mr Barford was the executive chairman of both shows.

Charles Gordon, 11th Marquis of Huntly, premier Marquis of Scotland, contributed a great deal through his timely Mastership of the Fitzwilliam and his enthusiasm for the new Foxhound show. He continued to work for many years with William Barford. The Marquis was a charming, sociable personality who was born in 1847 and died a nonagenarian in 1937 when he was succeeded by a nephew. His royal

The Marquis of Huntly in 1896 and hunting in 1912 on his chestnut mare, Lucky Sixpence.

*We Plough the Fields and Scatter, History of Peterborough Agricultural Society, John Knight and David Brandon, 1999.

The Prince and Princess of Wales, later King Edward VII and Queen Alexandra, enjoyed hunting as a young married couple.

connections must have been helpful for Peterborough. He was a Lord-in-Waiting to Queen Victoria from 1870-73, and was said 'during a long life in the ballroom, danced with Princess Charlotte and Queen Victoria.' Sir William Fraser unkindly imputed to him 'as acute an interest in the suppers, as in the dancing, since he was very poor'*. The Marquis was a bold horseman in the Shires when riding to hounds was at its most competitive. He was reported to be among an intrepid group who leapt in and out of five feet high oak rails by the new railway line near Twyford during the Cottesmore's famous 'Ranksborough Gallop' hunt of 1877.

Peterborough's splendid agricultural show by 1878 had already been established for eighty-one years as a popular annual event. The historic Cathedral city benefited from local agriculture, including the increasingly prosperous Fens since they were drained, and associated farm machinery manufacturing in Peterborough. Its main line railway station, and location near the Great North Road, later the A1, made the city an ideal venue for visitors from all over Britain.

At that time there was no bigger draw for mass spectator attendance than a royal visit. After Victoria's long period of mourning following the death of her consort, Prince Albert, the flamboyant personality of the pleasure-loving Prince of Wales (King Edward VII from 1901-10), attracted huge public interest. Edward adored country house parties, and although shooting became his major sporting interest, he was always entirely supportive of foxhunting, and rode to hounds with great enthusiasm.

Debrett's Handbook, 1982.

The Chase was enjoying its second golden era of national popularity in the last quarter of the nineteenth century, continuing into the Edwardian years up to the Great War, despite increasing competition from the growing sport of game shooting. New Hunts were formed in that period, and existing ones saw their support and popularity expand as never before. Although the hunting field was still considered by some areas of society not to be an entirely respectable place for ladies to appear, more female riders were attracted to the Chase late in the century, elegantly riding side-saddle. The invention of a safety-release riding habit reduced somewhat the dangers of riding to hounds side-saddle, but ladies who 'went well' across country were regarded in late Victorian England as rather admirable.

Royal patronage helped to encourage more recruits to the hunting field, and the Shires packs, based on Leicestershire, were a highly fashionable winter fixture in the Season. Foxhunting was by no means exclusive to the upper-classes. Over two hundred packs provided sport for all stratas of society in town and country throughout most of Britain. As well as those riding to hounds, many followed on foot, bicycle or horse drawn vehicles. Special trains took foxhunters on day trips from the City of London to hunt in the Home Counties and Midlands. Motorised traffic was still in its infancy: in 1878 the 'Red Flag Act' was passed, whereby mechanical road vehicles were limited to four miles per hour!

In the Shires in 1878 the most famous huntsman of his day, Tom Firr, was hunting the Quorn, the Yellow Earl, Lord Lonsdale, was Master and sometime

The Yellow Earl, Lord Lonsdale, in kennel, sketched by Cuthbert Bradley.

huntsman of the Cottesmore, and the acclaimed Frank Gillard was hunting the Belvoir for the 6th Duke of Rutland, a devoted foxhunter but steadfastly averse to Foxhound shows, a view he shared with the Duke of Grafton, Master of his family pack in Northamptonshire. Stallion lines from their kennels were so widely sought by other packs that neither Duke felt it necessary to prove anything 'on the flags'.

Sport in Leicestershire, and elsewhere, was reported regularly in London newspapers as well as a growing plethora of sporting magazines, most of which died early in the next century. *Horse and Hound* and *The Field* notably survived.

The Prince of Wales hunted carted stag with the Royal Buckhounds from Windsor in the country west of London, once finishing a hunt in the railway goods yard at Paddington station, and rode to hounds in the Shires, especially with the Quorn and Belvoir. In 1871 he planted seeds to create the Quorn's Prince of Wales covert at Baggrave where he was staying with the Master, Major Algy Burnaby.

Somewhat to Queen Victoria's alarm, Prince Albert hunted once with the Belvoir, in 1843. In a letter to King Leopold, Queen Victoria wrote: 'One can scarcely credit the absurdity of people, but Albert's riding so boldly has made such a sensation that it has been written all over the country, and they make much more of it than if he had done some great act.' Although the Queen was not anti-hunting, she was 'not amused' by the sport, and disapproved of the Empress of Austria's much publicised hunting visits to Leicestershire where she amazed the locals by her riding skills.

News spread that the Prince of Wales was to be accompanied to Peterborough Agricultural Show by the Princess of Wales, the former Princess Alexandra of Denmark, whom he had married in 1863. The royal visit was an irresistible attraction for all sections of Victorian society to flock to Peterborough from far and wide. It was fortunate the agricultural show was experienced in handling distinguished visitors and large crowds, but it was a considerable undertaking for those running the new Foxhound classes. Fortunately, the weather smiled, the organisation survived a severe test, and the first Peterborough Foxhound Show, in 1878, was to prove a winner.

3. First Peterborough Foxhound Show, 1878

I n the presence of their Royal Highnesses the Prince and Princess of Wales, and on a perfect summer day – warm, yet cloudy and fresh – this show took place on Thursday last, July 4, the York Hound Show having been given up.

That was how *The Field*'s reporter commenced his lengthy account of the first 'Peterborough Hound Show', in 1878. Twenty-one packs competed, an excellent start for a new venture.

Most significant amid the plethora of names in the report was surely that of Tom Parrington who was to be a regular attender and leading light of the show in its new setting. Not only had he guided the Peterborough committee in organising the first show, he appeared in the full authority of a judge. He was in exalted company: his co-judges were two Earls, Lord Coventry, Master and huntsman of his own pack in the West Midlands, to become the Croome from 1882, and Lord Macclesfield, who hunted his own pack, later the South Oxfordshire.

The following excerpt from *The Field* report gives a flavour of the leading foxhunters from far and wide who felt it worthwhile to attend the first show at Peterborough: 'Among the many Masters of Foxhounds watching the proceedings with the keenest interest were Capt. Anstruther Thomson, Messrs Lane-Fox, and Fenwick, Lords Willoughby de Broke,Valentia, Worcester, Fitzwilliam, Waterford, Galway and Carrington, Messrs Arkwright, Coupland, Gosling, Hamond, Langham, and Colonel Fairfax. Lady Yarbourgh, too, was there to see the triumph of her favourites.'

The show continued to appoint three judges until 1886, and Parrington was to judge twice again at Peterborough, in 1885 and 1890. No champion cup was presented during the first six years, but by 1884 a cup was given for the best hound of either sex.

It was a wise decision to ensure Mr Parrington officiated in the ring in 1878, for however knowledgeable were the many Masters present at Peterborough, very few had experience of judging Foxhounds at public shows. *The Field*'s correspondent remarked: 'Masters of hounds were present by the score, and great numbers of the hunting world were there to acquire a knowledge, or an inkling, of hounds on the flags.'

The 6th Earl Fitzwilliam was firmly behind the enterprise as the first President, but on this occasion he had to pay assiduous attention to the royal visitors. The Prince and Princess enjoyed a lengthy luncheon at Milton Park, and reached the show about three o'clock, and left for London soon after five.

The Field gave much credit to the Marquis of Huntly, describing him as 'the

One of the early Peterborough Hound Shows, held in the grounds of the Ice Rink. Terrier classes were included until disbanded in the 1890s.

promoter and leading genius of the undertaking', and declaring 'a marked success has crowned his efforts.' It is clear, however, that he was working closely with William Barford who organised the practicalities of the shows at Peterborough.

Two Secretaries were appointed to the new Foxhound Show, Andrew Percival and John W. Buckle. The latter continued as sole Secretary until 1882, when he was succeeded by Peterborough's only chartered accountant at that time, John Rich Smart.

Peterborough Agricultural Show had moved locations several times since its inception in 1797 at the Wagon and Horses Yard – a site of about four acres, nowadays the BT car park a the rear of Woolworths in the City Centre. Since 1865 the show took place at the Broadway Boroughbury ground, just north of the City centre. It was an eight acre site, part of it made available to the show by the Hon. Charles Fitzwilliam on behalf of the family at Milton. The annual Show offered entertainment to the townspeople as well as livestock classes for the farming community. There was a horticultural show, displays of newly invented farm machinery made in Peterborough, firework displays, hot air balloon flights, and cricket matches. The show executive had an excellent record of seeking innovation.

The new Foxhound show took place on the second day of the Agricultural Show. It was held at Peterborough's privately owned Skating Rink, which may seem a curious choice of venue, but the royal visit had much to do with this. The grounds outside the rink were made available for the show, and according to *The Field*, 'the inner part was fitted up by the proprietors, with tasteful and liberal hand, for the reception of the Prince and Princess.' A royal visit was an especially heavy responsibility in Victorian England.

Mr Parrington's advice on running a hound show had been well executed. According to *The Field*'s report: 'The arrangements throughout were admirable. Hounds were excellently housed in a quadrangle of roomy kennels; the space in which lot was in turn brought before the judges and the public, was easy to view; and hounds and huntsmen met with every facility and comfort.

'The latter, in most cases accompanied by their first whips, were in newest pink and neatest boots, with white ties of volume and intricacy, such as only a huntsman is educated to achieve.

'They brought their hounds by the early morning trains, all returning the same evening, each huntsman receiving a gratuity of two pounds and a dinner.'

The report noted: '...it was hoped at one time the Dukes of Grafton and Rutland might be induced to break their rule on this occasion and for once send hounds to compete. But though neither of these celebrated packs was entered, a great number of the leading kennels took part in the show, and such an opportunity of comparing high class hounds has seldom been given to hunting men.'

Some of those who were later to become frequent champions at Peterborough were also absent from the first show. For example, neither the Duke of Beaufort's nor the Heythrop found their way to Peterborough in 1878, although the Earl of Yarborough sent his Brocklesby pack, and Earl Spencer entered the Pytchley, shown by the legendary Will Goodall. Lord Portman brought hounds up from Dorset, and the Southdown came from Sussex.

Lord Willoughby de Broke, the 18th baron, showed his Warwickshire hounds, but as we shall see later, his successor in the early twentieth century was an outspoken critic of hound showing. There were two MPs among the Masters, an indication of Foxhunting's widespread popularity in the latter nineteenth century. Its interests were well protected then at all levels of government.

Packs competing were:

The 18th Lord Willoughby de Broke, Master of the Warwickshire.

Atherstone, Master, Mr W. Oakley; (huntsman, George Castleman.)
Old Berkeley, Mr A.H. Longman (Robert Worrall)
Blankney, Mr Henry Chaplin MP, (H. Dawkins)
Brocklesby, Earl of Yarborough (Alfred Thatcher)
Burton, Mr F.J.S. Foljambe MP (William Dale)
Cheshire (North), Capt E.P. Yates (John Jones)
Cottesmore, Lord Carrington (W. Neal)
Fitzwilliam (Milton), Marquis of Huntly (George Carter)
Earl Fitzwilliam's (Wentworth), (E.Christian)
Hurworth, Major A.F. Godman (W. Brice)
Norfolk (West), Mr A. Hamond (R. Clayden)
Oakley, Mr R.J.W. Arkwright (T. Whitemore)
Lord Portman's, Hon. W.H.B. Portman MP,(Joseph Moss)
Pytchley, Earl Spencer MFH (Will Goodall)
Quorn, Mr J.Coupland MFH (Tom Firr)
Rufford, Mr Chas. A. Egerton (Fred Gosden)
Southdown, Mr J. Streatfield (G.Champion)
Tynedale, Mr George Fenwick (N.Cornish)
Warwickshire, (North), Mr Richard Lant (W. Wheatley)
Warwickshire, Lord Willoughby de Broke (Charles Orvis)
York and Ainsty, Col. Fairfax (Charles Hagger)

PROS AND CONS

Tom Firr, renowned huntsman of the Quorn for twenty-seven years (1872-99) showed at Peterborough regularly, but he was one of those who doubted the value of showing hounds. He believed an emphasis on prize-winining characteristics could be detrimental to working hounds'*. Coupland, who was a shrewd, successful Master, encouraged showing, understood its values, and had instituted the Quorn Puppy Show in 1870.

The value of hound showing was a live issue even at the first Peterborough show. The argument was basically about conformation or work: are these issues compatible?

The Field correspondent found it necessary to defend showing at some length at the start of his report: 'Much has been said from both points of view with regard to hound shows. That they do not necessarily induce breeding from the best hounds in the field – and from them only – is an argument against shows which we are neither able or desirous of contradicting. But that they insist upon all outward points which are needful for work, and that they frame their standard of excellence only with a view to attaining those essentials most needed in the hunting field is, we fancy, equally undeniable.

'Moreover, if our Masters of Hounds, and still more their huntsmen, are to have a type in their mind's eye, that type must be acquired by comparison more extended than is likely to be found in their own kennel doors. Few Masters, and no huntsmen, are likely to afford

A Vanity Fair *cartoon of Tom Firr, the famed Quorn huntsman, who showed at Peterborough – but did not like hound shows.*

*Tom Firr of the Quorn, Roy Heron, 1984.

time and trouble to travel over the country from kennel to kennel by way of extending their knowledge, or of forming mental models of the Foxhounds.

'Even if they did, they would have no means of framing their ideas, or correcting their half-formed opinions, except at the prompting of those most biased in favour of the particular kennels visited. At hound shows they, and all of us, have an opportunity of comparing notes and, it should be, of attaining knowledge, such as we could have under no other conditions.'

Although unsigned, *The Field's* senior hunting correspondent at that time was Cuthbert Bradley, who sometimes wrote as 'Whipster'. His father was a parson in the Fitzwilliam country and passed on a passion for hunting to his son. It is probable Cuthbert reported the first Peterborough show. He hunted frequently with the Fitzwilliam (Milton) and was a warm admirer of this pack. He was a worshipper at the shrine of Belvoir breeding, and wrote fulsomely of the virtues of that kennel. He was a passable artist and illustrated his articles and books with drawings, often depicting the upright stance and huge bone of the Belvoir type.

One suspects the introductory essay extolling the virtues of hound shows was written shortly before the reporter visited the first Peterborough show, and had been well briefed by the organisers, perhaps Tom Parrington. The show report, probably handwritten at great speed, was then tacked on to the essay, and sent in a parcel by train to London for publication in *The Field* only two days later. It was an example of the Victorians' ability to achieve high levels of production through sheer application and a great deal of manpower.

The Field reporter's dissertation on the value of hound shows is worth quoting fully because the issue was debated at varying levels of intensity for so many years ahead. Since Peterborough was to be essentially involved in the impending revolution in Foxhound breeding the 'bred for work' issue was of prime importance. Cuthbert was a profound admirer of the Belvoir pack owned by the Dukes of Rutland. Generations of Dukes staunchly refused to show them in open shows, and Cuthbert endeavoured not to offend either side by stating: 'Belvoir gives us a sight of the ideal, and Peterborough sets the standard of type; both of which are institutions that should be visited annually by the student of Foxhound breeding.' He was referring to the Belvoir's annual puppy show which was attended by an even larger gathering than that at Badminton to-day.

The Field correspondent gives both sides of the argument at that time, but it is unlikely it would have been read with much pleasure by the ageing and infirm 6th Duke of Rutland (1815-88) at Belvoir Castle, who at this stage did not appear in the hunting field, but guarded the pure English breeding of his hounds assiduously. One cannot avoid the suspicion that one reason he firmly avoided hound shows was in case they rubbed some of the lustre off the huge reputation of his hounds as the most sought after sires in Britain.

The Field reporter explained the controversy which was to rage intermittently in the sporting press for years after Peterborough's inception: 'It has even been urged by those who set their faces against hound shows, that on their account huntsmen may be led to retain, and breed from a hound who, beyond his fashionable appearance, has nothing to plead against being knocked on the head as useless.

'That is, to say the least, an extreme argument. It states indeed, a case that *might* occur, but it accepts a contingency that no Master of Hounds is ever likely to allow. And, granting that breeding from appearance alone is to be strongly repressed, it surely yet remains that good-looking hounds should be the aim rather than illfavoured ones; that what experience has taught the eye to esteem as correct shape and make is desirable; and that the higher the standard we can arrive at this direction, without detriment to other qualities, the better.'

Having made his points, however ponderously, the first Peterborough reporter concludes his argument triumphantly: 'At any rate, the present venture met with strong support, and consequent success, much enhanced by the personal patronage of their Royal Highnesses.'

Peterborough's first hound show established that a national show was to be considered 'a good thing', and well worth repeating. The presence of the Prince and Princess ensured that strict standards of dress and deportment were in place from the start, and the royal patronage began a link with royalty which has remained unbroken throughout the show's history, although it was to be another fifty-six years before the 'Royal' prefix was officially granted.

FIRST JUDGEMENTS

So much for the pros and cons, but what of the judging at the first Peterborough. Did that set any precedent or pattern? The trio of judges had only six classes before them. There were only two placings reported in each class. The results are translated here in modern format, giving the dam's sires as well:

Class 1, Unentered doghound couples:
1, Fitzwilliam (Milton) Somerset (by Hermit out of Harriet, dam by Ossian) and Selim (Somerset-Benefit, by Bluster); 2, York and Ainsty.

Class 2. Two couples, entered doghounds:
1, Brocklesby Glider (Aider-Gaiety, by Mr Scratton's Gimcrack), Alfred (Ambrose-Garland, by Random), and Armlet and Aimwell (Ambrose-Gaiety)*.

Class 3. Stallion hounds:
1. Brocklesby Glider; 2, Pytchley Comus (Mr Parry's Blucher-Comedy, by Duke of Grafton's Chorister)**

Class 4. Unentered bitch couples:
1. Fitzwilliam (Milton) Harebell (Somerset-Harriet, by Ossian) and Sarah (Somerset-Benefit, by Bluster); 2, Fitzwilliam (Milton) Rosebud (Wrangler-Rivulet, by Rubicon) and Sunbeam (Somerset-Saphire, by Silence.)

Class 5. Two couples, entered bitches:
1.Fitzwilliam (Milton) Rachel (Rubicon-Rumsey, by Roman), Blameless (Selim-

* Mr D.R. Scratton hunted the Essex Union Country 1848-69.
** Mr Nicholas Parry hunted the Puckeridge country 1838-75.

Barley, by Bentinck), Rhetoric (Ransack-Benefit, by Bluse); and Skilful (Stormer-Social, by Sailor).

Class 6. Champion Cup, presented by the Marquis of Huntly, for the best three couples of any age:
Brocklesby Glider, Alfred, Armlet, Aimwell, and Gambler (Aider-Gaiety) and Mallard (Marplot-Gaudy).

BONE AND SUBSTANCE

What were the judges looking for in selecting winners from the twenty-one packs on show? It was made abundantly clear in *The Field*'s report that Peterborough opened in the age when size and bone in the English Foxhound were so much prized, the cause of intense controversy later.

The Fitzwilliam (Milton) winning unentered doghound couple were described as 'remarkably strong, thick-set young hounds, of enormous bone and showing unmistakably the stamp of their famous sire (Somerset) who at the present time has probably more progeny in existence than any other hound in England.' Somerset was overlooked by the judges in the stallion hound class, according to the report, because of his age.

The Brocklesby's winning two couple had 'strength and substance to fulfil all requirements...looked perfectly majestic, carried themselves as kings,and made all else seem almost plebian.' Was it a hint, or simply factual reporting, that the Oakley, placed second, were referred to as 'full of quality, and looked the type of quick, active work'?

There were fifteen entries for the stallion hound class, and there was a final tussle between Brocklesby Glider, Quorn Governor, Pytchley Comus and Fitzwilliam Somerset. Glider, a six-year-old, was described as a 'truly lovely hound with light tan marking'.

Three out of four bitches among the winners in the unentered bitch couples class were by the Fitzwilliam's Somerset, underlining the huge influence of that kennel in English Foxhound breeding. The Belvoir were believed to be the most influential of all, but gave much credit to Fitzwilliam blood for the foundation of the kennel at Belvoir Castle.

The 3rd Duke of Rutland used Fitzwilliam blood extensively in the late eighteenth century. It was believed the Fitzwilliam (Milton) blood 'sprung from one of a different type to that which was the root of the Belvoir race. A larger, bigger-boned hound, the doghounds standing perhaps 25 inches, but full of drive and dash, for though big, they were never heavy or slow*.

Cuthbert Bradley elsewhere stated the Fitzwilliam, under the management of their huntsman George Carter 'reached a very high standard of excellence, sweeping the board of prizes at Peterborough year after year'**. Carter had whipped-in to Sebright, and learned his role thoroughly before being promoted to huntsman.

---

* *The History of the Belvoir Hunt,* T.F. Dale, 1899.
** *Foxhunting from Shire to Shire,* Cuthbert Bradley, 1912.

Fitzwilliam (Milton) Hounds Potent (centre) with LEFT TO RIGHT: *Plato ('07), Saladin ('06), Rector ('06), and Glatton ('05), painted by Miss F. Jay.* (From the Milton collection.)

According to the Fitzwilliam Hunt history by Ralph Greaves, during George Carter's forty years at Milton up to 1888, the kennel produced hounds of 'a distinctive sort – big, powerful, slashing hounds, the doghounds particularly, coarse of coat, and with brushy sterns – "George Carter's shaving brushes", as they were termed. The predominating colour was a silver-pie. Their savage temperament earned them renown, and they were devils on the line of a fox.'

Carter was a very large man, tactfully described as 'portly' in Peterborough show reports. He had an expansive, outgoing personality, and was highly popular, but in later life was accused of occasional outbursts of petulance and bad temper. His friend and rival was Tom Whitemore, the smaller, wiry huntsman of the neighbouring Oakley.

In the bitch two-couple class the Oakley were clearly popular, but not quite level, and therefore the Fitzwilliam prevailed. Eight packs took part and this was said to be the competition with 'probably more interest to onlookers than any of the day'.It is still an outstanding class in every Peterborough show.

The three-couple class was reported as being judged 'in the presence of the of their Royal Highnesses' which indicates they did not spend all their time at Peterborough observing the Foxhound Ring. Nevertheless it was well understood that the Foxhounds were a considerable attraction for the Prince of Wales.

The Fitzwilliam brought forward for the champion cup only the young hounds with which they had already won prizes, but it appears the Brocklesby

George Carter, Fitzwilliam huntman for forty years (1848-88), successful at the early Peterborough shows.

augmented their winning two couple of doghounds with another couple which had not been in the ribbons, specially 'brought from home with a view to this prize'.

The Field report declared the Brocklesby hounds who won the championship were 'level, true and fashionable; and we may well carry them in our mind's eye as the type of what high bred foxhounds should be.'

Bone and size therefore prevailed at the first show. Such a pattern of championship judging standards was to remain fairly constant in Victorian and Edwardian Peterborough shows, giving rise to the 'Peterborough Type' jibe by those who wanted hounds of a lighter, more athletic type .

However much its critics might huff and puff, it became increasingly clear that Peterborough's influence on Foxhound breeding was to be considerable, as a mirror of current types, and through the decisions of judges in selecting what they considered the best. Once the judges accepted new types of Foxhound conformation, Peterborough would help to accelerate change from the type which so dominated its early years. The new Foxhound show was to prove a thoroughly worthwhile annual enterprise fulfilling all the hopes raised in its first year.

4. Victorian Showpiece – Peterborough 1879-1901

Seventeen packs, four fewer than the inaugural show, attended the second Peterborough Hound Show in 1879. They represented mainly the hunting Midlands, and East Anglia.

Packs such as the Southdown and Lord Portman's did not make the long journey up to Peterborough in '79. Early in the next century southern and western packs were to be served by a new hound show at Reigate, succeeded later by a show at Aldershot. Neither survived into the late twentieth century, and never achieved the prestige of Peteborough. The opening of new regional hound shows became a controversial subject for leading Masters of Foxhounds of a more conservative view, some whom still doubted the value of hound showing, even at Peterborough.

Taking part in 1879 were: South Berks, Burton, Brocklesby, Cheshire, Cottesmore, Fitzwilliam (Milton), Earl Fitzwilliam, Holderness, Lord Middleton's, Grove, Rufford, Oakley, Pytchley, North Shropshire, Warwickshire, Sir Harcourt Johnstone's, West Norfolk, and Tynedale.

'The Peterborough show has quite taken the place of the great Yorkshire gathering…it has succeeded in bringing together hounds from kennels that were never represented so far north,' *The Field*'s reporter commented.

A small drop in entries after the first show was not a setback. The Grove, Rufford, and Sir Harcourt Johnstone's were all appearing for the first time. The last mentioned was a private pack hunted in Yorkshire; Harcourt Johnstone, later the first Lord Derwent, and his son took over the Pickering country from 1862. Additional visitors, some of them highly influential, brought to Peterborough by the Foxhound Show were highly welcome. The farming industry had benefited from comparative prosperity in the mid-nineteenth century. By the 1880s the industry found itself staggering under the impact of competition from low-cost producers. Add this to capricious weather in the last years of the nineteenth century, and it can be seen that show organisers were having a difficult time, despite Victorian industrial prosperity, and overseas income from the British Empire. The Prince of Wales re-visited Peterborough Agricultural Show in 1879, and attended the Foxhound show briefly.

The show's fame had spread far and wide among the hunting fraternity already, for among the visitors this year was Parson Jack Russell, aged eighty-five, West Country breeder of the terriers bearing his name. According to the *The Field* the famous hunting parson had 'lost little of the stalwart sturdiness of frame, keenness of eye, or richness of voice that distinguished him in youth, and whose pleasant weather-beaten face beams still with a boyish enthusiasm'.

The Rev. Jack Russell, founder of the famous terriers, who judged at Peterborough in 1879.

The following year the Rev. Jack Russell appeared at Peterborough as a judge, probably because at that time the Foxhound show was accompanied by classes for Foxhound Terriers. They were usually judged by professional huntsmen, but the hunting parson was included on this occasion. The terrier show was dropped in the 1890s, and the absence of the 'yapping noise' was much welcomed, reported Cuthbert Bradley.

Frank Goodall, huntsman of the Queen's Buckhounds (1872-88) was at the 1879 show to support his younger brother, Will, who was showing the Pytchley. Retired veterans George Beer from the Grafton, Stephen Dodson from the Essex and Nimrod Long from the Brocklesby were among huntsmen attending. Judges at this second show were experienced former Masters representative of the British Isles: the Marquis of Waterford from Ireland, Colonel Anstruther Thomson, from Scotland (Fife), and representing England, Thomas Tyrwhitt Drake (Bicester and Warden Hill).

The Fitzwilliam (Milton) had a great day, and their portly huntsman George Carter's performance in the hound ring indicates it must have been somewhat less formal at that time. Carter was at liberty to greet victory with grins and merry quips to all and sundry.

When Fitzwilliam (Milton) won a strongly contested unentered doghound couples class, George Carter said triumphantly to the Master of the runner-up, the neighbouring Oakley: 'Now I'll run you Mr Arkwright.' There was much laughter when Arkwright responded quickly: 'You must find the fox in your country then, George.'

Carter beamed broadly when the Fitzwilliam won the entered doghound couples class, with the Oakley again second. Fitzwilliam won the stallion hound class with their Spanker, and reserve with Sultan.

'Rightly judged, thank you gentlemen,' said George. Modern society is believed to be less formal, but just imagine the frosty reaction in twenty-first century Peterborough if a huntsman loudly congratulated the judges as he left the ring.

Ribbons were attached to the huntsmen's button-holes at that time, rather than attached to one arm, the fashion today. Carter joked that his button-holes were so full of ribbons he would need a new Hunt coat for the next show.

The Tynedale won the unentered bitch couples class, but Carter had plenty to smile about, since they were sired by Fitzwilliam (Milton) Richmond, with the Grove couple in reserve. The Oakley won the entered bitch couples class, with Milton second. This year a special prize was awarded to the best individual bitch, precursor to a bitch championship, and the Oakley triumphed again, with a bitch named Flighty, a daughter of Fitzwilliam (Milton) Furrier, with the Brocklesby reserve with Wanton, by Belvoir Warrior.

The Belvoir. Brocklesby, and Fitzwilliam continued to be major influences on hound breeding for the next fifty years. Writing in 1947, Major Maurice 'Mo' Barclay, esteemed Joint Master of the Puckeridge for 52 years (1910-62), asserted*

> Brocklesby Rallywood 1843 is virtually the father of the Foxhound to-day…the greatest of Rallywood's descendants was Belvoir Weatherguage 1876…he had five lines back to Brocklesby Rallywood '43, three on his sire's side and two on his dam's; five lines to Drake's Duster 1844 and one to Lord Henry Bentinck's Contest 1848.

As we have seen, these lines were among early winners at Peterborough, and remained in the ribbons for many years. Charles Richardson, Hunting Editor of *The Field*, wrote in 1908**

Brocklesby Rallywood – 'father of the Foxhound'.

*The Lonsdale Library's *Foxhunting*, 1947.
** *The Complete Foxhunter*, Charles Rich Richardson, 1908.

...the best hounds of 30 years ago were of much the same stamp as the best hounds of the present day – from the onlooker's point of view. Peterborough does not, cannot in fact, point out which in every class are the best workers, but it can indicate year by year the type which breeders should aim at, and this is what it faithfully does.

Richardson strongly defended the so-called 'Peterborough type' in controversial statements which were the basis of sometimes heated debate up to the second world war:

Some critics there are who affirm that too much attention is paid to bone and straightness, but bone means strength and constitution, and these are absolutely necessary if a hound has to go through a long day, and travel home at night with his stern up...

There are those who urge that the lighter-built Welsh hounds can travel faster on a hot scent than the Foxhound which is used in other parts of the kingdom, but this has yet to be proved, and meanwhile it may confidently be stated that the modern Foxhound goes quite fast enough. Indeed, some will have it that nose has been sacrificed to speed...

PETERBOROUGH – PART OF THE CALENDAR

In the last two decades of the nineteenth century Peterborough Foxhound Show achieved the stability needed to become an important annual fixture for the foxhunting world.

Thanks to the organising ability of the secretary Mr Smart and his officials, the showring continued to run smoothly, and Peterborough's reputation grew as an enjoyable meeting place. The link with the agricultural show remained crucial. Successful show secretaries know all about the importance of lunch-time. Peterborough Foxhound lunches soon became a 'must' for most leading Masters throughout the country, usually ending with rousing speeches which indicated the importance of foxhunting in country life.

For example, at the 1888 lunch the President, George Lane Fox, declared:

Happy is the man that has his coverts full of good wild foxes, for he knows that England's greatness will never go down.

There is another place for those slipshod landed proprietors who wink at unnatural destruction of foxes, or keep them shut up in pigstyes; and as for those who set up barbed wire...'. The Horse and Hound reporter, seated somewhere at the far back, commented – 'would that they could have seen the brave old squire's face of disgust as he said what should be done with them, and he was too lenient in ladies' society. The cheering was long before it subsided, and it is to be hoped that someone better situated for hearing this speech noted it down for the benefit of malefactors.'

During the eighteen eighties and 'nineties the Fitzwilliam continued to appear frequently among class winners, George Carter's coat festooned with rosettes. He retired in 1888 after forty-three years' service, and died the following year, reportedly leaving £17,000, a considerable sum at that time.

George Fitzwilliam came of age in 1887 and started a great Mastership which lasted forty years, apart from three years' Army service from 1892-5. He bred Harper ('03) by Atherstone Harper ('97) who won the 1905 doghound champion and became a leading stud hound. In 1906 the Fitzwilliam bitch Sanguine ('04) by Analyst ('98) won the bitch championship. The Fitzwilliam were champions again in 1908 with the doghound Donovan ('05) by Dorset, a big tan and white hound.

One of the greatest of foxhunters, the 9th Duke of Beaufort, took office in 1899, but he had hardly missed attending Peterborough during its thirty-two years. He hunted hounds for thirty seasons before he

Mr George Fitzwilliam, Master of the Fitzwilliam (Milton) for forty years up to 1935.

Fitzwilliam (Milton) Sanguine, Peterborough bitch champion 1904.

The 9th Duke of Beaufort enjoying lunch at Peterborough Hound Show in 1923, and talking to Lady Diana Somerset; (RIGHT), Lady St Germans and Mr Bill Harford.

succeeded to the title, and when he became a very large man in later years he was driven all over the country in an open Ford to watch his son hunt hounds. The 9th Duke was photographed sitting down to a substantial lunch at a special table provided for him at Peterborough.

When in 1900 his son was born – always to be known as 'Master' – the news was brought to the 9th Duke in the hunting field. It was suggested by the huntsman, Will Dale, the field might like to give three cheers. 'Certainly not,' said the Duke. 'It might upset the hounds.'

The 9th Duke was described by Cuthbert Bradley as 'the tallest Master of Hounds on the active list', and 'the first gentleman huntsman of his time,' sharing the hunting with Will Dale, one of the tallest professional huntsmen of his day, previously with the Brocklesby.

In 1898 the Duke of Beaufort's, listed in the results as 'Badminton', won with their sire Governor one of 'three premiums for dogs which have never won a first at Peterborough'. The other winners were the East Essex with Goblin and the VWH (Cricklade) with Paradox.

There was great joy the following year at Badminton when the newly succeeded 9th Duke won his first Peterborough championship with the unentered bitch Rapture, the stallion hound class with Vaulter, and the three couples doghounds class. It was the Duke's first year as Master, and the start of Badminton's remarkable tally of Peterborough championships, well ahead of any pack in Britain, totalling fifty-one at the 2005 show.

At the turn of the century, Badminton blood nicked in well with Belvoir, Brocklesby and Fitzwilliam lines. In the 1899 show the Duke's three couples winners were all sired from the Belvoir kennel. His stallion hound class winner, Vaulter ('97), was by Belvoir Vaulter.

The Oakley continued among the ribbons in the late Victorian and early Edwardian shows. Oakley Dancer ('88) by Grafton Dancer won Peterborough's 1891 doghound championship. Tom Whitemore, latterly with snow white hair, often showed the Oakley hounds in competition with his son, George, who hunted Mr Austin Mackenzie's Woodland Pytchley Pack, later going to the Atherstone under Mr Gerald Hardy who also won at Peterborough.

The Atherstone captured Peterborough's doghound championship in 1902 with their Challenger ('98). When the Whitemores appeared together in a championship, if the old man's hound was beaten by his son's, 'much to the merriment of the huntsmen looking on, he used to say "Ah well, I had to let the boy have it this time."'*

The 9th Duke of Beaufort's Vaulter ('97), winner of Peterborough stallion hound class in 1899.

*Good Sport 1881-1909, Cuthbert Bradley.

Gerald Hardy was later associated with the reappearance at Peterborough of excellent young doghounds from the Meynell kennel, said to go back to the bloodlines of old Hugo Meynell, the 'Father of Foxhunting' who founded the Quorn in the mid-eighteenth century. The Meynell Hunt in Hugo's native Derbyshire, was founded by his nephew. The Meynell won couples classes in 1907 and 1908 with Warrener, by Belvoir Warlaby, and Why Not by Belvoir Vagabond ('99), a somewhat appalling example of the heaviest type of over-knuckled Old English.

At the end of the nineteenth century Lord Willoughby de Broke's Warwickshire pack were prolific winners. With Jack Boore as huntsman, Lord Willoughby was advised by the great pundit on foxhound pedigrees, the Rev. Cecil Legard, in building up the kennel with liberal infusions of blood from Belvoir, Milton and other 'proven sources'. They won both championships in 1887, the doghounds in '96. '97, and '98, and the bitch championship in '88, '93, and '98.

In 1901 the Warwickshire won the doghound championship with their unentered Pedlar ('01) by Tuscan from Heedfull, going back on both sides to the famous Belvoir Weatherguage, shown by their new huntsman Jack Brown, 'a noted hard rider from Lord Harrington's country', succeeding Jack Bore.

Cuthbert Bradley reported Pedlar as 'standing 23½ inches, with muscular back and quarters...lacking the elegance of neck and shoulders which distinguishes Warwickshire winners...the 18th Lord Willoughby de Broke pointed this out as he painted Pedlar's portrait...the noble Master was a confirmed invalid, wheeled in a bath-chair to the kennels.'

The 19th Lord Willoughby de Broke won Peterborough doghound championship in 1904 with Traveller ('03), by Belvoir Handel out of Tragedy, by Talisman. Three years later the Warwickshire won the championship with their Wizard ('06) by Tuner, and Traveller ('03) was contesting a highly competitive stallion hound class.

According to Cuthbert Bradley: 'Jack Brown, wearing one boot and one legging, stood chewing a bit of biscuit, smiling into the hound's face, Traveller giving a marvellous show of his blood-like quality in a statuesque pose.

The hunting writer 'Pomponious Ego' in *Vanity Fair* provided a delightful vignette from the 1907 show:

Personally, I should have bestowed the sire's prize upon the Warwickshire Traveller, because he raised a rippling laugh, and bent a beam of humour upon the scene – no hound at Peterborough has ever before realised the true dignity of the occasion as Traveller did. For minutes he stood as a statue graven in stone, with never a movement in his taut-drawn muscles. The best sire of our generation was magnificently upheld in the noble dignity and serene contempt he displayed for the other 'dogs' who brushed his flanks and with inquisitive nose examined this mould of fashion and glass of form.

The judges – Charles McNeill MFH (North Cotswold) and Gerald Hardy MFH

(Meynell) – were unable to decide who was the winner between Traveller and the Atherstone Conquest. So Mr John Watson, Master of the Meath, was called in as referee. Cuthbert Bradley reported: 'After bestowing critical glances on the couple, he slapped Traveller with his catalogue and said "I go for this dog" – confirming his opinion of 1904 when, with Mr W.M. Dunn, he awarded this Warwickshire dog the championship.'

The Pytchley was to make crucial changes in its pack in the twentieth century which dried up its remarkable record of Peterborough championships. During the Mastership of Mr William 'Willie' Wroughton (1894-1902) hounds were bred on old English lines, but Wroughton was a keen student of hound breeding, and endeavoured to improve the speed and drive of the Pytchley pack. He borrowed two Welsh-cross bitches from Col. Frederick Lort-Phillips of the Pembrokeshire. Dimple, by Llangibby Danger out of Taunton Verity, 'was there from find to finish, she leads from first to last'*.

Peterborough Hound Show 1899 – winning two couples.Will Goodall shows the Pytchley, left. In the white coat is the bearded Merthyr Guest, Master of the Blackmore Vale.

Officially, Dimple was not used to breed an out-cross in the Pytchley Kennel, but one wonders if she was used 'unofficially'? Wroughton's breeding, with John Isaac as huntsman, saw the Pytchley win at Peterborough the doghound championship in 1897 with Potentante, and again in '89 with Marquis (99) by Belvoir Dexter. The Hunt scored three firsts in 1901, and more prizes in 1903-4.

*The History of Foxhunting, Roger Longrigg, 1975 from 'Dimple, a Memory of 1894', H. Cumberland Bentley.

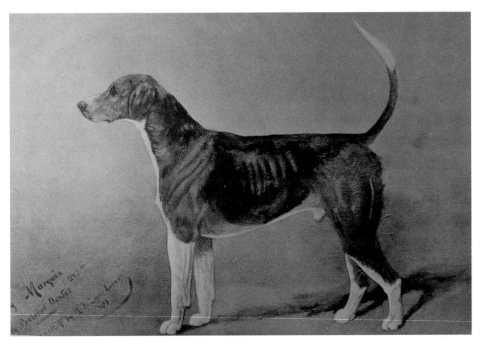

Pytchley Marquis, by Belvoir Dexter, doghound champion, 1889. (from a picture by H.F. Lucas Lucas)

Cuthbert Bradley reported Potentate was 'an upstanding, determined-looking dog, with good shoulders, and well ribbed up, in Belvoir tan, and that kennel used him as a stallion hound.' Isaac, the Pytchley huntsman was sometimes criticised in the hunting field, but he was excellent on the flags. He was praised by Cuthbert Bradley for his prowess...'all the action of a conjurer or a mesmerist, a marvellous knack of bringing out the best points of a hound.'

Lord Annaly who succeeded Wroughton as the Pytchley's Master (1902-14) had the good fortune to engage Frank Freeman, widely acknowledged as the greatest huntsman of his time (1906-31). Freeman quietly changed the Pytchley old English pack, full of bone and substance, to a much lighter, athletic type, and they produced superlative sport. They were not all bred in kennel; more than a few were carefully selected by the huntsman from hounds offered at the annual Foxhound sales at Rugby. Was excellent sport produced because the type of hound was altered, or was it due to Freeman's acknowledged genius in handling hounds in the field? Contemporary reports seem to indicate it was 'a bit of both'.

According to Guy Paget in his entertaining, warmly recommended *History of the Pytchley Hunt*: 'Freeman did not like the big turned-in-toed Peterborough Champions of his day. He absolutely believed in breeding only from the very best workers, both male and female. Though naturally he liked a hound to be plumb straight, he did not consider it a *sine qua non*. He thought good shoulders, loins, and neck far more important.'

Ronnie Wallace was a great admirer of Frank Freeman, and recalled: 'There was a famous story that one of the hound experts of the day, the Rev. Cecil Legard, saw the Pytchley hounds at the meet at Daventry in 1911. As he turned away, he remarked: 'Pack of harriers.'

'The meet was followed by the famous Badby Wood run in which hounds achieved a 14-mile point, running about 22 miles, and catching their fox.

'On Sunday morning, Legard came to the kennels and said: "Freeman, you had a great hunt."

'Freeman replied: "Yes sir. Not bad for harriers."*

The Pytchley won their last Peterborough doghound championship at Peterborough in 1901. It could hardly have been a coincidence that, with their lighter style of hound, they did not win another Peterborough championship during Freeman's twenty-five years as huntsman, gaining their next championship in 1948.

Mr Fernie's pack, originator of the modern Fernie in south Leicestershire, used Atherstone and Belvoir blood in the kennel, and had a succession of winners at the turn of the century, including the bitch championship in 1901. Yet one has to agree with Cuthbert Bradley's verdict on the Leicestershire packs in the showring:

> One might imagine that Leicestershire, the first hunting county in the world, portioned between four or five different Hunts, would have the hounds to sweep the board of prizes. But, excepting Mr Fernie's, Leicestershire does not count on the flags. As is well known, the Duke of Rutland's, the acknowledged premier pack of the day, has never shown away from Belvoir, though all the Masters and experts in breeding spend a day on the flags of that kennel, 'to tone up a Foxhound eye and a Foxhound memory', before visiting Peterborough. Though Belvoir does not enter into competition, it is their blood which wins the majority of prizes for other kennels. The Quorn and Cottesmore have been seen out very seldom, and the same may be said of Lord Harrington's hounds hunting a slice of Leicestershire country.

The Quorn won a championship, with their somewhat reluctant showing huntsman Tom Firr, in 1890 when they achieved the champion cup with Dreamer ('87) a lemon and white coloured hound, 'built on racing lines, and showing elegance of neck and shoulders,' according to the show report.

It was rare at that time for a lemon and white hound to be in the ribbons, let alone winning a championship from hounds in the much admired Belvoir tan livery. Tom Firr, like Freeman in the Pytchley, was experimenting quietly with Quorn hound breeding to develop a lighter framed, faster pack. He believed pace was highly important when hunting hounds in front of large well-mounted fields on the light going and fly fences of High Leicestershire, north and south of Melton Mowbray. Part of Firr's famous repertoire was the 'galloping forward cast'.

Let us not forget, however, that the neighbouring Belvoir to the east was renowned for consistent, excellent sport for generations, whilst firmly adhering to traditional English hounds. Hunting the strong hedge and ditch country in the

*Ronnie Wallace, *A Manual of Foxhunting*, 2003.

Belvoir Vale, climbing the hills above, and hunting the extensive ploughlands of the Belvoir's Lincolnshire country, was – and still is – a test of strength and substance for hounds. The Belvoir's old English pack satisfied generations of mounted fields who were equally as keen on galloping and jumping after a flying pack as followers of the Quorn – indeed many Meltonians hunted regularly with both packs.

GOLDEN JUBILEE – AND A NEW HOME

The 1887 Foxhound Show occurred during a highlight of the Victorian period, the Golden Jubilee year marking the fiftieth anniversary of the Queen's reign when the whole of Britain celebrated. That year, after nearly a decade at the Rink, the Foxhound Show joined the Agricultural Show in a major move to a new venue.

The site of a new, larger showground was at Millfield, known as Sexton barns, between Westwood and Millfield, all to be absorbed by the spread of the late twentieth century city. The wisdom of holding the early shows on permanent sites within Peterborough became apparent as land values increased spectacularly, allowing the show to fund its later moves to more spacious grounds further out. Millfield was near a much loved Peterborough local landmark, a spectacular windmill with six sails in Lincoln Road, regrettably demolished in 1937.

The new showground, purchased by the agricultural committee, comprised two fields, one containing a grandstand, a jumping course and horse boxes. The second field was occupied by judging rings and implement stands.

The Foxhound enclosure was similar to that at the Rink, but it was regarded as an exceedingly important part of the layout, and great care had been taken in organising its new home, with improved cover for ladies among the spectators. According to Horse and Hound's report in its June 18 issue, 1887:

> In the new enclosure prepared for the hound show everything had been done by the committee to ensure comfort for hounds, huntsmen, judges, and visitors, and it is not saying too much that nothing was left undone. The enclosure is very much on the old lines as in the well-known rink, but one improvement is that kennels, with a covered passage in front of them, are in the same yard as the judging ring and pavilion.
>
> Flagstones are laid on the turf, so as to set off legs and feet, and the turf ring allows liberty of action as before. An awning protected the judges from sun or rain, and the pavilion afforded seats under shelter for ladies. So from all sides it was a very pretty scene, and as usual, one that sportsmen love to look upon.

At the 1887 Agricultural show there was a fine firework display, a Golden Juibilee tableaux, and a display of machinery including a vertical-boiler agricultural steam engine, then the largest ever constructed by Barford and Perkins at their Queens Street Works*.

We Plough the Fields and Scatter, History of Peterborough Agricultural Society, John Knight & David Brandon.

Judging at the showground at Millfield, called Sexton Barns, used from 1887-1911. (etching by John Charlton, from the Milton collection)

There was considerable interest from visiting Masters of Hounds in Barford and Perkins' new hound kitchen, which cooked flesh and meal by steam, and saved a great deal in fuel. It was already in use in the Cottesmore and Sir Bache Cunard's kennels, and the one on show had been purchased by Captain Cheape of the Linlithgow and Stirlingshire.

With fewer entertainment distractions such as television, Victorian society at all levels attended outdoor events with great enthusiasm. The 1887 Foxhound Show, set amid the excitements of a new showground and the Golden Jubilee celebrations, was memorable. The *Peterborough Advertiser* gave a flavour of the atmosphere:

> The City had more gay bunting than usual, and was in a state of animation throughout the day. The flys, wagonettes, horse buses and other vehicles plying to and from the Great Northern and Great Eastern railway stations went as fast as the horses could travel.

In grand summer weather, fourteen packs showed hounds before three judges: Sir Reginald Graham, Mr T. Harvey D. Bayly, and Mr R. Chandos-Pole.

Hunts exhibiting were: Atherstone, Badsworth, Old Berkeley, Blackmore Vale, South Cheshire, Cleveland, Fitzwilliam, Mr Gosling's, Mr Jarvis's, Lanarkshire and Renfrewshire, Pytchley, Tynedale, Warwickshire, and the Earl of Yarborough's Brocklesby.

Lord Yarborough was the 1887 President, and the Foxhound show committee comprised: Mr William Barford, chairman, Lord Burghersh, and Messrs Beecroft, Bird, Buckle, Edwardes, Fabling, F. Gordon, H. Little, Percival, Staplee, Stones, and Walker, and J.R. Smart, Secretary.

The Secretary clearly understood press relations: *Horse and Hound*'s correspondent Mr Miles, who used the nom-de-plume 'Dragon', described Mr Smart as 'the ever courteous secretary who may well be pleased with the general praise that everyone gave their arrangements.'

However, 'Dragon' may not have been invited to lunch, or perhaps he found the tent too hot. He reported tactfully: 'Then came luncheon in the great tent, with the scarlet table bright as usual, and as much fun going on; but we could not hear any speeches, preferring a cigar in the cool breeze until it was time to settle down again to see the ladies judged, which was a greater treat than before.'

The 'scarlet table', referred to in various reports at that time, was a central table where the professional huntsmen in livery were seated. It was considered indelicate to mention 'bitches' in the Victorian press, and they were invariably referred as 'ladies', although the word was of course used in hound catalogues.

The Warwickshire won the overall championship cups, but other prizes in the six-class show were shared widely. The schedule was still markedly different from modern Peterborough. There was one overall champion of either sex and any age, and this was won by the Warwickshire with their unentered doghound Trueman, by Brocklesby Tapstery out of Roundelay who was by Belvoir Fallible.

He was clearly a strapping example of the 'upstanding type' so popular at the time; the report said 'it would be hard to find a handsomer hound'. He won a special prize for best single hound in the unentered doghound couples class, although first prize went to the Brocklesby's Smoker, by Fitzwilliam Solomon, and Clinker by Rubicon out of Countess who was by Lord Coventry's Cardinal. The Atherstone were second.

The Warwickshire won the two couples of entered doghounds class, and the stallion hound winner was Badsworth Advocate, by Fitzwilliam Spanker, out of Abigail by Quorn Alfred, a favourite sire among the English bred packs of the time. The Tynedale on the unentered bitch couples class, with the Brocklesby second. The Fitzwilliam won the two couples bitch class, with the Blackmore Vale in second place.

The Warwickshire brood bitch Delicate, by Belvoir Fencer by Duchess who was by Quorn Dexter, with the Blackmore Vale Romance second.

They also won the classes for three-couples, and couples (dog and bitch of any age). The important link between the Foxhound Show, the Agricultural Show and the City was emphasised by the Mayor of Peterborough, Mr H.P. Gates, presenting the champion cups.

It may seem a long way in Victorian England, for the Blackmore Vale to have journeyed from Dorset to show hounds in Peterborough, but their exceedingly wealthy Master from 1884-1900, Merthyr Guest, was accustomed to visiting Leicestershire with hounds, staff, and up to 100 horses, travelling by train and renting the great manor of Burley-on-the-Hill in the Cottesmore country. He took no subscriptions from his followers in Dorset, and the Hunt was known as 'the Queen of the West'.

Peterborough's position as the premier hound show, and its increasing value as a guide for hound breeders was emphasised at the 1887 show by the sale of bound copies of the show catalogues since its commencement. There were also on sale the new edition of the Foxhound Kennel Stud book, containing pedigrees from the complete lists of fifty-three packs, from 1865.

The 1895 show saw a royal visit on an especially grand scale. The Prince of Wales announced he would be attending the second day of the show, Wednesday 10 July, and 'was particularly keen to support the Foxhound Society's display.

> It was decided to make this an occasion the city would remember. The Prince and the Royal entourage arrived from London at the North Station aboard a train for Scotland... The Prince was met by Lord Burghley, and they transferred to an open landau, hauled by four magnificent greys and complete with postilions in fawn and gold livery. They made their way through streets lined with well-wishers...to the Showground at Millfield where they were greeted by the 6th Earl Fitzwilliam and escorted to the Royal marquee close to the main ring, where luncheon was served...the Prince was driven in leisurely fashion around the various areas of the Showground in a horse-drawn carriage...*

Once again the Foxhound Show had been of some help in gaining a royal presence at Peterborough, and the link was to prove invaluable in the next century.

The Warwickshire had a great morning at the 1895 show, winning all doghound classes except the stallion class and the championship, both captured by the Oakley's Dandy. The Cheshire excelled in the bitch classes, winning every class except the championship which went to the Warwickshire's Seamstress.

The Earl of Coventry, Mr A.W. Carnegy and Mr C.W. Wicksteed judged both sections in '95. Three judges prevailed the following year, but from 1897 Peterborough began using four judges, two in each section, which is still the practice.

Peterborough on the surface was sailing on serenely through Victorian and Edwardian England, but the background debate about showing versus work would not go away. The *Peterborough and Huntingdonshire Standard's* report of the 1902 show gave a hint of the underlying controversy. Sir P.A. Muntz MP, from Waarwickshire, at lunch proposed a Toast to 'Success to the Peterborough Hound Show'.

> He remarked upon the immense good the shows had done. Some few years ago gentlemen were fond of writing to the papers – many gentlemen were fond of writing in the papers: foolish gentlemen! (laughter) – and saying that the hounds shown at Peterborough were no good except on the flags. He thought they had demonstrated since then that hounds which appeared at Peterborough and won the prizes were also hounds which could hunt over a big country and

* *We Plough the Fields and Scatter – History of Peterborough Agricultural Society.*

hunt very fast too. (Applause) He was pleased to know that some of the prizes that day were going to his native county. (Hear, hear) Long might they continue to do so! (Applause). Not only had the hounds distinguished themselves at the show, but also in crossing the Shuckburgh vale. (Hear, hear and applause). Sir P.A. Muntz in conclusion, euologised the daring with which the young men of today followed the packs, and warmly the condemned the use of barbed wire in fences!

Far more severe challenges were to face foxhunting and country life in the twentieth century. Peterborough would be heavily involved in the further development of the Foxhound – and in the fight for survival of the greatest of all country sports.

5. BEFORE AND AFTER THE 1914-18 GREAT WAR

Although Millfield proved a happy home for Peterborough Agricultural Show and the Foxhound Show for twenty years, the growth of the former made another move necessary. Plans were made in 1910, and the new showground was ready the following year.

The Agricultural Show committee purchased outright a twenty-four acres site at Eastfield on the northern edge of the city. It was nearly ten acres larger than the Millfield site, had a frontage onto Eastfield Road, and access from the centre of Peterborough by electric trams.

The Foxhound Show erected a permanent building, described as a 'new shed' in its committee minutes: 90 by 56 ft, 28 ft to the ridge, and 10ft. 6ins to the eaves. The Foxhound Show's independence was emphasised by 7ft high fencing surrounding its site, and a gate to the showground. The hound shows continued to be run with separate admission charge of one shilling, and subscriptions from its Vice-Presidents who represented Hunts all over Britain.

Seats reserved for Vice-Presidents and their friends were covered, and a section at the west end of the south-west side was reserved for Hunt servants. Front rows on the long sides of the ring, and two front rows at each end, were to be reserved for Vice-Presidents.

An early Hound Show show at Eastfield, the new venue from 1911.

Vulgar details such as the cost of the new building were not recorded in the minutes which were dry, minimalist, and reflected deeply conservative policies. Whenever a change of venue occurred, the Foxhound Society committee endeavoured to recreate the hound building as nearly as possible a replica of the previous one. There were drawbacks, but the positive result was that members felt comfortably at home at the Foxhound Shows no matter what developments occurred in the Agricultural Show outside their compound. Changes in the management of the Foxhound Show usually occurred gradually after much consideration.

By 1884 a Cup was given for the best hound of either sex, won in three succsssive years by the Oakley, with Feudal ('82), Rhymer ('82) and Graceful ('82). Warwickshire Trueman ('87), an unentered doghound, was champion the following year, and Quorn Warrior ('84) won in 1888*.

In 1889 began the practice of awarding Challenge Cups for both doghounds and bitches, and in this year the Warwickshire gained a double victory with Stentor ('85) and Factious ('85).

An important innovation from 1889 was the annual Harriers and Beagles Show, using the same showring the day after the Foxhound Show, but retaining the advantages of the accompanying Agricultural Show. From 1892 the new show was held under the auspices of the Association of Masters of Harriers and Beagles.

There have always been strong links between the hound sports – many Masters of Foxhounds have learned venery skills by hunting beagle packs – and the new show provided another reason for hunting people to flock to Peterborough during the Agricultural Show. The Hound Shows remained firmly independent, and resisted suggestions they take place on the same day – until 2005, the year hunting with hounds was banned.

The growing importance of Peterborough's hunter showing classes was another incentive for hunting people to attend the annual fixture in July. Competing Masters and other keen hound enthusiasts were rooted to their seats throughout the show, but some of their wives and friends were known to sneak out of the compound to watch horse show classes, and browse through trade stands during the day.

William Barford, instrumental in bringing the Foxhound Show from Yorkshire to Peterborough, retired in 1894 as joint chairman of the Foxhound and Agricultural Shows. Three hundred members of both societies subscribed to the presentation of an album bearing their names, with wooden covers made from replaced choir stalls in Peterborough Cathedral. They expressed appreciation of the progress of the shows with a presentation of a silver bowl, tea and coffee service, and a sum of money which, at Mr Barford's wish, was invested in the purchase of votes in the Royal Agricultural Benevolent Institution.

The Sporting Times reported on the presentation on July 12, 1894:

It was a thoroughly representative company of sportsmen that met round the Judging Ring at Peterborough Hound Show yesterday – all the principal Hunts being in evidence, and perhaps there was never a more enthusiastic company in

The Book of the Foxhound, Daphne Moore.

the Luncheon Tent than that which assembled under the Presidency of Mr Parrington. The presentation was made in suitable terms by the Marquis of Huntly who has worked for many years with Mr Barford in the interests of the Peterborough Agricultural Society and Hound Show.

George Charles Wentworth Fitzwilliam, current owner and occupier of Milton, and Master of the Fitzwilliam, succeeded as chairman. William Barford died in 1898 and warm tributes were again paid to his crucial achievements for the annual shows. The Hound Show suffered a sad blow on 7 August 1913 when its secretary, John Rich Smart, collapsed with 'a seizure' while walking in Queen Street, and died that evening, aged fifty-eight. His death as senior partner of John R. Smart and Co., accountants and auditors, shocked Peterborough and there was a large turnout at his funeral. He was secretary also of the Harrriers and Beagle Show, and had many important functions in the city.

John Smart was succeeded as Foxhound Show secretary, at a starting salary of 30 guineas a year, by his business partner, Joseph Stephenson, who remained in office for the next fifty-two years, retiring in 1965. He was a tough, astute Yorkshireman with a formidable personality, who gave the Society

George C.W. Fitzwilliam, Master of the Fitzwilliam (Milton), Chairman of the Foxhound Show from 1894.

considerable stability and continuity. He was accustomed to hold meetings in his large office in Queen Streeet, seated at a large desk surrounded by the black metal deed boxes of his clients. Others attending the brief, business-like meetings, including the Earls Fitzwilliam, used to perch on the deed boxes.

The Foxhound committee listed in the minutes in 1913 comprised George Fitzwilliam as chairman, the Marquess of Exeter, Lord Southampton, Mr E.E. Barclay (first of the dynasty of Barclays who were Masters of the Puckeridge), Mr Percival, Mr Walker, and Mr Maxwell. William Barford was still a committee member, but was indisposed.

Peterborough Foxhound Show's income from its 1912 show was, in pre-decimal figures £28.19s.0d – 579 admissions at one shilling each. The entire cost of the luncheons, from Messrs Phillips and Co., was £28.9s.8d. It cost £3.7s.6d to advertise in *The Field* and only £1.18s.9d. to advertise in *Horse and Hound*. The Foxhound Show society at that time was paying the Agricultural Society a nominal five shillings per year for rental of its site.

The twentieth century up to the Great War saw social life led with new vigour and opulent style in the reign of Edward VII, from 1902-10, but it was still a nineteenth century English society, respectful of elders and betters, mainly ordered by birth and occupation. Many certainties were to be shattered by the horrors of 1914-18 warfare when 'the flower of the new generation' was decimated.

Peterborough Foxhound Show amply reflected Edwardian confidence and serenity. Lord Lonsdale, the 'Yellow Earl', celebrated Master of the Quorn and the Cottesmore, entertained 200 Masters of Foxhounds to dinner at the 1912 Peterborough show, described as 'the zenith of pre-war foxhunting'*.

The type of hounds winning prizes was the subject of a controversy still growing. Foxhounds winning at Peterborough up to the Great War were condemned by radicals among hound breeders as gross examples of the 'Shorthorn era': full of bone and substance. There were unproven accusations that certain Masters were breeding for prizes rather than work.

Sir Gilbert Greenall, Master of the Belvoir (1896-1912), was pleased to announce at his puppy show that nearly all Peterborough winners in 1899 were by Belvoir doghounds.

Although the Belvoir Mastership was relinquished by the Dukes of Rutland from 1896, the new Master, Sir Gilbert Greenall was reported in *Horse and Hound* that he announced with satisfaction at his puppy show in 1899 'every single hound that won a prize at the Peterborough show that summer, with one exception, was by a Belvoir dog'. The Rev. Cecil Legard endorsed this, adding 'the success of the Belvoir sires showed the absolute importance of maintaining the highest state of excellence'.

It was no wonder that Sir Gilbert, a Cheshire brewing tycoon, adhered firmly during his Mastership (1896-1912) to the ducal policy of confining their pack strictly to old English hound breeding. Succeeding Dukes of Rutland kept a watchful eye on

*English Foxhunting, Raymond Carr. 1976.

Atherstone Challenger ('98), doghound champion 1898,

their kennel at Belvoir Castle to ensure this was the case in the prestigious pack they continued to own.

From 1900 to 1914 the Fitzwilliam won four Peterborough doghound championships, the Warwickshire three, and the Pytchley two. Bitch championships were more widely spread: the Fitzwilliam and the Cattistock from Dorset each won two, and the Duke of Beaufort's won the last bitch championship before the war, at the 1914 show, with their Caroline ('13). Fitzwilliam (Milton) achieved the bitch championship with Wiseman ('10). Belvoir, Brocklesby and Fitzwilliam breeding lines continued to predominate among winners.

Few at first believed the Great War, which erupted after 28 June when the Archduke Ferdinand was assassinated at Sarajevo, would last long, nor that it would greatly affect British life. Peterborough Agricultural Show took place on 7 to 9 July and the Foxhound Show on 8 July, and they were well attended. It was reported as a 'very happy show'. Foxhunters who attended that year must have looked back on it with nostalgia during four long years of trench warfare. Britain entered the war on 4 August, and many from the hunting community were soon among those volunteering to fight in France.

TOO MANY FOXHOUND SHOWS?

A report of the annual meeting of the Masters of Foxhounds Association on 30 May 1914, understandably contained no reference to impending war. Peterborough Foxhound Show was, however, one of its preoccupations – and the subject was raised in critical fashion by the 19th Lord Willoughby de Broke who had succeeded to the title in 1902, and was Master of the Warwickshire from 1900-24.

He questioned whether Peterborough Hound Show was 'a good thing'. His remarks give more than a flavour of the disquiet in some areas of the foxhunting world over the prospect of yet more hound shows, seeking to emulate Peterborough in the regions.

Lord Willoughby told the MFHA annual meeting – as reported in *Horse and Hound* – that

> …in common with a great many other gentlemen present, I view with considerable alarm the tendency to multiply foxhound shows. (Hear, hear)
>
> We have got Peterborough Hound Show, and it is not at all certain that even Peterborough Hound Show is altogether a good thing. (Hear, hear.) We do not want to be ungracious about that, because my father and I have always sent our hounds there, and we have had our share of prizes.
>
> Well, there is Peterborough, and there is Reigate. The idea of Reigate was that it would be valuable for Masters of Foxhounds in the South of England who could not send, owing to the long distance and that kind of thing, their hounds to other parts of the kingdom.
>
> Then the next thing we heard was that a pack of hounds came down from Linlithgow and Stirlingshire to Reigate – I am sure Mr Meldrum [Master of that Hunt] will forgive me saying this – going straight past Peterborough on the way. (Loud laughter.) As this Reigate Show has been patronised, and is under the presidency of a sportsman who has done so much for the south of England, as Lord Leconfield has done, I will not pursue it just now.
>
> But, gentlemen, if this Association thinks that a Foxhound show is undesirable, do not you think that we could come to some decision about it, and express our minds on the subject?
>
> My mind is already made up, and it is that Peterborough and Reigate are quite enough, and perhaps they are a bit too much. (Hear, hear). Then there is Exeter, where some of us I think, want to compete. Now we were told the other day, as well as Peterborough, Reigate and Exeter – and perhaps other places we do not know anything about – that there is going to be another foxhound show for the north of England at Darlington.
>
> My Lord, I do not know what you think about this, but I hope the weight of your opinion as Chairman of this Association will be thrown against any proposal of this kind, the multiplication of foxhound shows, and I think we ought to express our opinion as to the undesirability of extending them.

The MFHA Chairman was the Yorkshire peer, Lord Helmsley, who replied: 'May I say how cordially I agree with Lord Willoughby de Broke. I think it rests largely with Masters of Foxhounds themselves, and that they should not patronise them. I may say there was some proposal a short time ago to have a show at York, and Mr Lane Fox and I and some other Yorkshire members discountenanced it so much that the idea was given up.'

The Chairman was clearly not a hound showing devotee, for he added: 'I cannot help thinking if that course was adopted generally throughout the country, we should not have any more than the two which are already in existence and which I agree with Lord Willoughby de Broke, are two too many already.'

Despite his condemnation of hound shows, the MFHA Chairman carefully avoided putting the matter to a vote. He was probably well aware that the Association had neither the power, nor the will, actively to interfere. The subject was not discussed further at this meeting, the war intervened, and Foxhound shows continued to proliferate. Reigate was to be succeeded by a show at Aldershot, followed later by the South of England Hound Show, nowadays a regular fixture at Ardingly, Sussex. By the 1920s there was a hound show at Colchester, a Fell Foxhound Show at Kirkby Lonsdale, and a Welsh National Hound Show. The modern MFHA has supported and encouraged the current range of shows at Ardingly, Builth, York, Honiton, Lowther and Rydal, but confirms Peterborough is the premier show by publishing its results in each annual edition of the Foxhound Kennel Stud Book.

In the background to the disquiet expressed at the 1914 MFHA meeting were increasing allegations in the sporting press and elsewhere that some Masters were breeding 'only for showing' at Peterborough. This was no doubt grossly exaggerated, and it was probably exacerbated by degrees of jealousy of packs dominating the prize-lists.

New debates would flare up after the war about showing in principle, and the sort of hounds chosen as winners.

WAR-TIME SHUT DOWN

A threat of war was not reflected in Peterborough Foxhound committee's meeting held in April, 1914. It was decided, after representations from the above mentioned Arthur J. Meldrum from Scotland, that in future two entries should be allowed for the champion cups classes, instead of one. There was discussion as to whether huntsmen should continue to be allowed to use 'meat and liver', as well as the traditional biscuit, in showing hounds to best advantage. Cautiously as usual, the committee decided 'it would not be advisable to do anything in the matter.' This subject was to return much later.

It was decided to do nothing about the question of packs showing draft hounds. But there were decisions indicating the show's growing popularity: seats were to be numbered in future, 'light luncheons' were to be provided by a Mrs Barton of Stamford, in addition to the large-scale lunch.

Most impressive, was the decision that the Station Master at Peterborough should be asked to ascertain 'whether a special train could be run from London on the morning of the show.' It was a sign of the amazing flexibility of the Edwardian railway system which already provided special trains for foxhunters to leave London for hunting accompanied by their horses, and allowed whole hunting establishments to attend far-flung meets by rail.

Alas, such pleasant plans for expansion, were to be shelved. At a special committee meeting in October 1914, the show for 1915 was fixed for 7 July, but the following March George Fitzwilliam held another meeting which resolved, in line with the Agricultural Show, that the 1915 fixture had to be abandoned in worsening war conditions. The Society had funds in hand of £156.5s.2d. The Secretary's fee was reduced to 20 guineas with his agreement.

A series of bleak minutes of annual committee meetings throughout the war charted the growing austerity on the home front. Many Hunts continued to operate limited fixtures, although packs were reduced due to shortages of oatmeal, rice and maize. Poultry were raised free-range at that time, lambs were at risk, and the war government officially recognised foxhunting as a practical aid to agriculture in 'controlling vermin', resisting calls from the Food Commission to order the destruction of all hounds. Food shortages for the human population became acute, and there was considerable malnutrition in some industrial areas.

The Foxhound population decreased mainly through smaller entries being bred each year, but thanks to the dedication of those running Hunt establishments few valuable breeding lines were irrevocably lost.

Many more women MFHs were in office, frequently taking over from husbands or brothers in military service. Peterborough Foxhound Show Society made donations to the Red Cross, and allowed the War Agricultural Committee to use its buildings for the storage of farm machinery.

There were tragic gaps among the ranks of Masters of Foxhounds, as among all other areas of society, when the 1918 Armistice arrived on 11 November. Yet there were plenty of returning servicemen in the hunting world who would have welcomed the resumption of Peterborough Foxhound Show in 1919, and the committee decided to go ahead on 9 July, with the Duke of Beaufort as President.

THE RABIES CRISIS

Sadly, the 1919 show was defeated by a new crisis. In May that year George Fitzwilliam as Chairman called a special meeting to give dire news of a 'serious outbreak of rabies'.

The possibility of rabies becoming endemic in British wild-life was a long standing threat to the continuance of all forms of hunting with hounds. It was widely recognised that rabies among British working and domestic dogs would completely alter the way of life of many, since the dread disease was communicable from canines to man, and to foxes and other wild mammals. Hounds were likely to contract the disease from foxes, the main carriers in the wild.

On the continent there were waves of rabies into the west from Eastern Europe, communicated mainly by foxes, at various times throughout the twentieth century, and Britain between the wars imposed stricter quarantine rules for the importation of dogs which have only been somewhat relaxed recently in line with EC regulations. Masters of Hounds have always been sensitive to the risks of rabies crossing the Channel.

Britain's rabies outbreak of 1919 – not specified in the Hound Show minutes – was said to be caused by dogs being smuggled home by servicemen from the continent at the end of the Great War. Prompt action by the authorities stamped it out quickly, and it was not transmitted to wild mammals. The Peterborough committee was absolutely justified in abandoning its show as a precaution, and in support of government action. Hunting in the following season was not restricted by the rabies outbreak, although the sport was to suffer intermittent regional stoppages between the wars, and disastrously later in the postwar years, due to outbreaks of foot and mouth disease in farm animals, especially in the Midlands and parts of the North.

Horse and Hound reported in 1920 'yellows' had been rife, and there had been 'serious losses from distemper in many Hunt kennels' at the end of the war.

Remarkably, the show was never to be halted again for canine disease, although distemper outbreaks remained a problem in Hunt kennels until effective vaccines were developed successfully after the Second World War.

1920 – FIRST SHOW FOR SIX YEARS

The resumption of Peterborough after the Great War was perhaps all the more successful because of the delay to 7 July 1920. New building work was carried out on the judging arena, and seating re-installed. The rabies outbreak had not prevented the 1919 Peterborough Agricultural Show taking place after a five years' gap, attracting an enthusiastic attendance of 20,000.

Eighteen packs entered the 1920 Foxhound show, only four less than in 1914. There was much rejoicing that such an array of hounds was available. *Horse and Hound's* reporter 'Swingletrees' observed: '...it was pretty evident there is no lack of hound meal in some kennels, as in several cases hounds were so full of pudding as to disguise their natural proportions.' This was probably due to packs hunting curtailed seasons in the latter years of the war.

The 9th Duke of Beaufort, President for the year, was in his accustomed place, with vacant chairs either side of him. According to *Horse and Hound* these 'reminded us of the loss we have sustained since we were last assembled in the Peterborough hound pavilion through the deaths of Lord Portman, Mr Fernie, and the Rev. Cecil Legard, among many others.'

Mr George R. Lane-Fox MP, and Mr J.E. Charleton, judged the doghounds. The Duke of Beaufort's won the unentered couples' class with hounds by Belvoir and Fitzwilliam sires. The best unentered single hound was Fitzwilliam Warwick.

The Linlithgow and Stirlingshire, a keen showing pack under Mr Meldrum, came down from Scotland to win the entered doghound class, with the Fernie taking the entered couples class, and the Linlithgow and Stirlingshire captured the stallion hound prize with their third-season Raider by Cheshire Sergeant. Raider was adjudged doghound champion, with Fernie Conqueror reserve.

Colonel H.A. Cartwright and Mr H.E. Preston judged the bitch section, and awarded the unentered couples prize to the North Warwickshire, the entered class to the Atherstone Ringlet, best two couples class to the Fitzwilliam, and the brood bitch class to the Atherstone Ringlet, by Sinbad out of Rosebud who was by North Warwickshire Rallywood. The Duke of Beaufort's Rumour, by Cardinal

The new Peterborough at Eastfield between the wars.

out of Belvoir Russet, won the bitch championship, with the Atherstone Ringlet in reserve. It was noted that leading packs absent from the first postwar show were the Brocklesby, Quorn, Cottesmore, Pytchley, Grafton, and Bicester.

As expected, traditional English breeding, largely from Belvoir sires, still dominated the top placing. The winners were overwhelmingly of traditional English type, and Otho Paget, who wrote as 'Q' in *The Field*, remarked: 'I imagine the crowd at Peterborough would be shocked if any pack were to show a light coloured hound now; but Quorn Dreamer won the Cup in 1890, and he was that colour.'

Massive change in colour and type was on a far horizon – largely due to the influence of an American-born Master of Foxhounds who never showed at Peterbrough.

6. 'PETERBOROUGH TYPE'? – THE GREAT DEBATE

P eterborough's outwardly formal atmosphere, like any contest where opinion matters, masks an array of ambitions and passions. No issue was fought with more heat than the introduction of Welsh outcrosses to the English foxhound between the wars, arising from fierce criticisms of the traditional bred English hound. The 'holy of holies' of the Peterborough show ring was a key element in the evolution of the type which nowadays wins Peterborough championships.

As we have seen in the earlier history of the show, some believed winning at Peterborough had become an end in itself for too many Masters of Foxhounds.

Peterborough winners for the first thirty to forty years were largely influenced by the Duke of Rutland's kennel which did not show. Ironically the Belvoir type was to be overtaken at Peterbough by hounds owing their evolution to a Master of Foxhounds, Mr Isaac (Ikey) Bell, who did not show.

Like all breeding evolution, it was not a simple, overnight change of direction. A group of Masters took part in the early use of Welsh outcrosses in English kennels, but Mr Bell was acknowledged as the instrumental figure in encouraging these changes. They were opposed with emotions ranging from anguish to fury among the conservative core of Masters of Foxhounds.

Ikey Bell, as he was usually known, was an American citizen, born in 1879, who spent his childhood in Paris with his widowed mother. He was sent to school at Harrow, and nurtured a passon for foxhunting. Ikey hunted in the holidays with the Warwickshire, North Warwickshire and Atherstone. He adored his early experiences of hunting and vowed he would hunt a pack of Foxhounds.

While Ikey was cramming for Cambridge entrance, he met Preston Rawnsley, renowned Master of the South Wold, who taught him a great deal about hound pedigrees. After University, the American hunted up to six days a week in the Shires, and visited other packs. He developed an intense interest in hound breeding, and was a disciple of the remarkable Lord Henry Bentinck, Master of the Burton for twenty-two years, 1842-64, who was renowned for breeding superb hunting hounds of an exceptionally athletic, active type, and contributed immensely to lines still existing in modern kennels.

Ikey had charm and wit, and became an amusing and perceptive writer on Foxhunting. He went to Ireland to become Master of the Co. Galway, and the Kilkenny from 1908-21. The new American MFH with a taste for experimentation used Lord Henry Bentinck's breeding in the Kilkenny kennel, and crucially introduced blood from the white hounds of the Curre where Sir Edward Curre, Master of his family pack at Itton, Montgomeryshire, from 1896-1930, earned a

Ikey Bell MFH, campaigner for the modern Foxhound, hunting hounds in Ireland.

great reputation as 'perhaps the greatest hound expert of the lot', according to Ronnie Wallace.

Sir Edward studied genetics and used selective breeding to produce active hounds, comparatively light of bone, crossing Berkeley with the best Welsh lines available, and breeding out to badger-pied strains at Badminton and Fitzwilliam (Milton). The Curre hounds were increasingly recognised for their marvellous working qualities.

From 1925, at the age of forty-six, Ikey Bell took the South and West Wilts Mastership where he continued his breeding policy started in Ireland. He took hounds from Kilkenny and purchased more from the Rugby Hound Sales, spending up to £1,000 a

Craven Vagabond (1893), Peterborough doghound champion in 1894 – sire of Duhallow Venturer, a stallion hound for Ikey Bell during his Kilkenny Mastership (1908-21).

An old print of Warwickshire Wizard ('05), doghound champion in 1906, an example of 'bone and substance' which some Masters sought to change, amid much controversy.

year, a great deal of money in the 1920s. He used more Welsh-cross hounds from the Brecon and the Carmarthenshire*. Most important of all, the 'new-look' South and Wilts hounds were credited with producing excellent sport, and younger Masters began to take far more interest in Ikey's breeding policies. His sociability, and his skills as a communicator with his pen helped greatly to spread his gospel, notably his book *A Huntsman's Log-Book* (1947). He became firm friends of the Duke of Beaufort, Sir Peter Farquhar and others who were willing to experiment in hound breeding to produce packs which hunted in a style they liked. They frequently referred to a hound's need to have 'fox sense', to run with the pack, but to show individual initiative in finding foxes – and above all to ensure that a hunt had a 'beginning, a middle and an end', resulting in the fox being killed by the pack above ground, or accurately marked to ground. These Masters abhorred the 'mystery tour' hunt in which huntsman and hounds galloped furiously about the countryside in runs which seemed to have no noticeable conclusion, the fox all too often being referred to as 'lost'.

Belvoir, 'pure' English breeding, continued to dominate Peterborough top placings in between the wars. The great nineteenth century Belvoir hounds Rallywood, Weathergate and Gambler, were by later Peterborough standards, small hounds at 23 inches; by 1900 hounds winning at Peterborough were nearer 25 inches. According to Daphne Moore, leading writer on Foxhound breeding after the second war, and an ardent disciple of the 10th Duke of Beaufort's breeding:

> The fashionable foxhound of the day (1900 to 1920s) was a massive animal with
> exaggerated bone, round 'cat-feet' which were anything but hard-wearing, and a general

*Famous Foxhunters, Daphne Moore, 1978.

lack of speed and activity which must have given great satisfaction to the foxes. Lord Henry Bentinck, whose skill as a Foxhound breeder Ikey greatly admired, regarded excessive bone as 'a useless appendage' and enquired if a hound had ever been known to break a leg through lack of it?

Though Ikey Bell met with violent opposition to his views which were like a red rag to a bull to the die-hards, he steadfastly refused to be ruled by foolish fashion and remained firm in his determination to breed a Foxhound more suitable for the purpose for which it was intended – namely, to hunt the fox.

Ikey Bell recalled after using the Curre hounds: 'Many Masters criticised me at the time, some actually declaring me to be "a menace to Foxhounds!" Many of these critics in years to come, bred to these lines, which certainly much amused me.'

He summed up what he believed to be the virtues of Welsh-cross hounds: 'Their necks and shoulders are generally very good, they hunt low on a weak scent, are remarkably perservering, try hard at a check, and continue to try under all circumstances. When cast for long distances, they continue to concentrate and do not suddenly get their heads up like many pure-bred hounds I have seen.'

With the benefit of hindsight, the condemnation of the traditional English hound seems excessive, but the critics were certain they were justified. The debate was trenchantly expressed in the sporting press, adding considerably to the heat of the dispute within foxhunting circles. Captain Charlie McNeill, Master of the North Cotswold (1901-6) and the Grafton (1907-13) wrote to *The Field*, complaining that if the best Belvoir stallion hounds sired as many litters as they were shown to have achieved in the stud book, they could not have done much hunting.

There was an angry response from others who said it was an impertinence to attack another Master's management of his kennels, and the Belvoir was performing a kindness in allowing bitches to be sent to their sires. Captain McNeill retorted that the Belvoir was a national institution, that hound breeding was of national importance, and therefore he was thoroughly justified in raising the matter. The debate wrangled on for some weeks, but of course reached no conclusion.

Otho Paget, one of the most perceptive hunting correspondents, commented more temperately: 'Belvoir blood, which had always been appreciated by other kennels, became in such demand that the stallion hounds were used rather too freely.'

In Leicestershire there was criticism from some that the Belvoir doghound pack was not performing at its best, and some 'experts' joined in the criticism with the futile remark that perhaps this was because they were doing too much work at stud!

Peterborough judges were conditioned to judging the old English type, and could only decide on the hounds exhibited. In the years following the Great War, large hounds of substance in Belvoir tan were still predominant. The Belvoir pack saw some change when it was hunted for the first time by an amateur huntsman, but on the Lincolnshire side only. He was the devoted foxhunter Major Tommy Bouch, Joint Master from 1912-24, who was a bold rider and an effective huntsman, receptive to modern hound breeding trends. 'Tommy didn't give a damn for appearances, but was all for sport', wrote Guy Paget*.

Bouch, who judged at Peterborough, tried discreetly introducing an out-cross into the Belvoir kennel, probably from the Curre, but it was reported to the ducal owner of the pack, and firmly eradicated.

The 10th Duke who succeeded to the title in 1940, recalled the outrage caused by the attempt 'to introduce an element of white Welsh hound into the breeding.' 'This caused great offence and immediately changed,' the Duke wrote in a booklet on the Hunt.

Bouch during his twelve years in office selectively reduced the substance of Belvoir hounds by using English lines available, producing more active looking hounds of somewhat less bone. They exhibited the English hound's virtues of drive and pugnacity, and produced excellent sport, especially in the 1930s under the Mastership of the second Lord (Toby) Daresbury.

The Belvoir's influence remained remarkably strong throughout the 1920s. The 1925 puppy show at Belvoir Castle was described in fulsome terms in *Horse and Hound*. The Duke of Rutland's kennel was 'the acknowledged purest source of foxhound blood,' said the report. The kennel was described as being 'of national importance to the future of foxhunting'.

Colonel R. Clayton Swann, ex-Master of the Morpeth, Sinnington and Blankney, was quoted as saying he travelled about the country a great deal judging hounds, and had seen a large number, but wherever he went he 'never saw anything like the Belvoir. They eclipsed anything in England.'

Some of the shine must have been taken off the occasion, however, when one of the judges, Willie Wroughton, ex-Master of the Pytchley, said of the entry 'he considered it very fair, but not up to the best Belvoir form.'

Several hundred of the hunting fraternity flocked from all over England to the 1925 Belvoir puppy show. The extraordinary swing in foxhound breeding and judging standards began to take some effect in the 1930s, accelerating greatly after the war, and resulting in 'pure' English breeding on Belvoir lines being confined to only a handful of kennels in the post-war years. All this was to be reflected at Peterborough where the main battleground for championship honours was to be fought out by the 'green coats', the Duke of Beaufort's and the Heythrop, both showing hounds of modern conformation – and mainly judged by a new generation of Masters of Foxhounds who believed firmly in the value of this change.

Despite the dramatic changes in Foxhound breeding elsewhere, the Belvoir's English pack continued to attract large mounted fields throughout the twentieth century. Belvoir Saturdays in the famous Vale were magnets for keen foxhunters from far and wide. The author was a subscriber and keen follower of the Belvoir for over twenty years from 1973, and can attest to the exciting, thoroughly enjoyable sport which the Belvoir achieved consistently with their pure English hounds, entertaining exceptionally hard-riding fields, hunted successively by Jim Webster, Robin Jackson, and Martin Thornton, their current huntsman.

*Bad 'Uns to Beat, Guy Paget, 1936.

An influential gathering of Masters and huntsmen at the Belvoir Puppy Show 1930,
representing both sides of the controversy of Old English versus new Welsh-cross Foxhounds.

STANDING: *W. Wilson, H. Lord (Blankney), Tom Down (Earl of Harrington's), Mr C. Hilton*
Green MFH (Meynell), Captain Hodgkinson MFH (Mendip), Lt.Colonel Lockett, Fred
Holland (Old Berks.) George Barker (Quorn), George Tongue (Belvoir), Will Morris
(Berkeley), and Tom Newman (Duke of Beaufort's).
SEATED: *Mr Ikey Bell MFH (S. and W. Wilts), the Duke of Beaufort MFH, Countess of*
Harrington MFH, Colonel F.G.D.Colman and Mr C.F. Tonge MFH (Belvoir), HRH the Duke
of Gloucester, Lord Conyers, and Captain F. Horton.

The modern Belvoir pack continues to exhibit great drive, running up
together remarkably well, and they are certainly good fox-catchers. The 'mystery
tour' accusation did not apply to the Belvoir pack which the author followed with
much pleasure, whilst at the same time having plenty of opportunity to compare
it with modern hounds also producing excellent sport.

The conclusion of the author as a widely travelled hunting correspondent –
visiting over 220 packs – is that although breeding and selection of the pack is
important, the handling of hounds by a huntsman, like the riding of a horse by a
consummate horseman, is the most crucial factor in maintaining consistent sport.
Hounds bred by Ronnie Wallace, but hunted by an inferior huntsman, were seen

to hunt well below the standards of the great Master of the Heythrop and Exmoor.

In the inter-war years, the evolution of the hound was mainly 'off-stage'. Lt. Colonel Sir Peter Farquhar, pre-war Master of the Meynell (1931-34) and Whaddon Chase (1934-38) and of the Portman post-war (1947-59), is credited with having the most influence on Foxhound breeding in the twentieth century. He was scathing in his analysis of the early problems of Foxhounds in an article in the early 1970s for *Horse and Hound*:

Towards the end of the nineteenth century and up to the 1914-18 war, there came a very sad period in the history of the Foxhound. Their breeding got into the hands of a few influential Masters who did not hunt their own hounds, but bred for fashion and the show ring. They created what was later to be known as the

Captain Ian Farquhar's father, the late Sir Peter Farquhar, a leading architect of modern Foxhound breeding, with Mrs Douglas-Pennant MFH, Master and huntsman of the Dartmoor (1946-55).

'Peterborough type'. They wanted a hound to be very big, very wide through the chest, which of course put the elbows out, and to have tremendous bone. Above all, he had to be plumb straight, which involved a short, rigid pastern, which nature intended to be supple so as to act as a shock absorber; with knuckling over knees and tight cat-feet all the stress came on the two front pads, the other three being off the ground. Such hounds were nothing more nor less than cripples; they could not gallop nor had they much inclination to hunt. The unfortunate Hunt servants had to do all the hounds' work for them, which is why galloping about all over the countryside, interpreted as brilliant casts, became the normal practice in fashionable countries. A few English packs, notably perhaps the Heythrop, Berkeley and Brocklesby, resisted this fashion, but of course their breeding policy became very limited and difficult. But there were none of these inhibitions in the Fell countries, nor in Wales.

Sir Peter Farquhar's son, Captain Ian Farquhar, Joint Master of the Duke of

Beaufort's since 1985, says his father remembered that 'between the wars, the dispute over hound breeding got so acute that at Peterborough, the faction supporting old English hound breeding sat on one side of the ring, glaring at the Masters sitting on the other side who supported using Welsh outcrosses...' Martin Scott, whose father Major Bill Scott was an apostle of Welsh-outcrosses before the war, says in London's club-land some Masters would cross to the other side of the street to avoid their opponents on the hound breeding issue.

One of the leaders of the traditionalists in hound breeding was the 7th Earl Bathurst, Master of the VWH, who was outraged by Welsh out-crosses. The hunting correspondent of *The Times* fuelled the flames by describing the English foxhound as 'as slow as the Durham Ox'. Among those who took him to task were the formidable Lord Leconfield, Master of his own pack in Sussex, and some of the Brassey family in the Heythrop country.

When Ikey Bell retired from the South and West Wilts Mastership in 1932, Lord Bathurst wrote: 'He has done no end of harm. Now that he has gone I hope that this propaganda will cease, and in time they will breed out the Welsh – the little sharp bitches that he likes will cure themselves by killing rats.'*

Sir Peter Farquhar paid great tribute to Ikey Bell's influence, and also that of Sir Edward Curre, Mr Jack Evans, Master of the Brecon, Lord Coventry at Carmarthen and Mr David Davies who hunted his own private pack.

Sir Peter recalled: 'By great good fortune, their hounds were entered in the Foxhound Kennel Stud Book which enabled us to use them, as well as numerous top-class stallion hounds from the South and West Wilts, without being completely ostracised; although many of the old guard believed we were ruining the Foxhound and said so – loud and clear!'

The conservative element struck back in 1928 when a committee of the MFHA, chaired by Lord Bathurst, decided to 'close' the Foxhound Kennel Stud Book to hounds not bred, entered and worked in recognised Foxhound kennels; or both their grandsires and both their grand-dams must have been registered in the FKSB. This excluded Welsh packs not registered with the MFHA and others, including Fell packs. Much concern was expressed that the trend towards using Welsh sires was already too much of a threat to traditional English Foxhound breeding.

After the war there was more debate about outcrosses within the MFHA, and thanks mainly to the influence of the Duke of Beaufort, Sir Peter Farquhar and Maurice Barclay of the Puckeridge, the Stud Book was opened in 1955. The MFHA ruled it was only necessary to prove that hounds had pedigrees going back five generations, later increased to six, to ancestors kept for hunting only the fox, and that they came from established packs of Foxhounds which had been hunting the fox only for at least ten years.

An accurate five generation pedigree would have to be produced, and Welsh hounds accepted only if approved by the Welsh Hound Association. All entries for the Stud Book had to be approved by the Committee of the MFH Association. Outcrosses from non-registered packs were entered in a section at the back of

*Ronnie Wallace – the Authorised Version, Robin Rhoderick-Jones, 1992.

The late 10th Duke of Beaufort at Peterborough with, right, Lord Bingley MFH (Bramham Moor).

the Stud Book. Fell Hound, Harrier, and American, outcross sires as well as pure Welsh are entered here in the modern Stud Book, indicating just how far the pendulum has swung from 'pure' English.

'Master', the 10th Duke of Beaufort, became one of Sir Peter Farquhar's closest friends. At first Master was cautious about changing the traditionally bred pack of large hounds he had inherited on succeeding to the dukedom in 1924. He had hunted a pack of smaller bitches as the Marquess of Worcester since the age of twenty before succeeding as Master of the remarkable family pack at Badminton, and he was to become the leading amateur huntsman, hound breeder, and head of the hunting community for most of the twentieth century.

After his accession to the Mastership he gradually set about breeding a lighter-framed, more active type of hounds. His first entry in 1925, was exclusively by home-bred sires; the next year saw the progeny of Berkeley Waggoner ('22), one of which, Wagtail ('26), became a notable foxhound and brood bitch, producing two Peterborough Doghound Champions.

Ian Farquhar says: 'My father said Master took a bit of persuading at first, but eventually he "crossed the floor" at Peterborough and supported the others involved in modern hound breeding. It helped a lot in healing the breach.'

It was by no means entirely Welsh blood which altered the shape of the English Foxhound. Through Ikey Bell, Master heard of a dog down in the West Country making a name for himself who might prove to be a useful outcross sire. He went down to see the hound, the famous Tiverton Actor ('22), and the Master, Sir Ian Amory, loaned him to Badminton for the 1928-29 season. Tiverton Actor had not a drop of Welsh blood, but he was a light-coated, almost pure white hound, who was to bequeath this colouring to many of his progeny. Master, having hunted Actor, knew he was good in his work.

Tiverton Actor carried the best Berkeley blood of the previous century, and revived a nearly extinct male line of Brocklesby Drunkard, 1748. Described as a very symmetrical, well balanced hound fully of quality, Actor produced a lasting male line which has contributed to many Foxhound kennels throughout Britain*. His grandsons, Autocraft ('32) and Fencer ('32) were probably the first light-coloured hounds to win championships at Peterborough since Milton Rector ('07) in 1910.

Sir Peter wrote that after the Second World War 'on the credit side I was delighted to find that the sometimes rather bitter Welsh-cross controversy was dead. Post-war Masters just wanted to breed the type of hound most suited to showing sport, and catching foxes in their particular countries. And catching foxes, which had previously only mattered much to hounds and huntsman, now became a valid justification for foxhunting.'

A reminder that not everyone felt the pre-war controversy had expired, was soon conveyed by a former long serving professional huntsman of pre-war years who wrote to *Horse and Hound* under the nom-de-plume 'Old Time Hunt Servant', declaring that criticisms of the 'old fashioned Foxhound' were unjust. He wrote:

> When I see some of today's prize winners I see them as the real 'cripple' – not their old-fashioned predecessors. Too often, the present-day hound is crooked back he knee, with feet like an Alsatian and hocks back in the next parish...Most old-fashioned hounds are straight, and may stand over rather than back, with their hocks in under them.
>
> Their cat-like feet will stand up to the wear and tear a damn sight better than the flat-footed, back at the knee specimens we see so much of today...For goodness sake, Masters and judges, come away from these Greyhound-Alsatian types that are so fashionable today...Your contributor's description of the Peterborough type simply is not true. They were not wide through the chest, big and out at elbow, and knuckled over on short pasterns. To say that they could not gallop, and had not much inclination to hunt is totally false, and I am surprised to read such a misrepresentation.

Lord (Toby) Daresbury, who took English hounds from the Belvoir to hunt the Limerick country with much success in post-war Ireland, remained a life-long opponent of the 'modern hound'. He used to claim they were 'self-hunting', far too inclined to 'beagle about' instead of running together in a pack, and that their conformation had a poor underline, without enough room for heart and lungs. The high standards of sport Toby Daresbury's pack produced over the huge banks and ditches of Limerick showed the Old English type as versatile and effective over a country far different to the Engish Shires where the breed had won its original reputation.

The background to the Foxhound breeding revolution is worth recounting not only because of its impact on the type of hounds shown at Peterborough. More importantly, the change had a major impact on the type of hounds which a great many non-showing packs were to use in the hunting field until this day.

The Book of the Foxhound, Daphne Moore.

LEFT:
Pytchley Potentate ('96), doghound champion in 1900 – an example of the Old English heavier type in this kennel until Frank Freeman became huntsman from 1906-31.

BELOW:
Tiverton Actor ('22), used extensively as a highly influential sire in the Duke of Beaufort's kennel.

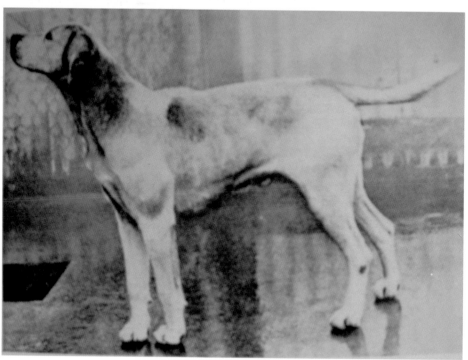

But there is nothing better than controversy to increase interest in the show-ring – and throughout the twentieth century Peterborough was to see plenty of controversy bubbling under its polite surface, all helping to ensure that it remained the summit of Foxhound shows.

RIGHT:
Belvoir Dexter (1895) one of the highly popular doghounds in the Belvoir kennel, used widely in other kennels throughout Britain.

BELOW:
Belvoir Primrose, a winner at the Belvoir puppy show in 1988 – still Old English in Belvoir Tan colour, but of the lighter type in the kennel today.

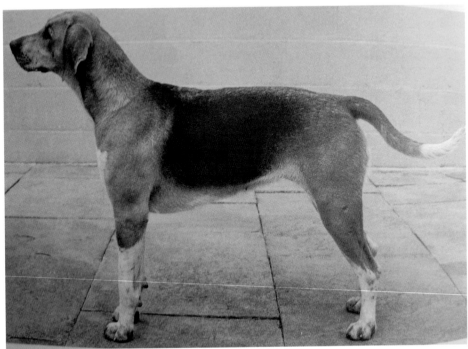

7. THE INTER-WAR YEARS

A notable achievement was begun in 1921 when the North Warwickshire Rally ('17) won the bitch championship as the start of a hat-trick – capturing the same prize again in 1922 and '23. She was a handsome, well balanced hound, but plumb straight in the old English mould, and she met the judging requirements of the day.

Peterborough made the sensible rule in 1924 that no winner of any class could be shown again in the same class, a rule followed by other leading hound shows. It was also ruled that all hounds must be bred by the present Master or his predecessors, thereby ensuring draft hounds could not be shown.

North Warwickshire Rally ('17) triple winner of Peterborought's bitch championshiip – in 1921-22-23. This feat is not possible under modern rules.

It is possible North Warwickshire Rally's triple championship victories reflected somewhat poorly on the standard of hounds before the judges at that time. There had been serious stoppages to foxhunting in 1921 due to outbreaks of foot and mouth disease in the Midlands and elsewhere, and this may have affected Peterborough entries. In the 1921 show the number of Hunts dropped to fifteen, although four packs had not appeared for many years previously: the

Lauderdale, Lord Portman's, Major Smith Bosanquet's and the South Durham. The Fernie won the 1921 doghound championship with their Conqueror ('17), but did not appear again in the championships lists between the wars.

The Rev. E.A. Milne, known to generations of Dorset foxhunters as Parson Milne, scored a triumph when his Cattistock David ('20) won the doghound championship in 1922. Milne was Master and huntsman of the Cattistock from 1900 to 1931. His Joint Master from 1930, remaining in office until 1939, was the American MFH Henry Higginson. He wrote excellent hunting books, including *The Meynell of the West*, the story of the Master of 'all Dorset', J.J. Farquharson.

Higginson was keen on hound showing, and wrote to the Peterborough committee from Lincoln, Mass., asking if he could bring hounds over from the US to compete at the 1914 show. After further correspondence, the committee decided they could not agree to entries from any overseas packs because 'it would place this show outside the jurisdiction of the MFHA.'

It was agreed by the committee in 1922 'that American Masters should be invited to attend the show in July next'. This helped to forge an Anglo-American link which has flourished until today.

There have been many trans-Atlantic visitors to Peterborough, and in 1946, the first show after the war, Henry Higginson was the first American to judge there. He had just retired as Joint Master of the South Dorset at the age of seventy, and on 10 July appeared in the ring at Peterborough, achieving a long held ambition, forty years after his first visit to the show as the guest of George Fitzwilliam. His co-judge in the doghound section was Major Gordon Foster, Master of the Sinnington.

Higginson was amazed to find himself judging hounds from thirty-three packs, and remarked in his memoirs: 'I have judged a good many hound shows in my day, in America of course, and several puppy shows over here, but never before have I been faced with such classes. There were over thirty unentered doghounds before us in the first class, and I confess I was very glad I had an experienced old hand like Major Foster with me.'

The second American judge to appear in the Peterborough ring was Mr C. Martin Wood, Master of the Live Oak pack, Florida, in 2001 (Chapter 9).

Frequent post-war links between US and British hound breeding added much to American interest in Peterborough as the world's premier show. Small decisions mattered too: Peterborough committee minutes of 1922 found room to record: '...at last year's show a mackintosh had been left which had not been claimed. It was resolved that if same was not claimed at this year's show it should be sold for the New Infirmary.'

A weightier decision in 1922 allowed that substitutions of entries would be allowed 'for any cause whatever', provided notice was given in writing by 30 June; the exceptions were classes one and five, for unentered hounds. A further sign of progress in these minutes was a resolution demanding that in future entrants should give the dates of sire, dam and dam's sire.

A Vice-President's subscription in 1922 was £3, and admittance was five shillings 'at the front gate', and two shillings and sixpence 'at the back gate', including entertainment tax. The back gate spectators occupied the upper rows, the front gate were in the middle rows and the Vice-Presidents in the reserved front rows. Early in the 1920s the show was operating on an overdraft due to postwar renovations and building works. The subscription was reduced to two guineas from 1924.

The major news in 1922 was that the Prince of Wales was to be invited to be President the following year, and would attend the show. The future Edward VIII, briefly a King before his abdication, began riding to hounds in the Shires in 1923, taking a suite at Craven Lodge, Melton Mowbray. He became immensely popular in Leicestershire and admired for his bold riding across country; he clearly liked all aspects of foxhunting.

A sign of the times – which saw the growing emancipation of women – was a committee decision that the names of 'Lady Vice-Presidents' be placed on the prize schedule in future – and the committee decided to spend £64 on two ladies' lavatories before the 1923 show.

The Prince had lunch in the Agricultural Show tent, and visited the Foxhound pavilion as President, watching the judging with great interest, attended by the Chairman, George Fitzwilliam, and other leading Masters. It was a great year for the North Warwickshire, whose Master was Mr J.P. Arkwright (in office 1920-29). He received both championship trophies, with the above mentioned Rally ('20) winning the bitch championship, and Lifeguard ('22) taking the doghound prize. The doghound judges were George Evans and Nigel Baring; the bitches were judged by Willie Wroughton, former Master of the Pytchley, and Mr W.E Paget MFH.

There were twenty-nine packs represented, no doubt encouraged by the royal presidency, and they included ten newcomers: Badsworth, Blackmore Vale, Cleveland, Croome, Dumfriesshire, Fitzwilliam (Grove), Holderness, South Dorset, West Kent and Zetland. The Cleveland and Zetland had appeared last in 1914.

While North Warwickshire Rally scored her third win as bitch champion in 1914, the doghound championship went to the South Staffs Denmark ('22).

The Prince of Wales, the future Edward VIII, in a Cuthbert Bradley illustration, is shown presenting a championship Cup at the 1923 show when the North Warwickshire won both championships.

Horse and Hound reported the 1925 show took place in 'continued glorious weather', with twenty-one packs participating. Belvoir sires were still succeeding: the Duke of Beaufort's Rustic ('23) winner of the doghound championship, was sired by Belvoir Wicklow ('16). Rustic was part of the two couples group placed second, and went on to win the stallion hound class before the championship.

The bitch championship went to Cleveland Tempest, a two season bitch by a Morpeth sire, who won the brood bitch class. She was praised for her 'balance and symmetry'.

WELSH TRIUMPH AT LAST

During the 1930s the Duke of Beaufort's kennel began to dominate championship placings at Peterborough in a manner which influenced Foxhound breeding widely. Their large type of hound with quality and activity became increasingly popular, and encouraged other Masters to follow Badminton when the Duke was seen to be using judiciously infusions of Welsh outcross blood. Badminton's ascendancy was signalled by the double triumph of 1932 (see Chapter 6) when his Autocrat ('32) and Peerless ('31) won the doghound and bitch championships respectively.

Colonel W.H.A. Wharton, whose family were long associated with the Cleveland, was Master from 1932-39, and achieved further lustre in 1933 when the Cleveland won the doghound championship with their Ranger ('31), the Rufford taking the bitch prize with Hebe ('30).

In 1934 the Duke of Beaufort's achieved another double championship, with Fencer ('32) and Pamela ('32). The following year the Duke won the doghound class with his Chaser ('30).

The HH won the 1935 bitch championship, plus the brood bitch class, with their Rarity ('33) – a victory with historic significance. It was the first evidence that a hound with Welsh outcross breeding could win a championship on the hallowed flags of Peterborough. Rarity had, in addition to a line to Mr Curre's Wonder ('08), another to Ystrad Watchman ('04).

Who were the open-minded judges prepared to award a bitch championship to a hound of Welsh lineage? None other than Master, the Duke of Beaufort, accompanied by Viscount Knutsford, Master of the VWH, one of the great characters of the foxhunting world, who in postwar years was to be known affectionately as 'Lordy' to generations of Whaddon Chase followers.

Welsh outcross breeding in hounds had already appeared in the morning when the Duke was not judging, and therefore able to show his hounds. Sir Harold Nutting and Colonel Lowther, prominent Shires Masters respectively of the Quorn and Pytchley, selected the Duke of Beaufort's Pelican ('35) as one of his winning couples of young doghounds. Pelican's dam, Petrel ('32), was a Brecon-bred bitch, full of the best Welsh strains intermixed with finest English blood, indeed her tail-female traces through generations of impeccable Brocklesby to their Cloudy (c.1743).

The following year, 1936, Pelican won Peterborough's doghound championship. The Welsh cross enthusiasts were elated. Here, at last, was recognition!*

* The Book of the Foxhound, Daphne Moore.

Duke of Beaufort's Pelican ('35), broke new ground as 1936 doghound champion containing Welsh breeding from the Brecon kennel.

As Badminton's indefatigable Foxhound scribe, Daphne Moore, pointed out, the Duke of Beaufort's kennel won the last bitch championship before the 1914-18 war, and the first after hostilities ended. By strange coincidence, the same happened before and after the Second World War: the Duke's pack from Badminton won the 1939 doghound championship with Darnley ('37), and the first after the war, in 1946, with Landsman ('45).

PETERBOROUGH BECOMES ROYAL

The 1932 show was notable for the presence of Their Royal Highnesses, the Duke and Duchess of York, the future King George VI and Queen Elizabeth. They were guests at the home of Lord Burghley, the future 6th Marquess of Exeter, heir to Burghley House and estates at Stamford, and one of foxhunting's most remarkable personalities. Born in 1905, he was a superlative sportsman of great charm and ability who won fame for his Olympic gold medal as a hurdler at the Amsterdam Olympics in 1928, celebrated in the film *Chariots of Fire*. He was often Field Master for the Fitzwilliam, and was Master and huntsman of his own pack at Burghley from 1935-9.

Thereafter he was Master of the East Sussex (1939-53) and the Old Berks (1957-66). He succeeded to the title in 1965, and founded Burghley Horse Trials at his historic home at Stamford. No better representative of foxhunting could have been found to escort the royal couple on this visit. The royal couple arrived

Their Royal Highnesses, the Duke and Duchess of York, the future King George VI and Queen Elizabeth, visiting Peterborough in 1932, with LEFT TO RIGHT *Mr W. Hemmant, Chief Steward: Mr I. Whitsed, Chairman, Peterborough Agricultural Society, and Mr Edmund Beck, Vice-Chairman.*

at the Foxhound Show at 11 a.m. and watched the judging for an hour before walking to the main luncheon tent of the Agricultural Show. After lunch, Lord Burghley proposed an eloquent toast to Peterborough Foxhound Show and Peterborough Agricultural Show, and there was a response from the Duke of York who was not fond of public speaking, due to his speech impediment, but was clearly at ease in this gathering.

The future King was a keen foxhunter, riding to hounds regularly with the Pytchley, over their formidable country. After their marriage in 1923, the Duke and Duchess took a hunting box at Naseby Woollies in the Pytchley country for some years. The Duke gave up hunting in the Shires on the 'advice' of his father, King George V, during the economic depression of the mid-1930s. Lionel Edwards painted Princess Elizabeth, the future Queen Elizabeth II, being led on a pony by her mother as Duchess of York, at the covertside when Frank Freeman was hunting hounds on his last day in 1931.

Since the 1932 visit, Peterborough enjoyed a long series of royal connections which have remained constant until the present-day. The committee received a letter from the Duke of York's secretary expressing particular satisfaction with his visit.

In 1933 the show updated its rules and constitution, on the advice of its shrewd accountant/secretary, Mr Stephenson, who pointed out various income tax advantages to be gained. At a meeting in September 1934 Mr Stephenson's office, the Finance and General purposes Committee approved a new draft constitution and rules, and there was another highly significant decision: '...it was resolved to recommend to the General Committee that the name of the Society should be altered to the Royal Peterborough Foxhound Show Society, if the necessary permission could be obtained from H.M. the King.'

The new 1934 constitution of the Society concluded with the announcement:

> Since the foregoing Constitution and Rules were passed by the Committee on the 15th day of October, 1934, H.M. The King has been graciously pleased to Command under date 5th November, 1934, that the Show shall henceforth be known as the Peterborough Royal Foxhound Show Society.

The change in the order of words from those recommended by the Finance and General Purposes committee should be noted. The title granted by the monarch placed the 'Royal' *after* the word Peterborough. This was almost certainly a condition made by royal advisors, to ensure there could be no misapprehension that the royal prefix had been granted to the city of Peterborough, but specifically to the Foxhound Show. Future generations of young foxhunters would have to be careful not to betray their ignorance by referring to the show as the 'Royal Peterborough'!

The 1934 Constitution and Rules listed a Vice-President's subscription as £1.10s.0d. Owners or Masters of Hounds subscribing this sum could enter all classes free of charge. Every huntsman in charge of hounds, not receiving a prize, would be presented with a £2 gratuity, and luncheon would be provided for all huntsmen and whippers-in.

The rules stated 'everyone showing hound in the ring must be dressed in proper hunting clothes (without spurs)'. All hounds shown had to bred by the exhibitor or his predecessors, and must be entered in, or eligible for entry in the Foxhound Kennel Stud book.

Under the Presidency of the Earl of Lindsay, the top dozen or so of the 1934 President's list certainly emphased foxhunting's links with the aristocracy. The remainder of the lengthy all-male list included many Masters without titles, although a great many military ranks were arrayed which was hardly surprising soon after the Great War. Leading the list were: HRH the Prince of Wales, the Duke of Beaufort, Marquess of Titchfield, Earl Bathurst, Earl of Dalkeith, Earl Fitzwilliam, Earl of Rosebery, Earl of Yarborough, Viscount Cobham, Viscount Milton, Viscount Mountgarret, and Viscount Portman.

A much shorter list of lady Vice-Presidents was headed by the Marchioness of Bute, the Hon. Anne Lewis, Mrs J.P. Arkwright, Miss D.L. Brackenbury, Mrs W. Hall, Miss R.M. Harrison, Mrs L. Lillingston, Miss M. Lubbock, Mrs A. Simmons and Miss A. Usher. The significance of these ladies at the top of the list was that they were Masters of Foxhounds, the first sizeable group of lady MFHs in the history of the sport, to be followed postwar by a huge increase in female Masterships.

While it was willing to produce a constitution and seek a royal pre-fix, the pre-war Peterborough committee was still highly nervous of such innovations as a microphone and loudspeaker. The show had quite enough trouble with the old fashioned method of shouting names from within the ring to the spectators around it. Back in 1913 they had instituted the fashion of a steward 'calling' the names of hounds. There were subsequent complaints from some Masters that a certain steward had called the names 'too loudly', and had frightened their hounds, causing them not to show themselves properly, a sure way of losing a prize. The committee stood firm in the face of this problem, and the 'calling' of hound names continued.

In 1935 the committee further emphasised its determination to preserve the Royal Foxhound Show's non-commercial character: a businessman wrote asking if they would be prepared to accept advertisements in the catalogue. The minutes noted bluntly: 'It was resolved that this application could not be entertained.'

After the 1932 royal visit the subject of a loud-speaker was raised again, but clearly it was still considered too daring in view of the risks of upsetting hounds, and it was deferred still further – until well after the Second War.

In 1936 Peterborough's general committee met in January to note officially their grievous loss in the death of George Fitzwilliam, their staunch chairman, and Master of the Fitzwilliam (Milton) pack for forty years. He was greatly admired and liked by many in the hunting community, and he had supported the Foxhound Show through the difficult inter-war years when England was beset with considerable change, and severe economic depression hit farming as well industrial cities.

No family was more deeply involved in foxhunting. The 7th Earl, on succeeding his grandfather in 1902, not only took over the Wentworth hounds in Yorkshire, but in 1904 he became Master of the Island country in Ireland, forming a new pack. Five seasons later, on the resignation of Lord Galway, Lord Fitzwilliam assumed command of the Grove country, known at that time as the Fitzwilliam (Grove). Thus the Fitzwilliam family were running four separate packs – three owned by Lord Fitzwilliam, and the Milton owned by his cousin George Fitzwilliam.*

Ralph Greaves recorded that between the wars the Fitzwilliam hounds continued to be bred on traditional Milton lines, with fusions from Badminton, Warwickshire and a few other kennels, and frequent recourse to Brocklesby. Unlike the early years of the show, the Fitzwilliam (Milton), retaining traditional breeding policies, did not figure in the championship results after 1914, nor in the early postwar years when 'modern' hound breeding began to hold sway. The Fitzwilliam family remained crucial to the late twentieth century survival and development of the great show they had helped to found. Their famous pack at Milton was regularly entered in the great annual show they had made possible, and figured frequently in prizes awarded for classes below the championship.

The 5th Marquess of Exeter, father of Lord Burghley, succeeded as Chairman of the Royal Foxhound Show in 1936, at the meeting on 21 January, and referred first to the death of King George V which had occurred only a few hours earlier. Then the meeting expressed sorrow at the passing of George Fitzwilliam.

*Foxhunting in Northamptonshire, Ralph Greaves.

The Marquess of Exeter, right, Chairman of the Royal Foxhound Show Society from 1936, talking to Show Secretary for fifty-two years, Mr Joseph Stephenson.

After a ballot, George Fitzwilliam's son, Tom Fitzwilliam, was elected to the new position of Vice-Chairman. This proved a vital appointment: 'Captain Tom' as he became known to many after the war, was to play a key role in the future of the show, and the preservation of Milton and the Fitzwilliam Hunt in the postwar years. (The 7th Earl died in 1942 and was succeeded by his son, Lord Milton. The 8th Earl died in a flying accident in 1948, and was succeeded as 9th Earl by his cousin, Eric Fitzwilliam, who died in 1951, whereupon Captain Tom Fitzwilliam, Master of Milton, became the 10th and last Earl Fitzwilliam.)

In 1938, the fifty-sixth show was honoured when HRH the Duke of Gloucester, another keen foxhunter in the royal family, agreed to be President, and presented the doghound champion cup.

The 7th Earl Fitzwilliam, one of the great foxhunters of the twentieth century, proved especially appropriate as President of the 1939 Foxhound Show since he could never attend another. Captain T. Wickham Boynton MFH and the Hon. Guy Cubitt judged the doghounds, and the Rev. E.A. Milne from the Cattistock, and Lord Grimthorpe MFH, judged the bitches.

The Duke and Duchess of Gloucester leaving the Royal Foxhound Show after their visit in 1938, with Mr I. Whitsed, Chairman, Peterborough Agricultural Society.

The international news was bad throughout the summer of 1939, and unlike 1914, most feared another war with Germany was impending. Like many other enterprises, Peterborough Royal Foxhound Show continued to plan ahead normally, and at a 1939 meeting made yet another of its splendid reactionary decisions: '…it was resolved that a loud speaker be not entertained.'

This proved just as well, for the loud speaker would have been silent for the next six years. Minutes of the later committee meeting on 21 October 1939, reported bleakly that 'next year's show would not be held if the War was still on.' It was decided to allow the use of the Foxhound grounds and buildings to the city authorities 'for war purposes' at a rent of £3 per month.

By the committee meeting of 2 November 1940, chaired by Lord Exeter, the phoney war was well over. The first deaths of Vice-Presidents on active service were reported: the Duke of Northumberland, the Earl of Coventry, and Commander C.H. Davey. There were to be many more.

As in 1914-18, the rural community ensured that a limited amount of foxhunting continued throughout the second world war. Farming gained renewed importance and the farming industry insisted that foxhunting should continue as an essential aid to vermin control

Limited feed rations were authorised by local War Agricultural Committees, and greatly reduced packs of hounds survived. Foxhunting was still a high priority for many thousands in the British countryside as a leisure pursuit, a way of life, and an occupation on which many depended. Despite many other pressures, there were enough devoted foxhunters of all ages and both sexes on the home front, prepared to make sacrifices and extra effort to ensure the survival of Foxhounds as part of the British way of life the nation was fighting to preserve.

Peterborough Royal Foxhound Show would revive after the war to delight many more who care about hunting – and once again the sweet cry of hounds in our countryside would refresh veteran foxhunters returning from war service, and capture the affection of new generations eager to explore the unique pleasures of the hunting field.

8. After the War

Foxhunting continued in limited fashion during the Second World War, but no-one foresaw how swiftly it would revive after 1945. For those who could hunt again there were to be at least two decades of traditional hunting on grassland before the terrain of many countries, especially in the Midlands, was drastically changed by huge increases in arable farming, and the arrival of motorways.

Foxhound breeding is extraordinarily elastic, because hounds are entered in their first year, and packs can be expanded remarkably quickly. Two couple classes were omitted at Peterborough just after the war, because packs were so reduced. Hunt staff showing hounds at the first two shows, 1946-7, wore white Hunt coats with bowler hats instead of full scarlet livery. Yet thereafter, the Foxhound Shows at Peterborough resumed their normal outward appearance. Pre-war standards of formal wear, bowler hats and dark suits for men, and summer hats and dresses for ladies, continued to prevail.

Hunt staff wore white coats at the first two shows after the 1939-45 war. Here, judging is taking place at the Eastfield hound enclosure in 1947.

Duke of Beaufort's Landsman ('46), dog-hound champion in 1946, still some way from the modern post-war type developed at Badminton.

Pytchley Crusty ('47), bitch champion in 1948.

The judging process continued to take place in a cathedral calm, although legend relates that on one occasion the atmosphere was dramatically rent when a senior foxhunting pundit from the north appeared to have lunched too well. He suddenly leaned forward from his front row seat, and vomited spectacularly into the ring. Unfortunately, he was seated next to Master, Duke of Beaufort, at the time, and their relationship was thereafter said to be more than a little chilly.

Despite outward appearances, the hounds judged at Peterborough were fundamentally altered in conformation and type: the war proved a catalyst for change in Foxhound breeding. It was estimated that up to seventy-five per cent of Kennels by 1945 had at least an element of Welsh outcross breeding, and hounds of this type increasingly won classes at Peterborough.

Even the pre-war mistrust of a loud-speaker in the Peterborough ring was overcome. In 1947 the Committee agreed that it should be 'tested' at the next show. In 1949, the chief steward, Lord Brassey, reported that hounds' reaction was satisfactory, and it was decided to install a microphone and amplifier – a facility which put it well ahead of most other hound shows.

NO MORE HOUND SALES

One of the most important changes in the foxhunting world, little publicised at the time, was the post-war abandonment of annual foxhound sales, conducted at Rugby by Messrs Tattersalls. Although Peterborough issued no prize money to Masters, only gratuities to huntsmen, the material value of a pack of hounds could be very considerably increased by victories at the premier hound show. The MFHA ruled firmly after the war that registered Foxhounds were not to be sold within the United Kingdom, although they could be sold abroad. This greatly facilitated drafting of useful hounds, and the use of notable stallion hounds in other kennels. Together with the opening of the stud book in 1955, it was one of the most important decisions in preserving the future of the breed as Britain's best example of an animal bred to the highest level for a genuinely demanding working role.

The nineteenth and early twentieth history of foxhunting shows some Masters willing to pay very large sums for packs of Foxhounds. It was the practice for many years for an outgoing Master to sell his hounds to the incumbent Masters, or put them up for sale at Rugby. New Masters could buy whole packs of hounds in this, or refresh their packs with selected hounds of a certain type which they liked. We have already noted the Pytchley changing their pack's style during Frank Freeman's term as huntsman in the 'twenties through buying hounds of lighter build at Rugby. Although later Pytchley Masterships in the pre-war years were among those who opposed Welsh outcrosses.

In the late nineteenth century Captain Percy Williams ruled the Rufford country for nineteen years, and when put up for sale by Tattersall's, they fetched £2,815, a very considerable sum if translated into modern monetary value. As far back as 1845 Mr George Foljambe sold the pack he hunted in the Retford country, Nottinghamshire, for the huge sum of £3,721.5s. – for five-and-a-half couple of working hounds, and forty-four couples of unentered hounds. At the time £115 was considered a good sum for a useful Hunt horse, although much larger sums into five figures were paid for blood horses in the Shires.

Badminton was not above buying hounds. The 9th Duke of Beaufort was reported to have paid 2,000 guineas for the doghounds of the Woodland Pytchley, sold by private contract in 1899 by Mr Austin Mackenzie, and Mr William Wroughton, Master of the Pytchley, gave 3,000 guineas for the bitches.*

Foxhound sales were still in full swing between the wars. The 1926 edition of *Baily's Hunting Directory* for example, lists two sales at Rugby, in April and May. Peterborough championships are named against some lots: in the dispersal of the Croome pack, owing to Mr Gresson giving up the country, the lots include 'Caroline, runner-up for the bitch championship at Peterborough in 1924, Dairymaid and Rushlight, the first-prize unentered bitches at the same show, and Credible, who won the previous year.'

There were quite a number of other smaller lots from Hunts, indicating that drafting hounds could involve significant transactions at that time. More than a few were sold abroad. In the 1926 second sale the best price was 110 guineas paid by the Marquis Casati 'for three couples from the Quorn Kennels, these going to Italy to hunt over the grassland of the Campagna Romana with the Roman Foxhounds.' Major Dermot MacCalmont sold fifteen-and-a-half couples of the Kilkenny Hounds for 134 guineas, and expended 100 guineas of it on the purchase of the three-year-old Brocklesby stallion hound Tarquin by Denmark ('19), out of Target ('14) by Heythrop Wildboy.

Since individual Masters at that time expended such large sums of their own money to run their Hunts, with subscriptions from their followers often making a contribution very far short of the cost of running the Hunt, recouping some of their outlay by selling their hounds at the end of their term of office seems perfectly reasonable.

Of course, Masters were buying hounds for work, but undoubtedly the lustre of Peterborough prizes added material value. It was said to be one factor in the

---

Baily's Hunting Directory, 1901, 'Hound Sales of the 19th Century', by W.C.A. Blew.

adamant opinion of some that nothing drastic must be wrought by Welsh outcrosses on the traditionally accepted type and size of the 'pure' English Foxhound. However, hound prices slumped during the economic depression in the 1930s, and the Rugby sales ceased.

The sales might have revived after the war when hunting had recovered, until 'Master', the 10th Duke of Beaufort, and other leading hound breeding friends in the 'modernist' camp, achieved the crucial decision to halt the practice within the United Kingdom, although hounds could still be sold abroad.

The basis of Mastership changed gradually in the post-war years: a new generation of Masters who hunted hounds were often sponsored by their fellow Masters, or other members of the Hunt. Increasingly larger Masterships of at least four people shared the duties and costs of this office, with subscribers encouraged to pay a far larger share of the costs of running Hunts. Many new Masters would have been unable to pay the sums of money expended in the past by incoming Masters, amounting in some cases to over £100,000 in modern monetary terms, in order to replace packs sold by the outgoing Masters.

BATTLE OF THE GREEN-COATS

If Ikey Bell was a great propagandist for his type of hounds, he was to be overtaken by the greatest communicator and persuader of all in post-war foxhunting, Captain Ronnie Wallace. His emergence as a huge influence on hunting, and hound breeding, was reflected at Peterborough where the 'battle of the green coats' characterised more than thirty years' of post-war judging: the Heythrop is a neighbouring offshoot of the original Duke of Beaufort's country, and therefore both retain the Beaufort green livery for their Hunt staffs, who compete side by side so often in the hallowed ring at Peterborough.

The young Captain Ronnie Wallace at Peterborough in 1957 with his second doghound champion, Heythrop Spanker ('56), with kennel-huntsman Percy Durno and whipper-in Sam Scott.

The last of Captain Ronnie Wallace's remarkable 33 championships at Peterborough: Exmoor Emperor ('97), doghound champion in 2001. LEFT TO RIGHT: *Exmoor huntsman Tony Wright, Edmund Vestey MFH, and the Captain's Joint Masters, Felicita Busby, and Liz Verity.*

Wallace spent the summer judging at puppy shows up and down the land, he attended all the other hound shows, and as the charismatic chairman of the Masters of Foxhounds Association for twenty-two years – nicknamed 'God' by many – he knew virtually every MFH and hunt servant throughout the United Kingdom and beyond. He was always generous with his own stallion hounds, and evangelised his type of breeding – hounds full of quality, highly active, and with beautiful, symmetrical conformation, excellent shoulders and strong backs. His writ extended to North America where he became highly popular as a hound breeder and judge, exporting some of his lines to US Kennels, and importing carefully selected hounds for use in his own pack.

Wallace blossomed from the 1950s as a hound breeder, moving from his Cotswold Mastership to achieve wonders as Master and huntsman of the Heythrop for twenty-five years (1952-77), followed by a further remarkable quarter century in the same role with the Exmoor, ending with his death in February, 2002.

Although a practitioner of modern hound breeding, Ronnie would not use fresh Welsh outcrosss, saying that modern hounds all contained enough blood from that source already. Unlike the Duke of Beaufort, he did not use the exceedingly popular New Forest Medyg ('69), bred by Sir Newton Rycroft from the pure Welsh sire Miller ('63) out of a small Welsh pack, the Plas Machynlleth, on to a New Forest bitch of English breeding. Medyg became a highly influential stallion hound throughout the United Kingdom. Wallace did, however, use

New Forest Medyg ('69), highly influential Welsh-cross sire, bred by Sir Newton Rycroft MFH, appearing at Peterborough in 1977, with huntsman Richard Perry.

outcrosses judiciously from West Country Harrier, American and Fell lines, and he went back to pure English lines to refresh his breeding; all these were to appear sometimes in the pedigrees of hounds he showed at Peterborough for nearly half a century.

The Duke of Beaufort was so pleased with the Medyg outcross that he organised a lunch at Badminton for other Masters who had used the now-famous hound. Over thirty attended and toasted the health of Medyg and his progeny. Ronnie Wallace was mildly amused, and remarked wryly to the author: 'Just occasionally there is an invitation when there is more distinction in not receiving it.'

In 1977, Sir Newton Rycroft, known affectionately to younger Masters as 'The Newt', was persuaded by Medyg's admirers to enter him in the stallion class at Peterborough, mainly to allow the hunting world to see him. It was surprising that Newton, took up the idea. As one of the greatest experimenters in hound breeding of all time – he used Bloodhounds, Harriers, French hounds and others as outcrosses – he had no great regard for Foxhound showing, although he did judge at Peterborough in 1970 with Martin Letts, as recounted by Tim Unwin (Chapter 10).

The night before the show, Medyg was housed at Whissenthorpe in the Cottesmore country, home of the late Mrs Betty Cross, who was related to the New Forest Joint Master Peter Cross. Betty gave one of her legendary Peterborough dinner-parties the night before the show, and one of the guests was Alastair Jackson, current Director of the MFHA, formerly Joint Master and

Huntsman of several packs, latterly the Cattistock. He reveals (Chapter 11) a hitherto little known story of Medyg's pre-night 'celebrations'.

The famous Welsh-cross hound was probably past his best, and was unplaced, although his presence caused much interest. The winning stallion hound was the Duke of Beaufort's Culprit ('75) by Crowner ('69), with Heythrop Pixton ('75) in second place.

THE COMPETITIVE DUKE

Wallace's perennial contest at Peterborough with the Badminton kennel sometimes seemed like the Hundred Years War, but if it encouraged increasing use of hounds from both green-coat kennels, the contest also evoked at times, some barely suppressed mirth.

This was largely because Henry Hugh Arthur Fitzroy Somerset, the 10th Duke of Beaufort increasingly relished the triumphs he had achieved at Peterborough for his Badminton kennel in the pre-war years, and was determined to ensure this remarkable record was not outshone after the war . He loved to win, and he simply hated to lose. As he grew older it became easier for his many friends and admirers to note the signs.

His delight was evident whenever another Beaufort victory was achieved at Peterborough; his barely hidden displeasure at a defeat, was just as easy to discern. Sometimes it would erupt in brief explosions of anger at examples of what he considered 'very poor judging'.

Queen Elizabeth the Queen Mother, presenting the trophy to a delighted Master, 10th Duke of Beaufort, on winning the doghound championship in 1976 with Culprit ('75). (CENTRE) Sir Rupert Buchanan-Jardine, MFH, Show President. The Duke's green-coat rival, Captain Ronnie Wallace, (RIGHT), won the bitch championship that year with Heythrop Flattery ('75).

Master was just leaving the ring-side at the end of the dog-hound classs at a 1970s show when the author remarked politely it had been 'a most interesting' morning.

'You think so, do you?' thundered Master. 'I have *never* seen such judging in my life!'

It was typical of the formidable Duke, tall and bespectacled, that when spoken to later in the day he was relaxed and beaming. Part of his charm was the complete honesty of his emotions.

Brian Fanshawe recalls that in his debut as a judge at Peterborough he 'got into trouble' with Master. 'He asked why I kept looking at a particular hound in his two couple', and I replied: 'We were trying to make up our mind about the bad one.' 'Master rose up from his chair, and enveloped me like an enormous bird of prey, and announced loudly and clearly that there are no bad hounds bred at Badminton! Incidentally, the Beaufort had already won the class – it's a hard life being a judge!'

Simon Clarke recalls that when he first judged at Peterborough, with Sir Rupert Buchanan-Jardine, they made the great Heythrop Craftsman ('62) champion above the Duke of Beaufort's Beadle ('66). Simon remembers: 'His Grace did not agree with this decision, and at the bar before lunch he was talking to a fellow Duke while Rupert and I were at the other end of the counter. 'Master said in a very loud voice: "I helped to get these young men into my Regiment; it did not do them much good." 'However, after a week or so it was forgotten.'

According to the Heythrop's whipper-in at the time, Hugh Robards, after one of Ronnie Wallace's early champion doghound victories, the Duke turned to Wallace and said: 'Of course, you young fellows are not worried if your hounds are not straight.'

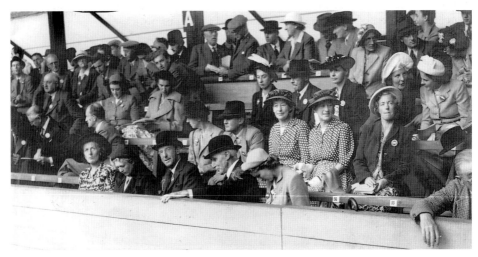

Master, 10th Duke of Beaufort, third from left in the front row at Peterborough, held at Eastfield in 1948. The two identically dressed ladies in the second row, centre right, were the celebrated twin sisters, May and Violet Wilson, Joint Masters of the Cotswold, and formerly the Woodland Pytchley.

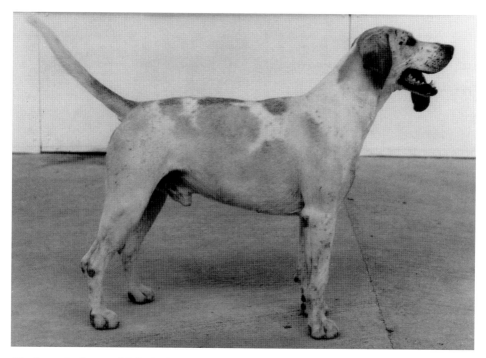

Heythrop Craftsman ('62), doghound champion in 1967.

One of the most celebrated incidents concerning Master at Peterborough occurred in 1981. A dreadful problem arose on the show morning when it was noticed in the office that the Duke of Beaufort's hounds had not been entered for the class for unentered bitches, second class in the afternoon.

The clerical work of drawing up the Beaufort pedigrees, and entering for shows was undertaken with elaborate care by Daphne Moore. The Duke and Duchess had invited her to live for some years at Pond Cottage, just by Badminton House. A tall, slim figure, of great dignity, Daphne could be seen wearing a headscarf as she rode a large, iron framed bicycle of ancient vintage around Badminton Park, and in pursuit of the hounds on hunting days. Daphne lived for the Duke of Beaufort's hounds, although she would admit to being an admirer of Ronnie Wallace's Heythrop kennel too. It was truly a labour of love for Daphne to be in any way associated with the hounds she adored. In the postwar years she became *Horse and Hound*'s acknowledged Foxhound expert, reported all the Peterborough shows until the middle 1980s, and many puppy shows in the summer.

The Foxhound world owes Daphne an immense debt. She was meticulously accurate, and her *Book of the Foxhound*, first published in 1964, with a later edition in the 1970s, is the standard work on Foxhound breeding. Daphne was inclined to be somewhat over-partisan in supporting the modern hound against the pure English, and some of her reports were over-full of glowing descriptions of virtually any Badminton hound, '...a great mover, with slashed shoulders.....'

However, she was devoted to her task, extremely knowledgeable, and Peterborough was fortunate to have her at the ring-side. She marked her catalogues in beautifully clear hand-written red ink notes, and they contained remarkably frank comments which did not always find their way into her published reports: '...quite the worst set of young hounds I have seen for a long time etc...' Daphne remained at Badminton well into the Mastership of the 11th Duke and his family. They were very kind to her until she died in her nineties in 2004 in a Tetbury nursing home.

Alas, in the doom-laden 'affair of Master's botched entries', Daphne had perhaps suffered a lapse of concentration, and apparently confused the first unentered class for which the Beaufort were ineligible, restricted to previous non-winners, with the second, open class for unentered bitches, failing to ensure the Beaufort were entered in the latter.

The Beaufort, as usual, had brought a wonderful array of unentered hounds, and when the difficulty was noted, and brought to his attention, Master was highly displeased. Although substitutions for existing entries were possible up to 9.30 a.m., no new entries could be made on the day of the show. He had already won the unentered doghound couples class, and no

Daphne Moore, Foxhound breeding authority, journalist and author, at a meet of the Duke of Beaufort's in 1974.

doubt expected their sisters to do as well in the afternoon.

Master demanded the omitted official entry should be overlooked, and his hounds included in the unentered bitch class. A hasty meeting of the Peterborough committee was held, chaired by the vice-chairman, Lt. Colonel Tony Murray Smith, former Master of the Fernie, and of the Quorn. He was given the unfortunate task of braving the wrath of the disappointed Duke.

Tony Murray Smith was notably 'steady under fire', but had to take a heavy ducal broadside when he explained the committee had decided the rules had to stand, and no exceptions could be made.

'I think that's *thoroughly* unreasonable,' exploded Master in a massive thunder-storm of rage, but his hounds were not shown in the class, and as usual it was not long before the storm gave way to clear skies when he won the bitch championship.

Poor Daphne, who could be highly-strung and inclined to weep at moments of crisis, was much mortified, and retreated to the car park to regain her composure. Dermot Kelly as steward, had earlier been upbraided by the Duke for a mistake by the 'hierarchy'. Later the Duke apologised to Kelly, saying he now understood that the fault was Daphne Moore's.

Dermot Kelly recalls the Duke saying, with perhaps a twinkle in his eye: 'My ancestors would have put her in chains and placed her in a dungeon, but I shall simply let her make her own way home on this occasion.' Legend says Daphne was so upset that she did not wait for the Duke's car to drive her back to Badminton, but went home alone on the train from Peterborough.

As usual, the Duke's ire was of very brief duration: Daphne continued to reside at Badminton, and was much valued by the Duke as the compiler of his hound pedigrees. Her beautifully annotated catalogue for the show noted in red ink on the last page: 'Many of the hounds here to-day were decidedly too fat, and need plenty of work before they will be ready to start cubhunting!'

Master – whose car number plate was appropriately 'MFH1' – was deservedly much loved, and admired by foxhunters everywhere for his great skills in hunting and breeding his hounds, his generosity in lending hounds to other packs, and giving superb leadership to the hunting world.

At Peterborough he achieved a legend of highly competitive hound showing which provided extra zest throughout his long association with the show. It was a magnificent example of innocent pot-hunting carried out completely unselfconsciously by a passionate enthusiast. Whenever a class involving Beaufort hounds was nearing completion, heads would turn discreetly to the seat always occupied by the Duke to the left of the Presidential box, unless he happened to be President.

Master would sometimes rock to and fro in his seat as judging approached a climax, exploding in a flash of fury if his hound was beaten. This much amused his close friend, Queen Elizabeth the Queen Mother, who asked those around her at Peterborough during a visit: 'Is it always like this?' She knew perfectly well that it was.* If his hounds scored a victory, the Duke would signal his pleasure with one of his long legs, pushing a foot forward to kick the ring boundary boarding in front of him. No doubt it could sometimes be heard by his huntsman in the ring.

When the new Foxhound enclosure was built at Alwalton, Peterborough's major change of venue in 1966, the plans were altered so that the gap in front of the Duke's seat at the ringside was large enough to allow His Grace to continue kicking the board, according to Roy Bird who became the Show's secretary for forty years, as recounted more fully later.

*Ronnie Wallace – the Authorised Version, Robin Rhoderick-Jones, 1992.

Duke of Beaufort's Pontiff ('70) champion doghound at Peterborough 1973 – and supreme champion at Honiton!

Master's senior henchman, his Joint Master with whom he shared the hunting of the hounds, the marvellously droll Major Gerald Gundry, sat to his left, observing the judging with equal attention. The Major remained sanguine even if the Beaufort were not winning, and he once remarked to the author: 'Hound shows are fun, but we mustn't get too excited about the results. After all, it's just "something to do in the summer".'

It was indicative of the Duke's attitude to showing, and the Major's success as his right-hand man, that at a West of England Hound Show in the '70s, the Duke was heavily downcast on winning neither championship, and announced abruptly: 'Right, we're going home!'

Gerald murmured to him: 'Remember, they have a supreme championship here, Master.' The Duke brightened immediately and demanded of his huntsman: 'Get Pontiff!'

Pontiff, a former Peterborough doghound champion, with a superbly masculine head, was rushed by the Beaufort huntsman Brian Gupwell from the hound lorry, where the illustrious animal had no doubt been kept as heavy reserves. Pontiff duly won the supreme championship, and the Duke was happy. Not everyone considers showing former Peterborough champions the best of practice at lesser shows, but Master was among those who would occasionally do so, and clearly regarded this as an emergency.

When the delighted Duke went to receive his trophy, it was to be presented by Gerald Gundry, that year's President at Honiton.

'Where's the cup?' asked the Duke.

'I'm sorry, Master, but the previous winner forgot to bring it back.'

'Really, who was that?' asked the Duke.

'You were,' said Gerald with a broad smile, and solemnly presented the Duke with a tin of Coca-Cola on a plinth. There was a momentary, black cloud of ducal displeasure, then sunshine broke, and the Duke roared with laughter, as did everyone else around the Honiton ring – with some relief.

RONNIE WALLACE – THE OPPOSITION

At Peterborough on the right of the Presidential box, but several seats further along, was the Duke of Beaufort's principal showing adversary, although a more tactful opponent it would be hard to find.

Captain Ronnie Wallace, ever more formidable as he grew physically in bulk, immaculately draped in a pin-striped suit, with a rose in his button-hole, would retain a studied expression of complete concentration throughout the show, altering little whether he won or not. Between classes he would lean forward and confidentially murmur orders to his green-clad huntsman who would come over and bend close to the Captain's ear, as if in conspiracy. In show business terms it was a class act, and it certainly produced results.

A scarcely noticed hound from the Heythrop's two couple entry would be selected by Wallace as the appropriate weapon in his armoury, and superbly shown in the championship judging where its excellence would suddenly become apparent to all and sundry. The Heythrop type became embedded in the consciousness of the modern Master of Foxhounds; more important, it became increasingly clear that Peterborough's younger, post-war judges were often among the most ardent admirers of this type, and the Heythrop tally of championships began to mount alongside those of the Duke of Beaufort's. Because he was not showing in the 1930s, he could never match the Badminton total, but Wallace was a genius who created his own legend.

The Captain would permit himself to smile on receiving championship cups, but there was never a hint of glorification. Let no-one imagine however, that his joy in victory did not exist, nor his angst if he lost.

Wallace had a talent for detail, and most years would phone the shows office to make sure he received a special pass for his car to be driven into the VIP area within the showground. Roy Bird recalls that one year, the Captain found all the VIP spaces taken so he drove his car up on the top of a bank in another grassy area. 'Unfortunately, it was the newly created Derby bank in the showjumping enclosure, and the jumping chief steward was absolutely furious,' said Roy.

Seated beside him at Peterborough, usually in a magnificent white summer hat of Royal Ascot style and proportion, was Ronnie's wife, the often amusing, unpredictable Rosie Wallace, much loved by many of us in the foxhunting world who appreciated her warm-hearted enthusiasm and generosity, as well as her outspoken wit which could be caustic. At Peterborough luncheons and in other eating places, Rosie was wont sometimes to put down her fork and remarkably loudly: 'I can't eat this. The food's simply filthy!'

Countess Fitzwilliam (LEFT), Chairman of Peterborough, with Rosie Wallace, wife of Captain Ronnie Wallace, at the 1989 show.

Sometimes at the Peterborough ring-side she would exclaim just a little too loudly her celebration of the Captain's hound breeding skills, when his hounds scored a victory, or her irritation if he lost.

'Do be quiet, Rosie,' the Captain would counsel quietly, but no-one could blame her, since she gave unremitting support throughout their marriage to her husband's Masterships and his brilliant hound breeding. There were many foxhunters who attended Peterborough for many years, at Rosie's funeral at Dulverton, Exmoor, in 2005.

The Duke of Beaufort and Ronnie Wallace became an integral part of the post-war legend of Peterborough, and their absence from the modern ring-side leaves irreparable gaps of formidable personalities. Peterborough survives and flourishes in the twenty-first century, but it will never be the same without the two twentieth century giants of Foxhound breeding

In the latter years of their long Masterships, when they became unable to hunt their beloved hounds themselves, Master and Ronnie Wallace became even more fervent about showing successes. The Duke of Beaufort achieved twenty Peterborough doghound championships, and ten bitch championships, in his first fifty years of Mastership.

By the time he died in 1984, Master's kennel had won another twelve championships. Captain Ian Farquhar, the brilliant amateur huntsman, who succeeded as Joint Master at Badminton, has maintained its Peterborough showing successes, with the whole-hearted support of the 11th Duke of Beaufort, and Badminton reached fifty-one championships by 2005.

Ronnie Wallace achieved thirty-three championships at Peterborough – seventeen with the Heythrop pack, and the remainder with the Exmoor. Although he took a nucleus of hounds with him from the Cotswolds to the moorlands of Exmoor, it was a truly remarkable feat to continue producing champions from a small kennel in an entirely different sort of country.

Roy Bird said he had not been Secretary of the Hound Show for long before he received a letter from Ronnie Wallace, pointing out that he had won the Duke of Beaufort's cup for three years in succession, and therefore wondered if he could make a request to keep it.

Earl Fitzwilliam, when advised there were no special conditions attaching to the cup, agreed there was no reason why Captain Wallace should not keep it, provided he gave another genuine silver trophy.

But Percy Leach cannily advised Roy Bird: 'I would not like to be in your shoes, or Lord Fitzwilliam's, if you give Master's cup away. I suggest you ask Captain Wallace to write direct to Master.' Roy Bird and Earl Fitzwilliam both agreed with this advice.

Two months later Captain Wallace sent Bird a copy of a letter he had received from Master:

> My Dear Ronnie, Delighted to know you have won my cup three times in succession,
> which means that you are entitled to ask if you can keep it, but I hope you won't.
> Yours ever, Master.

The Duke of Beaufort's Cup is still awarded annually for the Champion Doghound today.

SKILLS IN THE RING

Although the hound's conformation and movement is paramount, as in a horse-show class, the skill with which the animal is shown to the judges is a huge factor in its success. It is essential that a great deal of work is done at home to ensure the hound gives the huntsman its full attention in the ring.

The hound must be confident, not at all abashed by the crowd of spectators so close to the ring. Showing young hounds at puppy shows is useful experience, but the most skilled professionals take much more trouble to ensure their hounds show properly at Peterborough. Even with good conformation, a shy hound with its stern down, which seeks to leave the ring and wanders away from its huntsman, is soon sent out of the ring and will not appear in the ribbons.

One of the major virtues of hound showing, as opposed to a dog show, is that hounds are judged as much as possible on movement as well as conformation. After being shown on the leash, the whipper-in is asked by the steward to release them, and they chase pieces of biscuit thrown across the ring by the huntsman.

One of the greatest hound showing artists of the post-war years was the late Brian Gupwell, huntsman to the Duke of Beaufort for seventeen years from 1967. Brian was elevated to the Beaufort after hunting the much smaller Eridge Hunt in Sussex. He was recommended to Master by his friend, the Eridge's Master and notable hound breeder, Major Bob Field-Marsham.

The Duke of Beaufort's huntsman, Brian Gupwell, an artist at showing hounds, receives a silver salver from the Prince of Wales at Peterborough centenary show, 1978, with Earl Fitzwilliam.

Gupwell, a slim, neat figure, with a great deal of charm, exhibited the art of totally capturing his hound's attention. His championship entrants would gallop across the ring exuberantly, and then stand perfectly still, showing themselves magnificently, as they gazed at Brian's hands, juggling the biscuits like a magician. He took great care to see they were standing at their best, and he retained a deadpan face at all times until a championship win when he would smile warmly. One lady in the tea-room confided to the author she enjoyed gazing at Brian Gupwell even more than looking at his hounds.

Hugh Robards, who was a whipper-in at the Eridge and Heythrop, remembers that Bill Lander and Brian Gupwell had their own ideas of showing hounds, even up to the point of how their whippers-in should hold the show leads. Also, a major factor was the bribe that would make the hound more attentive.

'Brian, when at Badminton, discovered that dried fish was the best. I am not sure which type of fish; I would imagine it was something like sardines. All I know is that it worked, although I am sure on a hot day his pockets would smell a little strong...myself, when showing hounds in Ireland, used the old fashioned dried liver.'

Master was delighted by Gupwell's showing skills, although he was sometimes inclined to give his huntsman rather too much direction and criticism in later years in the hunting field. At Peterborough Master was highly pleased with Gupwell's star quality. He continued as kennel huntsman for Ian Farquhar from

1984, and helped show the Badminton hounds in further Peterborough triumphs. Later he was succeeded by Charles Wheeler, and nowadays by the tall, slim Tony Holdsworth who keeps alive the Badminton traditions of showing hounds impeccably.

Ronnie Wallace was equally keen that his hounds were shown well. He ran MFHA seminars for many years on hound judging, which no doubt assisted many younger judges, and he coached – or instructed – his own huntsmen in the art of showing when necessary.

At the Heythrop he inherited as kennel-huntsman the splendidly imperturbable Percy Durno, who was succeeded in 1964 for six seasons by Bill Lander, later the highly successful huntsman of Sir Watkin Williams Wynn's pack. Bill is renowned for a dry sense of humour. He is enshrined in hunting history for telling an inquirer he had never had a chance to hunt the Heythrop hounds when the Captain was ill, because 'I've been here nearly six years, and the bugger hasn't coughed once yet.'

Bill Lander recalled: 'Every Sunday afternoon there would be as many as twenty or thirty visitors to the Heythrop kennel to see the hounds. So that was a great chance to rehearse showing them. 'Our hounds soon got used to being looked and shown. That was how we trained them to show, and it worked well. The same was true of the Beaufort's and the other big showing kennels.'

Bill, now in retirement in Melton Mowbray, confirms that underneath the formality of Peterborough there was often a more light-hearted atmosphere among the Hunt staff. He recalls Dermot Kelly, ring steward at Peterborough, jokingly betting his former kennel huntsman Johnny O'Shea £5 he would be out

Bill Lander, kennel huntsman of the Heythrop, later huntsman of Sir Watkin Williams Wynn's, with the Heythrop's winning two couple at Peterborough, 1969.

of the ring with his Cheshire hounds before Lander with the Heythrop. The judges made their perambulation of hounds on the couples, and decided the Heythrop and the Cheshire should leave the hounds at the same time.

When Dermot Kelly approached O'Shea, he asked: 'Am I out too, sir?'

Kelly assented, and the Cheshire's Irish huntsman said with a grin: 'Well how about a pound bet on which of us gets to the gate first?'

Bill Lander says that he achieved the closest attention from hounds he was showing by using small chunks of boiled cow's udder instead of biscuit. 'It looked like biscuit, but it smelled better, and it bounced across the ring when you threw in front of a hound; it worked wonders' Bill recalls.

Bert Pateman, the Duke of Beaufort's kennel-huntsman for thirty years up to 1967, was especially popular among the other hunt staff at Peterborough. He established a favourite corner for standing with his hounds in the ring at the old hound enclosure at Eastfield, and no other huntsman tried to usurp it. Bill Lander recalls that Pateman was often 'refreshed' during the day's showing by small glasses of gin surreptitiously passed over the barrier by a friend.

The huntsman would gulp down the gin, palm the glasses and stack them on a convenient ledge in his corner.

'Bert had a marvellously strong head for gin. By the end of the day you would never know he had taken a drink at all, except there were a lot of glasses on that ledge' said Bill.

Hugh Robards, later a brilliant huntsman of the Limerick, and nowadays Master and huntsman of the Rolling Rock hounds, USA, recalled going to Peterborough in 1964 as the Heythrop's second whipper-in, with Bill Lander as kennel-huntsman. Hugh was born in Kent and started Hunt service with the Eridge, under Brian Gupwell. In his memoirs* Robards provides a young whipper's-in memory of showing at Peterborough, and reflects on the difference between showing and performance in the hunting field.

> The big day arrived and Tom Bailey drove the horse-box. Bill came along later in his car, looking very smart. This was my first time at Peterborough and I was very nervous. I was very surprised to see Brian there with the Eridge hounds. In their eighty-five-year history, this was the first time they had shown at Peterborough.
>
> Brian started the ball rolling by winning the first class. He was also second in the fourth classes. Both classes were for novices, which was not bad at all; this was Peterborough. Bill won the unentered couples, the best young with Cardinal and the best two couples. This was good, but much to the Captain's delight, he won the championship with Cardinal and the reserve with Brewer.
>
> Major Victor McCalmont MFH (Kilkenny) and Mr Anthony Hart MFH (Albrighton) judged the doghounds. There was not a shadow of a doubt from some critics that an unentered dog should not be awarded the championship, but there was no rule against it, and it was generally accepted that the best dog won.
>
> Daphne Moore later wrote of Cardinal in Horse and Hound that 'this dog is a great showman and looks as if he enjoys every moment of a show. He appears to be difficult, if

*Foxhunting – A Life in Hunt Service, Hugh Robards, Derrydale Press, 2000.

not impossible, to fault, and is extremely deep and mature for his seventeen months. A creamy lemon pie of superb quality, graceful in action and with perfect balance when stationary, he was an obvious winner.'

In his first season, Cardinal never entered. He would run behind the pack, taking no part in the proceedings at all. The following summer we took him again to Peterborough. We could not show him in the championship because he was a previous winner, but Brewer went on to win it that year.

This was to be the last show at the Peterborough venue [Eastfield], so at the end of the show, there was a special class for hounds, dogs and bitches, which had previously won a Peterborough championship. The Captain entered eight ex-champions in this class and Cardinal won. The trophy was a silver hunting horn on which the Captain blew 'home' to close the show.

Cardinal was given a second chance the next season, but he still would not enter. The Captain sent him to the South Shropshire, where his sister-in-law was Master, but he did no better there.

Brian again opened his account at Peterborough in the afternoon by winning the first class in the bitches. This time the judges were Captain Evan Williams MFH (Tipperary) and Colonel Murray Smith MFH (Fernie). Bill won the unentered couples and the best single hound. No less than twenty-three brood bitches were shown in their own class. Eridge Freedom, champion bitch at Aldershot, won it easily.

Silence fell over those assembled around the ring as the judging for the bitch championship took place. The judges slowly whittled down the numbers, until there were just two bitches left – Eridge Freedom and Heythrop Lottie. The two finest showmen in the world were showing those bitches. There was much deliberation, and then the roof of Peterborough was lifted with the cheers of the spectators as the Earl Fitzwilliam Cup was awarded to Freedom. Major Field-Marsham's view holloa rang out above the cheers, and his face as he received the trophy, said it all.

Captain Ronnie Wallace blows the 'Champion of Champions' horn trophy, won by his Heythrop Cardinal, in front, at the last Peterborough at Eastfield in 1965. LEFT TO RIGHT: *Bill Lander, Heythrop kennel-huntsman; Bert Pateman, Duke of Beaufort's kennel-huntsman; Earl Fitzwilliam, Show Chairman; Mrs Pam McKinnon MFH, Heythrop; and Hugh Robards, Heythrop whipper-in.*

Hugh Robards wrote that Freedom 'ran mute' in the hunting field, and was inclined to leave the Eridge pack to hunt on her own. She was killed on the road while doing so.

He commented: 'This example of two hounds with outstanding conformation that did not live up to expectations in the field cast doubts for me about the value of showing. I enjoyed it, but I never took it seriously once I had left the Heythrop. Naturally, as we drove home from my first Peterborough, I felt proud to have been at the Eridge and also proud now to be at the Heythrop.'

Fortunately, there is ample evidence of many Peterborough champions proving brilliant in their work, the acid test of a hound's real worth. Because the Foxhound is a genuine working animal, any hound consistently poor in its work, is not used for breeding, so that this trait is not transmitted to its stock. Those Peterborough winners later to prove stallion hound or brood bitch winners would all have shown themselves effective in the hunting field before they were used for breeding purposes.

Other huntsmen in the post-war years who were exceptionally effective in the Peterborough ring were Tony Collins who showed for Captain Wallace, and later as his successor as huntsman; Anthony Adams, who showed the Exmoor superbly as Wallace's kennel huntsman, next, when he was huntsman of the Warwickshire, and later as huntsman of the Heythrop; and Tony Wright who succeeded at the Exmoor, and continued the tradition of showing the Captain's winners.

Mr Goschen's huntsman, Ted Rafton, 'showing' Heythrop huntsman Tony Collins the biscuit!

Michael Rowson was notable for his skills when showing the Shropshire hounds, and today Julian Barnfield (Cotswold, and nowadays Heythrop), and Patrick Martin (Bicester with Whaddon Chase) are among those showing hounds exceptionally well. There are many other professional huntsmen and whippers-in who make Peterborough possible.

They stand in the ring all day, uncomplaining, in heavy hunting coats, breeches and boots, even when July temperatures are boiling; or put up with heavy rain 'back-stage' when they are collecting their hounds from the outside hound pens. Many leave home before dawn to drive hound lorries to the showground, and they do not get home until late at night. Often they are supported by their wives and families who sit with them in the special rows of seats for Hunt staff at the hound entrance end of the show building. The bowler hatted ranks of older professionals, many of them retired, seldom betray much emotion when results are announced by the ring stewards, but no-one is analysing the quality of the classes more shrewdly.

EARLY POST-WAR SHOWS

Daphne Moore reported enthusiastically in *Horse and Hound*'s 13 July issue, 1946, that the first post-war show broke all records – thirty-seven packs entered, and thirty-three actually exhibited. Entry levels were settle down to around twenty for some years afterwards.

She remarked: 'It was nice to meet all our old friends again, but there were many old and family faces we sadly missed, such as Square Wharton and his huntsman Frank Morris, who have both passed on since 1939, and who showed the Cleveland hounds with great success at Peterborough for many years. The show this year has certainly been a very great success and a better lot of hounds we have never seen.'

It was, in fact, a restricted show of eight classes: unentered, entered couples, stallion or brood bitch, and champions. The committee omitted the two-couples classes on this occasion, no doubt a reflection on the greatly reduced packs still left in Hunt kennels at the end of the war.

Prizes were widely shared: the Rufford won the unentered doghounds class; the couples class was won by Ikey Bell's former pack, the South and West Wilts; the West Dulverton won the stallion hound class, the champion doghound was the Duke of Beaufort's Landsman ('45).

The Bicester took the unentered bitch class, the Quorn won the entered couples, the Middleton won the brood bitch class with Ripple ('44) who went on to take the championship, with the Quorn Seldom ('44) in reserve. The Quorn pack, like many others, had survived the latter years of the war largely on a diet of vegetables, grown by its veteran huntsman for thirty years up to 1959, George Barker.

The Quorn has not been regarded as a keen showing pack, but George Barker, enjoyed showing, being something of a natural showman. 'He used to stamp about and make quite a lot of noise,' Albert Buckle recalls.

The Quorn won the doghound championship in 1947 with their Raglan, the last time this was achieved, since for many years later in the postwar era they did not show at Peterborough, although they have appeared again recently.

Middleton Ripple ('44), bitch champion at the first post-war show in 1946.

The 1947 bitch championship was an unfortunate decision. The pure English bitch Middleton Ripple ('44), by Ranger ('40) out of Ringlet ('39), made history by winning the bitch championship for the second year running – despite the Society's Condition Four stating 'No entry or part of an entry in any of the classes which has won a first prize at a previous show can be shown again in the same class'. There was presumably confusion as to whether a championship amounted to a 'class'.

The committee discussed the 'difficulty' over the bitch championship at their meeting in October 1947. They resolved to bottle up the loop-hole by adding 'no hound which has won a Champion Cup at previous show can be shown again for a Champion Cup', a rule which stands. No champion has ever showed again in a Peterborough championship, although champions have reappeared as stallion hounds or brood bitches.

The South and West Wilts' victory in the doghound championship in 1948 was another significant sign of the entry of the new-style breeding, since the pack had received so many Welsh outcrosses in the Ikey Bell Mastership. Their 1948 winner was Porlock ('48), a grandson of Ikey's Kilkenny Grasper ('29). Porlock was bred by the Master for thirty-four years from 1932, John Morrison MP, later Lord Margadale. He had been Ikey Bell's Joint Master for two seasons.

'Since the war, Peterborough championships containing no Welsh blood have been extremely few; at least a dozen have a male line to Glog Nimrod, ('04), through Meynell Pageant, ('35), and almost all the rest contain a percentage of Welsh strains far back in their pedigrees,' wrote Daphne Moore in 1964.*

---

*The Book of the Foxhound, Daphne Moore.

South and West Wilts Porlock ('48), doghound champion in 1948, deriving from Ikey Bell's breeding containing Welsh out-crosses.

The Beaufort won a triple sequence of doghound championships from 1950-51, and from this period modern Foxhound breeding could be said to dominate top placings at Peterborough. By 1951 hunt staff were wearing full livery again, and the Eastfield show ring was a wonderful spectacle, especially during the group classes.

The royal link was emphasised in '51 by a visit to the Agricultural and Foxhound Shows by HRH Princess Elizabeth. She spent the previous night with the Duke and Duchess of Gloucester at nearby Barnwell Manor, their family residence, and travelled into Peterborough in a motorcade along the Oundle Road. Huge crowds turned out to cheer the heir to the throne. The Princess, soon to become Queen on the early death of King George VI, was escorted

Princess Elizabeth, the future Queen, visits Peterborough in 1951, greeted by the Mayor of Peterborough, and by (left) Lord Halifax and the Marquess of Exeter.

into the Foxhound Show by the President, Lord Irwin, and the Duke of Beaufort, who held the ancient post in the royal household of Master of the Horse.

The Duke won the doghound championship with Rector ('47), and the Puckeridge had their first Peterborough championship victory since 1937, winning the bitch championship with their Poetry ('51).

Queen Elizabeth the Queen Mother visited the Foxhound Show in 1956 when the Duke won the doghound championship with Dresden ('53), and there was a 'turn up for the book' when an 'outsider' from Cornwall, the Four Burrow, won the bitch championship with their Pasty ('54). It was a great triumph for a small kennel, but their Master Percival Williams from 1922-64 had already won much renown as a remarkable hound breeder. His son John Williams was to succeed him successfully as Master and huntsman, and his daughter, Venetia Williams, is nowadays an acclaimed National Hunt trainer.

Daphne Moore wrote in her catalogue next to the bitch championship 'Tense moment...terrific applause...' The Judges 'had difficulty'...there was 'great deliberation'...Major Maurice Barclay (Puckeridge) and Sir Rupert Buchanan-Jardine (Dumfriesshire) were the bitch judges, and they whittled the championship class down to Four Burrow Pasty, the Duke of Beaufort's Pansy ('54) by Portman Playfair ('51) and Ronnie Wallace's Heythrop Lesson, an unentered bitch, also by Portman Playfair.

Four Burrow Pasty, a delightful badger pie bitch by South Dorset Vulcan ('50) had already won the brood bitch class, and was in illustrious company. She was shown by John Williams – believed the first time an amateur had shown a champion – with the kennel huntsman, Tom Bunch, and Daphne noted that in the championship John ran out of biscuit, and had to borrow from the Duke's

Four Burrow Pasty ('54) scored a great triumph for this Cornish pack as bitch champion in 1956, showed by an amateur huntsman, John Williams MFH.

Portman Wizard ('55) won the 1958 doghound championship for Sir Peter Farquhar, confirming his breeding policies.

kennel-huntsman, Bert Pateman...'even the judges were convulsed', Daphne wrote in her catalogue.

Giving the championship to the Four Burrow, the judges placed the Duke's hound reserve, and he was among the first to congratulate the Four Burrow Masters. Martin Scott recalls the Four Burrow had an eventful time travelling to Peterborough: several hounds escaped from their trailer in Uppingham. (Chapter 10)

Sir Peter Farquhar, one of the great architects of modern hound breeding and a season short of retirement as a Master, won the 1958 doghound championship with Portman Wizard ('55), who Daphne Moore reported 'combines compactness, depth and quality with the delightful light blue-pied colouring seldom seen to-day.' Wizard won the stallion hound class as well, beating his kennel-mate Prompter ('56). Portman Wizard, by Sailor ('52) out of Widgeon ('52), was a male descendant from the great Heythrop Chorister ('06) who was responsible for every doghound champion at the English Hound shows of 1958.

Wizard was an example of champion who was an excellent worker in the hunting field, leaving a beneficial legacy in the Heythrop kennel where his son Blackcock won the Peterborough championship of 1961. Sir Peter previously won the doghound championship in 1953 with Portman Latimer ('51) and the bitch championship in 1955 with Portman Planet ('54), emphasising further the success of modern hound breeding on the flags.

The Duke of Beaufort's scored a remarkable run of championships in the 1950-60 decade, winning six with doghounds, and four with bitches. At three shows – 1953, 1959 and 1960 – Badminton gained both championships. During that decade Ronnie Wallace scored his first championship, and the stallion hound class, with Heythrop Harper ('53) in 1955. The green-coat contest was on the way: the Heythrop and the Beaufort each won sixteen Peterborough championships in the years from 1955 to 1977, establishing a green-coat dominance. Martin Scott refers to these championship victories in more detail in Chapter 10.

MOVE TO ALWALTON

The major change of the postwar years was the 1966 move of Peterborough Agricultural show and the Foxhound Show to Alwalton, outside the City to the west, and bordering on the A1 main road, later to become a motorway.

As referred to in Hugh Robards' memoirs, the 1965 show concluded with a special supreme championship to commemorate the last year of holding the show at Eastfield Showground. Heythrop Cardinal ('65) referred to above by Hugh Robards, had a remarkable array of past championships: Peterborough, Great Yorkshire and Royal Counties. The Duke of Beaufort's bitch Posy ('63), Peterborough champion that year, was runner-up as supreme champion.

The Duke was President of the Show and remarked in the catalogue foreword that '1965 marks the end of a tradition that has increased in popularity during almost a century, and it is sad to think that we shall never again meet our friends on this acre of ground that has known so many triumphs and disappointments.'

Peterborough 1965 – the last year at Eastfield, before the move to Alwalton. Judging are Lord Margadale MFH and Sir Peter Farquhar, with ring steward Marcus Kimball MP, now Lord Kimball.

However he looked forward to a great future at Alwalton, and Earl (Tom) Fitzwilliam, still Chairman of the Society's committee, promised: 'The new ground will possess many of the amenities which are lacking here and, with the increased seating and car parking facilities, we can look forward to a bright and prosperous future.'

After war service, Roy Bird joined Peterborough Agricultural Society as assistant to the popular, hard working secretary, Robert 'Bob' Bibby, until his sudden death in 1957. Roy succeeded immediately as secretary of the Agricultural Society, and in 1965 became only the third secretary of the Royal Foxhound Show, succeeding Joseph Stephenson.

Roy recalls that after being secretary of the Agricultural Society for a few years, he was invited into the Hound Show by Mr Stephenson, who added: 'You will of course come in through the back gate.'

Roy remembers: 'I was only in my early thirties, and he was very kind, introducing me to many of the famous Vice Presidents of the day. Although he said he would invite me again, he never did, and if he had done so, I hoped it might have been through the front gate.'

The Earl and Countess Fitzwilliam,and Mr Stephenson, always took lunch with the President of the Agricultural Society in their President's dining area. Mr Bird recalls that Joseph Stephenson was the accountant for the Agricultural Show's long-standing and highly influential Chairman, Mr W.S. Smith OBE.

'Joseph Stephenson somehow found out that the Chairman was being paid in cash for the straw which he provided for Peterborough Show,' Roy remembers.

'Mr Stephenson insisted, much to my Chairman's annoyance, in declaring the value to the revenue. My Chairman was naturally upset, and told me to cross Joseph Stephenson off the Agricultural Show President's luncheon list, which I did.

'About two weeks before the show, Mr Stephenson rang to say that he and his wife could not find their invitation to the President's lunch. He thought there was either a mistake in the office, or it had been lost in the post. He went on to say they both always looked forward to escorting the Foxhound Show President and Chairman to the Agricultural Show lunch.

'I apologised, and said I would make sure they were both included on the top table as always.

'When I told the Agricultural Show Chairman, he said: "You didn't tell him I had crossed him off?"

'"Of course not," I replied. The Chairman just said: 'Well done.'

Joseph Stephenson, who lived in Peterborough's Cathedral Precincts, died in office at the age of eighty-three, having served fifty-two years as Secretary of the Royal Foxhound Show, while still working as senior partner in the chartered accountants firm, Stephenson, Smart and Co. His pragmatic guidance had helped keep the Society afloat during two wars, and difficult post-war years, and he deserved the warm tributes paid to his contribution.

He was of the generation who tended not to know about retirement. After his death at the time of the 1965 show, Lord Fitzwilliam asked the Agricultural Society if it would look after the administration of the Foxhound Show, with Roy Bird as its secretary.

Roy Bird, Show Secretary, with Percy Leach, retiring as secretary's assistant in 1969, after forty-one years. In the background is Mrs Leach.

This was agreed although Roy admits that at time 'I knew nothing about organising or running the Hound Show. Fortunately for me, Percy Leach who had for many years carried out the Hound Show work for Joseph Stephenson said he would be pleased to carry on, and I jumped at the opportunity.

'He and Mrs Leach, who worked from home, became great friends of mine. 'Percy was very meticulous; he told me how Vice-Presidents should be addressed, and that they should never be moved from their usual seats. Some seats have been in a family for three or four generations.

'At Eastfield, which was much smaller than the present Fitzwilliam Enclosure at Alwalton, Vice-Presidents sat in the front row, with their wives and friends in the rows further back. Percy warned me to be very particular if a Vice-President and his wife had parted, not to sit them next to each other.

'His knowledge of the Vice-Presidents was unsurpassed. He stayed with me until after the 1969 Show, by which time the Society's offices had moved permanently from Priestgate, Peterborough to the present showground.'

Soon after the move to Alwalton, in 1966, Roy was walking from his office to the grandstand when a senior land agent put his hand on his shoulder, and introduced himself by saying: 'Of course, you don't know who I am.'

'Yes, I do, Roy replied, 'You are a Vice-President of the Foxhound Show.'

'What a memory,' he said.

Roy recalls: 'What I did not tell him, was that he was the only Vice-President who had not paid his subscription for the current year. He went on to say he had a complaint about the Hound Show because we had moved his seat. I apologised and asked if we had moved it very far.

'He said we had only moved it "one along", but added: "I like to turn round to those at the back and say my Grandfather sat in this seat, my Father sat in this seat, and I have for the last thirty years." I promised to move him one seat back the following year. He wrote and thanked me.'

Roy Bird says that throughout the post-war years few, if any, Vice-Presidents attended the Society's Annual General Meeting, content to leave it to the general committee to run the society's affairs, and the show.

Percy Leach told him there had been a ritual that at the end of a general committee meeting, Lord Fitzwilliam always announced: 'Would you now let in the Vice-Presidents for the Annual General Meeting.'

Joseph Stephenson used to walk to the door, open it and shout in a loud voice: 'Would all the Vice-Presidents now enter the room for the Annual General Meeting?'

Roy says: 'There was, of course, never anyone there, and so he would return and say to Lord Fitzwilliam: "There are no Vice-Presidents waiting for the Annual General meeting."'

However, on one occasion, a Vice-President did arrive. As he walked past the window, Lord Fitzwilliam declared: 'It looks as though a Vice-President has turned up for the AGM – he must be new. I suppose we must let him in.'

'They did so, but first Lord Fitzwilliam asked Mr Joe Odam if he would go outside to make sure the Vice-President had paid his subscription.

'When it came to the re-election of the committee, the new Vice-President asked if he could propose this, and also that Lord Fitzwilliam should carry on as chairman. The Earl thanked him, and declared the meeting closed.

'On his way out from the meeting, the new Vice-President said to Lord Fitzwilliam: "I promise not to come again."'

Lord Halifax, President, and Earl Fitzwilliam making a presentation to Percy Leach with Mrs Leach at the 1969 show.

Mr and Mrs Leach retired in 1969, after forty-one years' service to the show. They were made Honorary Vice-Presidents, and presented with a testimonial in the ring at the 1969 show by Lord Fitzwilliam, accompanied by the President, Lord Halifax. In the testimonial Lord Fitzwilliam praised the couple as 'a pillar of strength in all the work connected with the show's organisation, in particular the allocation of Vice-Presidents' seats for some thirty-five consecutive shows.'

After Mr Leach's retirement, the administration of the Foxhound Show was passed entirely to the Agricultural Show. The entries and catalogue preparation was undertaken in the Livestock Department, and the Vice Presidents' records in the membership department.

Roy Bird says: 'The staff were totally devoted in maintaining the high standards and great traditions, to ensure the administration carried on smoothly; equally, they all enjoyed the Hound Show work. In later years two of the staff, Sue Chamberlain, now Fox, and more recently Jayne Bailey, now Bradshaw, have done the entries and prepared the catalogues at their homes, particularly since the Agricultural Show moved its own date earlier. These two ladies showed the same dedication as when they were on the permanent staff.'

Until the retirement of Mr and Mrs Leach, the show's minutes were beautifully hand-written. Later minutes were type-written, but in 2005 the Royal Foxhound Society's records were not on computerised record, and this remained a task for the East of England's chief executive, Andrew Mercer, who that autumn succeeded Roy in the secretaryship of the Foxhound Show.

THE MOVE FROM EASTFIELD

Roy Bird, always cheerful and highly efficient, was appointed chief executive of the newly created East of England Agricultural Society from 1970, following the arduous move to Alwalton in which he had played a major role. The East of England was formed by the merger of the following long-standing agricultural societies: Cambridgeshire and Isle of Ely, Huntingdonshire, Peterborough, Bedfordshire, and last to join, Northamptonshire, in 1972.

Roy was awarded his MBE in 1979 for his services to agriculture,and retired from the Agicultural Society in 1992 when he had been involved in the organisation of over forty annual shows. Roy's enthusiasm and attention to detail in his other role at the Foxhound Show was deeply appreciated. He was additionally Secretary of the Shire Horse Society from 1963-91.

It was fortunate that a prominent local businessman and farmer, Mr Joe Odam, chairman of the Site Development committee at Alwalton, took considerable interest in the Foxhound Show, and served on its committee as a representative of the Agricultural Society, providing valuable liaison. His role was officially recognised when he was appointed President of the Royal Foxhound Show in 2004.

Joe Odam and Roy Bird pay warm tribute to the involvement of the Fitzwilliam family throughout the history of both societies. When the Agricultural Society decided that it had outgrown Eastfield, where there was no permanent car-parking (show visitors were allowed to use a nearby school playing field), the City Council wanted the site for a technical college and playing field extension.

The 10th Earl Fitzwilliam, still chairman of the Foxhound Society, was instrumental in arranging that the Foxhound Show site at Eastfield could also be made available to complete an attractive land package. This was important because the Foxhound site had an important road frontage. Ultimately the Eastfield site was purchased by the City Council on behalf of their Joint Education Board.

Lord Fitzwilliam was further crucially involved in negotiations ensuring the Society was able to move to the new site on Milton Estates land at Alwalton. He instructed the Milton Estate to negotiate with the Church Commissioners for the purchase of Glebe Farm, south of the A605 which was farmed on a tenancy, and adjoined other land owned by the Milton Estate.

The Commissioners agreed the land could be sold to the Milton Estate, and it was then conveyed to the Agricultural Society by the Estate at the original purchase price. The Earl arranged for the tenant of the farm, Mr Robin Waterworth to give vacant possession to the Society, also selling them a twenty-seven acre field along the frontage to the A605. Lord Fitzwilliam made available to the Agricultural Society a further forty acres of land on a long lease at a peppercorn rent, and after his death Lady Fitzwilliam generously gave this land to the Society.

Plans for the new 210 acres agricultural show site, including extensive car parks, included a new enclosure for the Foxhound Show, permanently named 'The Fitzwilliam Hound Enclosure'. The enclosure was permanently fenced, and had its own entrance, where an additional fee was charged to visitors, emphasising the Hound Show's independence. Although a new structure was erected for the judging ring and collecting ring, the Eastfield Road kennels were dismantled and re-erected at Alwalton, with new buildings provided for offices, sloakroom, toilets and Hunt Servants' dressing room. There was room for a Vice-Presidents' car park next to the Enclosure, a much needed improvement on the Eastfield site.

Roy Bird recalls that in driving wind and rain, during the early planning stages at Alwalton, Earl Fitzwilliam visited the site of the new Fitzwilliam Enclosure with the Foxhound Show general committee members. The Earl was somewhat concerned about an old, and dangerous, oak tree which happened to be in the area of the proposed Foxhound show enclosure.

'The committee duly made their visit, having already expressed a view that the new layout should be exactly the same as the one at Easfield, the judging ring surrounded by kennels in the same positions, but giving slightly larger space for judging,' said Roy.

He placed pegs to give a rough indication of the site, but Lord Fitzwilliam asked: 'And where will Master sit?' Roy did his best to point to a position.

'And where will I sit?' asked the Earl. Roy indicated again, as best he could, and also showed where the collecting ring would be. The Earl asked two committee members to take position on their shooting sticks in the two premier 'seats'. Then he declared 'It looks fine'.

The committee returned to their cars, and did not visit the site again until it was completed for the first show. The only modification was a slight increase in dimensions to allow room for the Duke of Beaufort's long legs, as recounted earlier.

The Agricultural Society recognised that to a large extent its new show ground depended on the generosity and goodwill of the Earl and Countess Fitzwilliam, and in its turn gave an undertaking to the Royal Foxhound Show Society that should the Agricultural Show ever move to another site, the Agricultural Society would maintain its obligation to provide on any new site a Hound Show enclosure at least as good as the present site and with similar offices and facilities. Improvements and refurbishments to the present Hound Show enclosure were made in recent years, and the Agricultural Society financially backed the new 'Festival of Hunting' in 2005.

The first Alwalton Show in 1966 was notable for the Agricultural Show and the Foxhound Show having the same President, appropriately the 10th Earl Fitzwilliam.

It was a close shave because workmen were still banging away on the site on the previous Sunday, two days before the show. About 1,500 people in unseasonably bad weather attended a dedication service. The Show included a pageant depicting the 'Cat and Custard Pot Day' from Robert Surtees' Jorrocks' *Jaunts and Jollities*, with the Fitzwilliam Hunt contributing some of the hunting characters.

As President and Chairman of the Royal Foxhound Show Society, Lord Fitzwilliam welcomed Vice-Presidents and other supporters to the new Hound Show enclosure at Alwalton. In the foreword to the catalogue he stated: 'The work of the Foxhound Show Society is now being undertaken in the offices of the Agricultural Socieity, Mr Roy W. Bird being Secretary of both Societies – which means a very much closer link exists between the two organisations.

'Over sixty new Vice-Presidents have been elected during the year and with the increased and better seating accommodation in the Enclsure, more Vice-Presidents can be elected among the many supporters of hunting – each one will be guaranteed a seat in the Enclosure.

'As your Chairman and President for the year I would like to pay tribute to the work of the Council of Peterborough Agricultural Society and those who have been engaged in the work of establishing the Foxhound Show on the new site.'

Nineteen packs were represented, and Major Bob Hoare MFH (Cottesmore) and Mr Dermot Kelly MFH (Meynell) judged the doghounds; Lord Halifax MFH (Middleton) and Major J.J. Mann (VWH) judged the bitches.

Lord Brassey was ring steward with Marcus Kimball MP, later Lord Kimball, who was a Joint Master of the Fitzwilliam, and later the Cottesmore, and performed great services for hunting as Chairman of the British Field Sports Society in the nineteen sixties and seventies.

The 1966 committee under Lord Fitzwilliam's chairmanship was Colonel Tony Murray Smith (vice-chairman), Captain Charlie Barclay MFH (Puckeridge) who represented the MFHA, Lt. Colonel Neil Foster MFH (Grafton), Major Bob Hoare MFH (Cottesmore), Major Tony Warre MFH (Fitzwilliam), Lord Brassey, Lt. Colonel Sir Henry Tate (former Cottesmore MFH), Mr E.T. Channel, Lt. Colonel J.E.S. Chamberlayne (Secretary of the MFHA), Lt. Colonel R.J.C. Crowden, Mr A.B. Gould, Colonel J.G. Lowther, Mr Joe Odam, Major H.M. Peacock, and Mr A.B. Wilkinson.

Long serving kennel-huntsman Micky Flanagan showing Tipperary Grizzle ('64) to win the bitch championship in 1966 for Master and huntsman, Evan Williams.

Joe Odam recalls: 'The committee meetings were very amiable and easy, mainly because the committee met beforehand for dinner with the chairman at Milton, and any contentious issues were thrashed out then.'

Daphne Moore reported the bitch championship in 1966 went to Ireland for the first time since 1928 when Carlow Vera ('23) had won. The 1966 bitch champion was Tipperary Grizzle ('64) by Heythrop Finder ('61) and a grand-daughter of Portman Grossman ('52). She was bred by the Tipperary's remarkable Master and huntsman, Evan Williams, who had preceded his hunting career in Ireland by riding the winner of the Cheltenham Gold Cup twice, and training the winner of the King George VI Gold Cup at Ascot.

Daphne noted in her catalogue: 'How I wish Ikey were alive to witness this triumph, since the Tipps were so largely built up by him at the start of Evan's Mastership. It is the first time the Fitzwilliam Cup has ever gone out of this country, but no-one can grudge it to the Tipps.'

It was another great day for Ronnie Wallace, whose doghound sired the bitch champion, and who won the doghound championship with Heythrop Clincher, an unentered hound, by Feudal ('61) – plus the reserve bitch championship for good measure, with Heythrop Frenzy ('63) his brood bitch class winner. The Duke of Beaufort had to be content that year with the doghound championship reserve, won by Falcon ('63), but he had many good years ahead in Peterborough's superb new setting.

9. The Alwalton Shows

The Beaufort/Heythrop axis continued to dominate championship placings in the 1970s, but there was a splendid victory in 1973 for a small kennel from the South-East. Applause and cheers nearly lifted the roof when West Kent Payment ('72) won the bitch championship.

Daphne Moore said it was 'a judgement of Paris', the judges having to decide between Payment and the Duke of Beaufort's Crimson ('72). By then, the West Kent huntsman Stan Luckhurst had only one rosette on his arm, a blue second rosette in the entered doghound couples class.

Payment was shown in the entered bitch couples, but the judges – Captain Ronnie Wallace and Martin Scott – did not like the other hound, and the couple was unplaced. The Heythrop were not, of course, showing because of the Captain's involvement.

Payment owed much to Bob Field-Marsham's breeding at the Eridge; she was by Eridge Painter ('66) and a grand-daughter of Eridge Choirboy ('60). Daphne Moore in her inimitable style described her as 'white, tan speckled ears, good back and long elbow slash, well muscled good body, and well let-down hocks...looks a hard sort.' It was the West Kent's first Peterborough championship, a great day for the Master, Richard Thorpe, and veteran huntsman Stan Luckhurst.

West Kent 'upset the form book' when their Payment ('72) won the bitch championship in 1973, shown by huntsman Stan Luckhurst.

HORSE AND HOUND CUPS

The author took over as Editor of *Horse and Hound* in 1974, and after that year's show the committee accepted his offer of two cups as special prizes for the champion unentered doghound and bitch, plus a donation for gratuities for Hunt staff.

Every year since 1975 Horse and Hound has been named twice on the black results board above the ring-entrance. It was a handsome recognition of the magazine's full coverage of the show since 1884 – and it was still on the board in 2005. *Horse and Hound's* 1984 centenary was celebrated at the East of England Show by a colourful foxhunting pageant, kindly arranged by Roy Bird in the main ring, and watched by many who were attending the Foxhound Show.

First winner of the *Horse and Hound* unentered doghound cup in 1975 was Crawley and Horsham Bandit, and the bitch winner was Heythrop Active, by Kilkenny Anthony ('68), bred by Ronnie Wallace's great friend, Victor McCalmont, one of the finest Masters ever to hunt hounds in Ireland. He hunted his superbly bred pack from Mount Juliet with great style and success, crossing his stone-walled Kilkenny country on top-class hunters. For ten years up to 1975 he also hunted the Wexford pack over their formidable country of stone-faced banks.

Peterborough was visited in 1974 for the second time by Queen Elizabeth the Queen Mother, and in '75 received a particularly popular visit from the Princess Royal who was already renowned as an international eventing rider, and rode to hounds with the Duke of Beaufort's. Members of the royal family were immediately at home at Peterborough in the company of Master whom they regarded as an uncle, and visited annually for his great horse trials at Badminton.

Princess Anne, the Princess Royal, visiting Peterborough in 1975, with Earl Fitzwilliam and, right, Show Secretary Roy Bird.

CENTENARY YEAR

The 1978 show to mark the Centenary year, was distinguished for the third time by the presence at Peterborough of a Prince of Wales. Prince Charles was a warmly enthusiastic foxhunter, and accepted the Presidency. He had only taken up the sport three years earlier, but he was already able at Peterborough to greet many foxhunters he had met in the hunting field.

The Queen gave permission for the reproduction on the front page of the catalogue of a painting, by the artist Susan Crawford, of Prince Charles in his distinctive Windsor Hunt coat, blue with scarlet cuffs and collar, and silver buttons bearing his crest. He was riding Candlewick, the seventeen-hands gelding bred by the Queen which had been ridden as an eventer by Princess Anne. The Masters of Foxhounds Association presented the painting to the Queen in 1977.

There was much joy in the hunting world over Prince Charles's passion for foxhunting, following his first day riding to hounds – as a guest of the Duke of Beaufort on 17 February 1975; hounds produced a wonderful five-mile point from Badminton and the Prince was converted immediately to the pleasures of the hunting field. He had ridden since childhood in the polo field, but now learned to become an excellent cross-country rider, and visited over forty packs throughout Britain, mainly in the company of the

Front page of the 1978 centenary year show catalogue, depicting the President, HRH the Prince of Wales, riding Candlewick in a painting by Susan Crawford, presented by the MFHA to the Queen.

Crown Equerry, Sir John Miller. The Prince proposed the health of foxhunting at the Masters of Foxhounds Association centenary dinner in 1981.

Prince Charles wrote the following foreword to the 1978 Catalogue, under his request, and signed Charles:

I am delighted to have been asked by Peterborough Royal Foxhound Show Society to be its President for the centenary year. Centenaries are always important occasions for any organisation and none more so for this Society which has become established as probably the greatest Foxhound show in the world, performing a major role in maintaining the high standards of hound breeding in this country.

Having heard so much about the Foxhound Show and the passions it arouses amongst the enthusiastic competitors, I look forward to seeing the whole thing for myself.

Daphne Moore wrote in *Horse and Hound*:

Someone once said: 'There are of course, other hound shows, but there is only one Peterborough.' And the fact that Peterborough has survived not only two world wars, but the experience of moving to fresh showgrounds no fewer than four times, speaks for itself. This year's centenary show was remarkable in a number of respects...

It is gratifying indeed that Prince Charles possesses such a genuine interest in the Foxhound that he was present during the greater part of the judging, intent upon all that occurred in the ring. He presented the major trophies, and gave great pleasure to the Hunt servants concerned, as well as others, by conversing with them at some length.

Horse and Hound contributed largely towards prize money and other items. A total of twenty-six packs exhibited; the greatest number for five years.

Earl Fitzwilliam as Chairman was pictured in the catalogue in a delightful photograph at the Fitzwilliam kennels where he is seen with Lady Fitzwilliam and a group of hounds. In his catalogue foreword the Earl wrote: 'Great changes have taken place in the foxhunting world during the one hundred years in which the Show has been in existence, none more striking than the quality of the Foxhound. Peterborough sets a high standard, and the Foxhound of today has probably reached a higher peak of excellence than ever before.'

The Foxhound Enclosure at Peterborough 1978 was painted by Terence Cuneo in a large-scale work showing Prince Charles in the President's box, between the Duke of Beaufort and Lord Fitzwilliam, with Ronnie Wallace sitting just behind. Prints were sold by subscription to Vice-Presidents and others, and proved popular, not least because Cuneo included miniature likenesses of many foxhunters present, with a key to their positions in the painting.

The Centenary Year committee, under Lord Fitzwilliam's chairmanship were: Major Tony Warre MFH, vice-chairman, Captain Simon Clarke MFH, Colonel Neil Foster MFH, Lt. Colonel Sir Henry Tate, Lt. Colonel Tony Murray Smith, Mr Marcus Kimball (later Lord Kimball), Mr Joe Odam, Major H.M Peacock, Mr H.M.T. Jones, and Mr C.E.W. Saunders.

Simon Clarke and Edmund Vestey judged the doghounds, and Ronnie Wallace and Ian Farquhar the bitch classes – so there was to be no green-coats clash in the afternoon. Daphne Moore pointed out that it was twenty-seven years since Ronnie Wallace was a junior judge at Peterborough with Ian Farquhar's father, Sir Peter...'continuity is another of the endearing features of the Royal Foxhound Show.' Dermot Kelly and Marcus Kimball MP, later Lord Kimball, were the ring stewards. Their impressions of Peterborough are included in Chapter 11.

The Heythrop won an impressive doghound two-couples class, but the Duke of Beaufort won the stallion hound class with his Clinker ('74), a son of the great Crowner ('69), and went on to win the doghound championship with Monmouth ('77). This was truly a sign of the changes since the early days of 'Shorthorn' English hounds in 1878 – for Monmouth was by none other than the famous Welsh outcross sire New Forest Medyg ('69). Daphne Moore ecstatically described Monmouth as 'a dream of a hound...clean lines, lovely neck, white with very light badger in spots...'

Terence Cuneo's painting of Peterborough's 1978 centenary show, with the Prince of Wales in the President's box between the Duke of Beaufort and Earl Fitzwilliam. Simon Clarke and Edmund Vestey are judging the doghounds.

Duke of Beaufort's champion doghound Monmouth ('77) in 1978.

In the afternoon the Kilkenny won the two couple class, with sisters all sired by Heythrop Foreman ('73). The Duke of Beaufort's Lucy ('76) won the brood bitch class – and then the Kilkenny made history when their bitch Famous ('77), one of their two couple winning group, took the championship. Daphne Moore described Famous as 'a well made, shapely bitch with size and scope, and plenty of heart-room, tan and red mottled'.

The reserve placing was a triumph for Marek Kwiatkowski, Joint Master and huntsman of the Meynell. He paid tribute to the previous long-term breeding at the Meynell kennel by Dermot Kelly who ceased his Mastership three years earlier. The prize went to the Meynell bitch Lesson ('77) by Growler ('74). Lesson 'had a lovely fore-hand, and was shown in impeccable condition,' according to Daphne. Miss Moore rather desperately explained the Beaufort's lack of a prize in the championship as 'a dramatic turn...the Duke of Beaufort's Lucy, who was one of the finalists, had the great misfortune to collide violently with one of her competitors and would not show thereafter...'

There was every reason for the Peterborough committee to feel the year show was a worthy celebration of the show's success since 1878.

In 1979, the year after the Centenary, there was a great loss for the Fitzwilliam family, and the Peterborough community, when the 10th Earl Fitzwilliam died suddenly of a stroke.

He and Lady Fitzwilliam had enjoyed a happy marriage for twenty-three years, sharing many interests – of which the Royal Foxhound Show and the Fitzwilliam Hunt were high on the list. 'Captain Tom', as he was at the beginning, had been chairman of the Foxhound Society for a remarkable thirty-six years, and

Kilkenny Famous ('77), champion bitch in 1978 – a rare victory for Ireland at Peterborough.

Prince Charles presents the cup to Major Victor McCalmont, Master and huntsman of the Kilkenny, for his triumph in winning the bitch championship with Famous ('77).

no-one could have been more assiduous in protecting the show's interests. Warm tributes were paid by everyone concerned with the Foxhound Show. Having died childless, Tom Fitzwilliam was the last Earl Fitzwilliam, an earldom created in the seventeenth century for William Fitzwilliam, 1st Earl 1643-1719.

A highly popular victory in 1984: Captain Charlie Barclay receives from Countess Fitzwilliam the championship cup for the Puckeridge bitch, Pigeon ('81). Show President Major Gerald Gundry, Joint Master of the Duke of Beaufort's, is in the centre.

LADY FITZWILLIAM – THE NEW CHAIRMAN

Fortunately, Joyce Countess Fitzwilliam, proved entirely equal to carrying on her late husband's great responsibilities, and she continued his support of the Agricultural and Foxhound societies, as well as the Fitzwilliam hounds.

Certainly, no-one who met Lady Fitzwilliam was ever likely to forget her forthright personality which cloaked much warmth and kindness. She took over as Chairman of the Royal Foxhound Show Society in 1980 immediately after her husband's death.

Lady Fitzwilliam was described in her obituary in the *The Times*, after she died aged ninety-seven, in 1995, as a 'tall, erect elegant woman of great presence, who entertained with flair and originality at two great houses, Milton Cambridgeshire, and Wentworth Woodhouse in Yorkshire.'

Fortunately the Fitzwilliam family was able to provide further excellent continuity. Sir Philip Naylor-Leyland Bt., grandson of Lady Fitzwilliam, is a keen foxhunter who joined the Mastership of the Fitzwilliam pack in 1987. He became Chairman of the Royal Foxhound Show Society in 1996, and continues to serve in that role.

Sir Philip's mother, Lady Hastings, was Joint Master of the Fitzwilliam from 1980 until her untimely death in 1997. Lizzie-Anne, as she was known to a host of friends, had a delightful personality, and as well as taking a close interest in all aspects of English country life, she was a distinguished Egyptologist. She was highly popular in the hunting world, and having inherited Milton, enthusiastically continued the Fitzwilliam hunting traditions on the estate. She married in 1975 Sir Stephen Hastings, MP for Mid-Bedfordshire, a keen hunting man who joined his

Countess Fitzwilliam escorting Princess Anne, visiting the show in 1989.

Sir Stephen and Lady Hastings, Joint Masters of the Fitzwilliam. Lady Hastings was posthumous President in 1997. Her son, Sir Philip Naylor-Leyland Bt., succeeded his grandmother, Countess Fitzwilliam, as Chairman in 1996.

wife in the Fitzwilliam Mastership, and shared her interest in hounds and hound breeding. Lady Hastings was to have been President of the Royal Foxhound Show later in the year she died, and the Show honoured her memory by retaining her name posthumously on the list as 1997 President. Sir Stephen served as Deputy President.

NEW WALLACE CHAMPIONS – FROM EXMOOR

In the 1979 show the Cottesmore won their first Peterborough championship, with their Baffle ('78), beating the Duke of Beaufort's Wamba ('78) into reserve place. Baffle was a grand-daughter of South Dorset Bridegroom ('70), and her earlier breeding was achieved by Simon Clarke who was Master of the South Dorset before taking the Cottesmore Mastership. He left the Cottesmore in 1976, but his good work in breeding their hounds was continued by Joint Master Mrs Tim Hellyer.

Daphne Moore, ultra loyal to Badminton, was notably disappointed, describing it as a 'very disappointing decision' by the bitch judges Sir Rupert Buchanan-Jardine, and Anthony Hart, Secretary of the MFHA. She conceded that Baffle 'showed a lovely smooth action and a great turn of speed, but Wamba also moved well and had that extra touch of quality which Baffle lacked.' The '79 doghound champion was Heythrop Draycott ('77) who had been reserve the previous year to Monmouth ('77).

Cottesmore Baffle ('78) scoring that pack's only Peterborough bitch championship in 1979, shown by huntsman Peter Wright and whipper-in John Seaton. The champion was bred by Joint Master, Mrs Tim Hellyer.

The current Duke of Gloucester presents Mr Ken Goschen MFH with an unentered hound trophy in 1979.

Duke of Beaufort's Whimsey, a rare example of an unentered bitch winning the championship, in 1982.

Ronnie Wallace moved to the Exmoor in 1977, and in 1980 he started his extraordinary run of Peterborough successes from that kennel. He won the doghound championship with Exmoor Fortescue ('77), by Meynell Growler ('77) and full of Heythrop breeding. Daphne Moore noted that Fortescue traced back in direct tail-male to Ronnie's first ever Peterborough champion Heythrop Harper ('53). But Daphne, loyal as ever to Badminton, thought Fortescue had 'not the best feet', whereas the Beaufort reserve champion, Midnight ('79), was 'well made, and very impressive…'

Passions were running high in the bitch championship, won by Heythrop Berry ('78). Beaufort Wamba, narrowly beaten the previous year, was reserve champion again. Daphne Moore wrote in her red ink: 'Always the bridesmaid – never the bride. It really was a bitter pill for Master to swallow'.

The Duke saw his bitch hounds win the championships in 1981 and 1982, with Ticket ('78), and an unentered bitch Whimsey by Carbine ('76). Ticket was evidence of the further experimentation at Badminton; she had some Fell blood, being a grand-daughter of Bellman ('70) from the College Valley kennel which has part-Fell hounds.

The 1982 championship was Master's last, but he was present at the 1983 show when Queen Elizabeth the Queen Mother made her third visit.

Master suffered a heart attack when following his hounds during a February afternoon, in 1984, in a vehicle driven by his great friend Peter Farquhar. The 10th Duke died peacefully next morning aged eighty-three, still Master of his own pack after sixty years, having hunted them for forty-seven years.

His cousin, David Somerset, succeeded as the 11th Duke, and has splendidly

Queen Elizabeth the Queen Mother visiting Peterborough in 1983, with the President, Mr Ken Goschen, and Lt. Colonel Tony Murray Smith, looking at Vale of Aylesbury hounds shown by Jim Bennett.

The 11th Duke of Beaufort, receives a champion cup from 1985 President, Ulrica Murray Smith, Joint Master of the Quorn for twenty-six years. The Duke of Beaufort's won both doghound and bitch championships in '85.

maintained the hunting traditions at Badminton. A keen hunting man, and a top-class eventing rider, he had been Joint Master since 1974, and served as a Field Master. His support for Ian Farquhar, Joint Master and huntsman since 1985, has ensured that breeding standards in the Badminton kennel have remained superlative, ensuring excellent sport – and more Peterborough championships.

Master left a huge gap at Peterborough where his competitive zeal added so much to the show for over half a century. The Duke was the staunchest supporter of the show and all that it stood for in raising Foxhound breeding standards; although he suffered defeats with such disappointment, he was always keen to return next year to achieve the victories he relished so much. No-one had a more expert eye for a good hound, and his total concentration on every class helped to concentrate many other minds, especially after a good lunch. He was a stickler for returning to his seat well before the start of the afternoon judging.

Sir Peter Farquhar's son, Ian Farquhar, who moved from the Bicester and Warden Hill to become the new Joint Master and huntsman at Badminton, now had to contend with regular jousts in the championships with the red coats of the Exmoor. Among other packs who intervened in the championships struggle were the Crawley and Horsham in 1983 who won the doghound championship with their Brandon ('80) by Heythrop Brimstone ('76), and the Cotswold who remarkably won the doghound championship two years in succession, 1987-88, with Cotswold Grappler ('85) and 'Grocer ('86) respectively. Their breeder, Tim Unwin, refers to their breeding in Chapter 11.

Triumph for breeder Tim Unwin, Joint Master and huntsman of the Cotswold, holding the trophy right, after Cotswold Grocer ('86) won the doghound championship in 1988, shown by kennel-huntsman Roland Sheppard, and whipper-in Richard Tabberer. Centre-left are judges David Herring MFH and Captain Charles Barclay MFH.

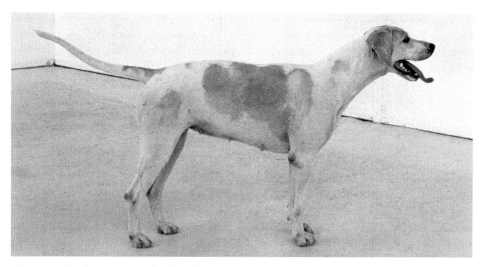

Champion bitch in 1994, Wheatland Rosebud ('92), bred by Captain John Foster MFH, Joint Master of the Wheatland for thirty-four years (1961-95).

The 1988 fixture was celebrated as the centenary of the shows, taking into account fixtures lost in world wars. *Horse and Hound* sponsored a special catalogue in which Lady Fitzwilliam paid tribute 'to our friends from the East of England Agricultural Society with whom we are pleased to have been so closely associated for so many years.'

Ronnie Wallace's younger brother Lindsay Wallace, breeder of the South Shropshire hounds, had a triumph in 1989 when their Crocket ('87) by Exmoor Bandsman ('81) won the doghound championship. The Puckeridge and Thurlow scored in the bitch section when their Devious ('87), by Portman Dayus ('82) was champion.

Ronnie Wallace proved fully the progress he had made in the Exmoor kennel by winning both championships at the 1990 show. Exmoor Daresbury ('87) won the doghound championship, and Exmoor Ripple ('89) took the bitch prize.

There was much joy among the many friends of Captain John Foster, Master of the Wheatland for thirty-four years (1961-95) when his Wheatland pack scored their first doghound championship in 1991, with Wheatland Glider ('87) by the much valued Cotswold sire Glencoyne ('84) bred by Tim Unwin. The Wheatland bred an attractive type of hound, and won significant prizes in Peterborough classes for many years before gaining their championship. John Foster's son, Edward, joined in the Wheatland Mastership from 1984-95.

The 1995 show benefited from major improvements in the Foxhound enclosure, paid for by the East of England Show, and caused mainly by radical alterations to the whole of the showground site. The enclosure position was much improved by being re-sited 180 degrees, and the ring was equipped by a new non-slip surface. The kennel fronts of black iron railings, the same as those used in the nineteenth century, were refurbished and improved, and new partitions provided with a top for each one.

Twenty-one packs competed, and although the sharing of the top championship honours was 'traditional' – the Duke of Beaufort's and Exmoor-they did not sweep the board in other classes,which included strong entries from two-day-a-week packs.

There had already been an unsuccessful anti-hunting Bill in the House of Commons in 1992, and another appeared in 1995. The hunting world knew it was facing its greatest challenge from the abolitionists, especially if Labour were to gain power. Dr Charles Goodson-Wickes MP, chairman of the British Field Sports Society, was especially welcomed at the 1995 show and sat in the box with the President, the Duke of Buccleuch.

For the student of hound breeding, the show was especially interesting when the judges – Sir Rupert Buchanan-Jardine and Sir Philip Naylor-Leyland – gave only third place in the stallion hound class to the Duke of Beaufort's handsome, part-mottled Mostyn ('92), by Baritone ('89). Only the previous week he had been stallion hound winner and doghound champion at the Great Yorkshire show. He was a highly popular stallion hound, used in many kennels with success,notably the Middleton and Cattistock, but some criticised the durability of his feet. One of his critics was Ronnie Wallace who rarely spoke openly about a specific hound, but certainly did not like Mostyn. After Mostyn's rejection, for the first time in memory, the Duke of Beaufort's did not enter a hound in the doghound championship. Ian Farquhar warmly defended his hound, who certainly proved pre-potent; his colour, his conformation and good working abilities were apparent in many hounds thereafter.

There were loud cheers at the 1996 show when the bitch championship was won by the North Cotswold – for the first time for ninety-two years. The winning

North Cotswold Grapefruit ('95) bitch champion in 1996, with LEFT TO RIGHT: *kennel-huntsman Charlie White, puppy walkers Mr and Mrs Charlie Warren, and Joint Masters Mr and Mrs Nigel Peel.*

Leading hunting photographer Jim Meads, surrounded by Hunt staff, in 1996 receiving a painting by Joy Hawken, front row, to mark his 50th year at Peterborough. He was due to reach his 60th year taking photographs at Peterborough in 2006.

North Cotswold bitch Grapefruit ('95) was a daughter of none other than the Beaufort's Mostyn. It was a great victory for the North Cotswold's husband and wife Joint Masters Nigel and Sophia Peel,and their kennel huntsman Charlie White who was retiring at the end of the season. The North Cotswold previously won the bitch championship in 1904 with a bitch named Pilgrim. The Duke Beaufort's Marlin ('95) won the doghound championship.

At the 1996 show there was a unique presentation in the main ring to Jim Meads who was attending his fiftieth consecutive Peterborough as photographer. Jim, who succeeded his father as Britain's leading specialist field sports photographer, earned special recognition from professional huntsmen for the superb quality and correctness of his pictures from the hunting field, and hound showing. Hunt staff presented him with a painting, by Joy Hawken, depicting Jim taking photographs of a Peterborough hound class. After the judging, Peterborough champions are taken to a corner near the kennels area to be photographed. Huntsmen know it as 'Jim's Corner.' The post-war photographs illustrating this book are by Jim Meads.

In 1997 there were twenty packs showing, fewer than usual, but many foxhunters had taken time off for the Countryside Rally only six days earlier, and not all could attend both events.

After twenty-five years as a ring steward, Dermot Kelly, former MFH of the Meynell, was presented with a silver photograph frame by Sir Stephen Hastings

MFH, Deputy President of the Show, to mark Dermot's retirement. As Joint Master and huntsman of the Meynell, he bred some lovely bitches as well as Meynell Growler ('74) who comes into many pedigrees today.

The main influence in the 1997 show was the Duke of Beaufort's somewhat controversial Mostyn ('92) who had sired twenty-one hounds placed. His nearest rival, Eggesford Danger ('91), had seven of his offspring placed.

Anthony Hart, secretary of the MFHA, judged with James Barclay, then starting his tenth season as MFH of the Fitzwilliam (Milton). His father, Captain Charlie Barclay, renowned Master of the Puckeridge, watched from a wheel-chair, having recently suffered several bone fractures.

The South Shropshire won the stallion hound class with their Sinbad ('95), a beautifully balanced hound, and he went on to win the doghound championship. The South Shropshire won this prize eight years earlier with Crockett ('87), a maternal grandsire of Sinbad, and bred from a male line going back to Exmoor Hackler ('78).

Ian Farquhar judged in the afternoon with Edward Knowles MFH South Dorset, and they ensured a great day for the South Shropshire by awarding their brood bitch Ginger ('92), by Berkeley Albion ('85), first place.

The run-off for the championship was between the South Shropshire's white hound, Sunbeam ('96), and North Cotswold Bowwave ('95). In the end Bowwave majestically glided across the ring to take top honours. It was the second year the North Cotswold had taken this championship. Bowwave was bred on Beaufort lines, and was by Berkeley Freshman ('84), who also comes into Mostyn's pedigree.

Ronnie Wallace left a legacy of great hound breeding in the Heythrop kennel, and since his departure to Exmoor in 1977, the Heythrop continued to feature in championship victories, although more sporadically. Richard Sumner joined the Heythrop Mastership in 1984, and took over the hound breeding, often advised by Ronnie Wallace. The result was a remarkable record of new champions; the Heythrop became the third side of a triangle of main protagonists at Peterborough, with the Duke of Beaufort's and Exmoor.

The Heythrop won the doghound championship two years consecutively in 1998-9, with Sandford ('97), a son of Exmoor Whinchat ('93), and Busby ('96) respectively. Ronnie Wallace judged the doghounds 1998, his last appearance as a judge at Peterborough – in his fifty-fifth consecutive year as a Master of Foxhounds. On paper, the Captain's decision in favour of the Heythrop, full of his previous breeding, may seem incestuous, but in truth the Heythrop kennel's success under Richard Sumner proved that a new creative hound breeder was in control.

Richard is the rare combination of a superb horseman, an excellent Field Master, and a top-class hound man. Sandford and Busby were to be used widely as stallion hounds, proving extremely effective in the hunting field and on the flags.

By the millennium, hunting had its back to the wall as a political issue. New Labour had been in power three years, and Tony Blair had promised on television legislation to ban hunting 'as soon as possible'. The Foster Bill to

Countryside Alliance President, Baroness Mallalieu, with Hunt staff at Peterborough, 1999, after she made a rousing speech.

enforce a ban had failed to become law, but it had raised the temperature ominously. The British Field Sports Society was reborn as the Countryside Alliance in 1998 and under Robin Hanbury-Tenison as chief executive, it engaged in a high profile battle to save the sport, with a Countryside March in London in 1998, and a political campaign in the Commons. In March, 2000 the Watson Bill emerged in the new Scottish Parliament, to ban hunting north of the Border.

At Peterborough in 1999 a sign of the times was the Alliance's President, Baroness Mallalieu QC, attending as show President. At the end of the morning judging, Lady Mallalieu, a Labour peeress who adores hunting, made a forthright speech in the show-ring, and was given a standing ovation by a packed Peterborough enclosure. She spoke of 'a sense of betrayal over a Prime Minister who said he would represent one nation, and govern on behalf of us all, and she promised: 'We will fight back, and we will win.'

1999 – A SEPARATE SHOW

Despite the acute political threat now reflected within the hallowed precincts of the show, the 111th Peterborough Show in 1999 was still outwardly calm – indeed quieter than for many years. This was because for the first time in its history it was held separately from the East of England Show, or the preceding Peterborough Agricultural Shows.

The East of England Show executive decided that diminishing attendances at the annual fixture in late July were due to many farmers in the predominantly arable East Midlands and East Anglia being heavily engaged in their harvest, not having time to attend the show.

The East of England therefore moved its date back to mid-June, and has remained at that part of the calendar since. The Royal Foxhound Show Society's committee felt they could not make such a move. Their show traditionally fits into a sequence of premier hound shows – the South of England and Wales and Border Counties in June, followed by the Great Yorkshire in mid-July, with Peterborough the following week. Masters show their hounds at one of the preceding shows only before appearing at Peterborough as the climax of the summer season. The season ends with the West of England four-ring outdoor show in Honiton in the first week of August, soon followed by the northern shows at Lowther, and Rydal in Cumbria, where Fell hounds predominate.

The committee of Harriers and Beagles Show, traditionally following at Peterborough, the day after the Foxhounds, took the same decision to adhere to their traditional date, and so did the Masters of Basset Hounds who were holding their show at Peterborough the day before the Foxhounds. Later the Bassets left Peterborough for another venue.

Unity is strength, and at this difficult time for hunting, it seemed a pity that the premier Foxhound show was now on its own at a time when other hound shows, such as the South of England and Great Yorkshire, were opening their doors as widely as possible to the crowds attending the agricultural shows of which they were part, and inviting them in, partly in order to spread the gospel that hunting should not be banned.

However, Peterborough had little choice in the matter, if the whole summer programme of hound showing was not to be disrupted. There were fears that the hound show attendances might suffer, but the 1999 Royal Foxhound Show still attracted a full and enthusiastic attendance. Without the attendant agricultural show, it was far easier to drive into the showground, and there was plentiful parking. Some appropriate trade stands remained with the Foxhound Show, and the lawns were a delightfully relaxing setting for afternoon tea. Roy Bird and his team continued to ensure the same high standards of organisation and attention to detail.

A popular innovation in 1999 was a parade of Foxhound sires, ranging from

A parade of Foxhound sires was a 1999 innovation: LEFT TO RIGHT: *Dumfriesshire, Brocklesby, Berkeley, David Davies, Belvoir, Meynell and S. Staffs, and Eskdale and Ennerdale.*

pure English to Fell, Welsh and French origins, from packs mainly unused to competing at Peterborough. At last the Belvoir hounds were at the show, but not competitively. Other packs included the Berkeley, Brocklesby, David Davies, Dumfriesshire, Eskdale and Ennerdale, and Meynell and South Staffs.

The far wider scope of hounds competing at Peterborough was emphasised in the unentered doghound couples class when the Cattistock were victors with honey coloured hounds who were grand-daughters of the sire Hardaway ('89). This stallion hound was bred in the Midland, Georgia, kennel of the famous American hound breeder, Ben Hardaway, who was at the ring-side with his Joint Master and son-in-law Mason Lampton. Ben is noted as an experimenter in hound breeding more daring even than Newton Rycroft, or Ikey Bell who had influenced Ben early in his Mastership of his own pack.

Horse and Hound's report on the show concluded: 'Altogether the Peterborough entries represented the cream of an irreplaceable British heritage of Foxhound breeding that must surely not be lost by government action based on prejudice, and ignorance of hunting's huge contribution to rural life.'

MILLENNIUM CELEBRATIONS

Against a darkening political background, the 2000 Peterborough was remarkably unchanged and confident. Veteran foxhunters admired the beautiful array of hounds in the ring as usual, and mainly kept to themselves their acute fears for the future of the breed.

There was, however, a reminder of the perils awaiting foxhunting and the future of its hounds, when Sam Butler, chairman of the Countryside Alliance's Campaign for Hunting, made a rousing speech in the ring to rally supporters of the sport. Sam bravely promised that a ban 'certainly will not occur', for which no-one could blame him; the positive result of the recent government inquiry into the sport, conducted by Lord Burns, gave every reason for optimism if there was a shred of tolerance and fair-play among the majority of Labour back-benchers. Peterborough Royal Foxhound Show made its own submission to the Burns Inquiry. (Appendix 5)

Sam was warmly applauded, and however inaccurate his forecast proved, it was a helpful message before lunch where appetites were not at all upset; it was the same affable, enjoyable get-together of hunting people which had been maintained since 1878. Foxhunting is a risk sport; resilience and optimism are essential equipment for the hunting field.

It was entirely appropriate that Sir Philip Naylor-Leyland filled the posts of President and Chairman at this millennium show, emphasising the vital connection with the Fitzwilliam family, and the Fitzwilliam pack. He warned in a special millennium catalogue that it was sobering to reflect how many years of careful thought and sustained endeavour were contained within the bloodlines of today's Foxhound, which would ultimately be lost forever were hunting to be banned.

Queen Elizabeth the Queen Mother, who celebrated her one hundredth birthday in 2000, sent a message in response to royal greetings from the show: 'I have much enjoyed my visits to Peterborough Royal Foxhound Society over the years, and I hope that your millennium show will be a most enjoyable occasion.'

Queen Elizabeth the Queen Mother visiting Peterborough in 1992, her 92nd year, with the President, Sir Watkin Williams-Wynn Bt, MFH.

Heythrop Chorus, champion bitch in 2000, another rare example of an unentered hound winning the championship.

Main topic of conversation in the show was the first victory for many years in the bitch championship of an unentered hound: Heythrop Chorus, another triumph for Richard Sumner's efforts to preserve the Heythrop kennel's position as one of the leaders of Foxhound breeding. Chorus, a superb example of the modern Foxhound was described by the author, reporting the show for *Horse and Hound*, as 'white with tan patches, a splendid mover, deep through the heart, and with a strong, slightly wheel back. She was beautifully shown by Heythrop huntsman Anthony Adams.'

The author's too hasty estimate that it was the first time for forty years that an unentered hound had won the championship was soon disproved. Brian Gupwell wrote to the magazine reminding us that he had showed the Duke of Beaufort's unentered Whimsey ('82) to achieve this in 1982, and another correspondent pointed out that the unentered Heythrop Clincher ('66) and their Cardinal ('64) had achieved the same in 1966 and '64 respectively. Foxhound showing is a paradise for those who enjoy statistics, and a minefield for anyone daring to report shows.

Doghound champion at the millennium show was the Duke of Beaufort's Foxham ('99), a grandson on the bottom line of the famously rejected Mostyn ('92) who had also sired Marlin ('95) as champion doghound in 1996.

2001 – FOOT AND MOUTH DISASTER YEAR

A terrible disaster struck the British countryside, and hunting inevitably suffered, when a major foot and mouth epidemic swept the land in 2001. It was a major tragedy for many live-stock farmers, especially in the West Country and the North-West. The Wales and Border Counties show, the Great Yorkshire, West of England, Lowther and Rydal hound shows were all lost. Hunting, as always, had voluntarily ceased immediately the outbreak was notified in February 2001, and fixtures were to be decimated in the 2001-2 season ahead. Among the casualties was the planned London March by the Countryside Alliance in spring to protest against Labour's avowed intent to enact a ban.

The South of England Hound show was postponed to take place on 4 July, and there was much relief when Roy Bird was able to announce that Peterborough would go ahead on 18 July. He said in *Horse and Hound*: 'We have certificates from all the entrants stating that they are not within foot-and-mouth infected areas.'

In these circumstances, it was remarkable that twenty-seven Hunts competed at Peterborough in 2001, five more than the previous year. 'We are very pleased with the response, and we hope it will be a real tonic for the foxhunting world', said Roy Bird. Such a tonic was certainly needed; resilience and optimism were being thoroughly tested.

The author wrote in *Horse and Hound*: 'The sport is facing financial pressures due to fixtures lost in last season's floods, reduced income due to the foot-and-mouth restrictions that are causing uncertainty about the start of hunting this autumn, and the threat of a new anti-hunting Bill from the re-elected Labour government. But the mood among devoted hunting people is defiant, and they are determined to overcome all obstacles to save their sport...Founded in 1878

Martin C. Wood II (LEFT), Joint Master of the Live Oak , Florida – only the second American to judge at Peterborough – with co-judge David Palmer MFH during the doghound couples class in 2001.

to become the world's premier hound show, Peterborough will this year symbolise the sport's continuity.'

The 2001 Peterborough Basset Hound show, and the Harriers and Beagles Show were cancelled.

C. Martin Wood, Joint Master with his wife Daphne of their own Live Oak pack at Monticello, Florida, appeared as the second American to judge at Peterborough. Marty and Daphne were disciples of Ronnie Wallace's breeding in developing their Anglo-American cross-bred pack

Mr and Mrs Martin (Marty) C. Wood, Joint Masters of their Live Oak pack in Florida, USA, with Captain Ronnie Wallace (RIGHT) at Peterborough 2001.

Torrential rain hit the 2001 show: Thurlow kennel-huntsman Chris Amatt and whipper-in Adrian Robinson lead hounds over flooded ground to the collecting ring.

in the northern Florida region of pine forests and sandy tracks thirty-one years ago. Both have served as Presidents of the Masters of Foxhounds Association of America, and have forged strong links with English foxhunting. They have entertained many English Masters at Live Oak, and came to London to support the Countryside Alliance Marches, as well as fund raising for the Countryside Alliance campaign.

Marty was judging the doghound section with David Palmer, a highly experienced Foxhound judge, and Joint Master of the Worcesteshire. Martin Letts, Master of the College Valley and North Northumberland, and Andrew Cook, Joint Master of the South Shropshire, judged the bitch hounds.

STORMY 2001 SHOW

As if the political climate was not bad enough, the English weather inflicted a dreadful day on the 2001 show: high winds accompanied a constant heavy downpour, flooding parts of the ground, and fusing one of the floodlights above the ring. At one stage, a downpipe was feeding gushes of water into the collecting ring, and spectators were advised there were only two exits they could use. On this occasion, Hunt livery with top-boots was ideal wear for the staff showing hounds, and men in bowler hats and woollen suits were well equipped; ladies in summer hats and dresses with light shoes, tackled the weather with foxhunting stoicism. No matter how the storms raged outside, the show continued without interruption in normal Peterborough calm.

Marty Wood said afterwards it was one of the 'greatest days of my life', but reflected wryly that his previous judging experience in England, at Honiton, had been attended by a heat wave, and now he had endured storms and flooding.

Despite fading light, and accompanying lightning and thunder with fierce rainstorms offstage, the two-couples bitch class was a remarkable sight, cramming the ring with hounds from fifteen packs, of superb quality. It was indeed a hound lovers' treat.

This was Ronnie Wallace's last appearance at the show. He died, aged eighty-two, the following February in a car accident in Somerset, driving himself to a Taunton hospital to visit his wife Rosie. It was a grievous loss for the foxhunting world, and for Peterborough in particular, the arena where he had contributed much, and played a large part in developing the modern Foxhound.

Ronnie Wallace's lemon and white doghound Exmoor Emperor ('97) won the stallion hound class against strong competition, in which the Heythrop were runners-up with Forger ('99) and the Bicester with Whaddon Chase third with their Miller ('99) a grandson of the Beaufort Mostyn ('92). Although they had not won a Peterborough championship, Ian McKie's breeding in the Bicester kennel produced a robust, well made type of Foxhound which many admired at the Peterborough ring-side, and which had frequently been in the ribbons.

Exmoor Emperor appeared again to win the 2001 doghound championship, amid impressive candidates from six packs in the final judging, with the reserve going to the Heythrop's badger-pie Grafter ('00), a grandson of Cotswold Pilgrim ('88) on the top line. After the show Ronnie sat in the Vice-Presidents' bar with his brothers, Lindsay and Vivian, quietly discussing the day, their last meeting at a hound show. The South Shropshire mourned the passing of Lindsay in 2004, and Rosie Wallace died later the same year.

The 2001 bitch champion, Cotswold Captive ('00) was a triumph for Tim Unwin, Joint Master and huntsman of the Cotswold for twenty-eight years until

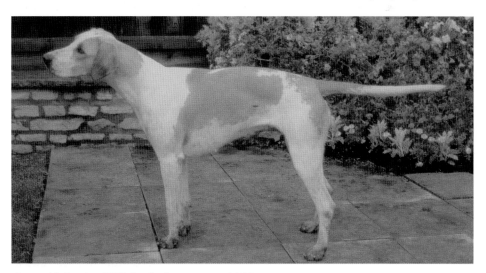

Cotswold Captive ('00), bitch champion in 2001.

1999, and for Martin Scott who bred Captive's sire, VWH Guinness ('92), one of the most influential stallion hounds of recent years.

Twenty-two packs competed at the 114th Peterborough in 2002. It was a 'traditional' show, but the Exmoor was a notable absentee, officially due to a kennel cough, and the Hunt was mourning the loss of its great Master.

GREEN-JACKET DUEL

Yet again there was a green-jacket duel in the bitch championship. Many at the ring-side believed Heythrop Poplin ('01) would win; she had been the Harrogate bitch champion, and had been unentered champon at Peteborough the previous year. She represented a shrewd use of refreshing Old English lines, since her sire was Belvoir Poacher ('98). However, the judges preferred the more substantial tri-coloured Duke of Beaufort's Galaxy ('01). It was a great show for Ian Farquhar: he had already collected the doghound championship with Whipsnade ('01), a grandson of Mostyn.

In the autumn of 2002, the Countryside Alliance held its second great March in London, magnificently supported by over 400,000 protestors. In December the government announced its own Hunting Bill, and although it was shelved during the Iraq War early in 2003, the Bill emerged on the floor of the Commons for its Third Reading on 1st July, and the political battle renewed.

The background for Peterborough in 2003 was therefore still troubled, but the atmosphere of the show was relaxed, mainly because it was a stifling, hot day. As

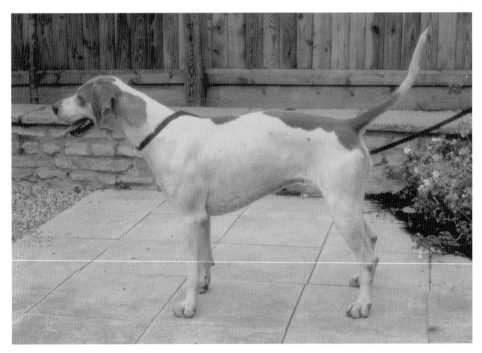

Heythrop Poplin ('01), by Old English sire Belvoir Poacher ('98) won the bitch championship in 2003, having been denied in 2002.

usual, there was no question of shirt-sleeve order at Peterborough, and none of the Hunt Staff requested it. Simon Clarke, who has devoted much of his life to the best interests of foxhunting, was President, and the Queen as Patron sent a message of thanks for the loyal greetings sent on behalf of the show which was celebrating its 125th anniversary.

The Queen's message in the catalogue was: 'As your Patron, I thank you for your thoughtfulness in writing, and send my warm good wishes to all those present for a memorable event.'

Baroness Mallalieu attended again, and on behalf of the Countryside Alliance delivered another 'we shall win' speech which was much appreciated, and warmly applauded. It was a vintage Peterborough, with twenty-four packs competing. Brian Fanshawe and Rupert Inglesant MFH (Ludlow) judged the doghounds. Ian McKie, who had made a move from the Bicester to join the College Valley, judged the bitch section with James Barclay, who moved from the Fitzwilliam to the Cottesmore and South Wold.

LAST SHOW BEFORE THE BAN

The 2004 Peterborough, the 116th show, paid tribute to the East of England show by appointing Mr Joe Odam as its President. He said in his presidential message: 'I would like to think as a representative of the East of England Agricultural Society since 1963, on the Foxhound Show Society General Committee, that my appointment reflects the closeness of the two organisations through their successive leaders. The East of England Showground could not have been located and created as it is today without the generosity of the Fitzwilliam family...The Foxhound Society was founded in 1878 – who dares to prevent it continuing?'

The 2004 Show was to be the last before the heinous Hunting Act was imposed at the end of the year, with the intention of making all forms of "hunting with dogs" illegal. Simon Hart, recently appointed chief executive of the Countryside Alliance, addressed the Peterborough gathering, urging hunting people to keep their nerve in the face of the political threat. He was previously director of the Alliance's Campaign for Hunting, a former Master and huntsman of the South Pembrokeshire, and as the son of the late Anthony Hart, Secretary of the MFHA for twenty-two years, he was 'at home', and among friends. Anthony Hart was elected President of the Show in 2001 in recognition of his many years service to hunting which included appearances as a highly effective judge at Peterborough, but sadly had been unable to attend through illness. His term was extended to 2002 in the hope that he would be able to fill the role, but it was not to be, and his wife, Judy Hart, attended as Deputy President.

Mr Odam had compiled statistics which indicated the Duke of Beaufort's had up to 2004 won forty-nine championships; the Heythrop were thirteen behind with thirty-seven the Warwickshire third with eighteen, and Captain Ronnie Wallace's last pack, the Exmoor in fourth place with fourteen. Sadly, the Exmoor were unable to show in 2004 due to an outbreak of kennel cough.

There was warm applause when the Duke of Beaufort's achieved their fiftieth championship victory with their doghound Bailey ('03), by Heythrop Busby ('96), who won the unentered prize the previous year. Reserve was Middleton Samson

Editor Lucy Higginson (LEFT) in 2004 presents Heythrop Joint Master Richard Sumner, accompanied by Libby Cooke, with the Horse and Hound *Cup for unentered champion.*

('03) who had also won the stallion hound class, a compliment to the breeding of Middleton Joint Master and huntsman Frank Houghton-Brown. There was some surprise in the brood bitch class when the previous year's champion, Heythrop Poplin ('01), was placed only second to the North Cotswold's Daytime ('01). The bitch section judges, Ian Farquhar and John Lockwood MFH (Burton) awarded the North Cotswold their third Peterborough championship, by selecting Daytime as the bitch champion; she was a daughter of Heythrop Busby ('96). The Heythrop gained reserve championship with their fine unentered bitch Greedy, by Governor ('01).

It was another great show, but huge changes were on the way. For Peterborough there was to be a special challenge the following year – the new Festival of Hunting, when at last, the Harriers and Beagle show would take place on the same day, with many other attractions for the hound lover.

10. THE POST-WAR CHAMPIONS

W e are indebted to Martin Scott for the following analysis of Peterborough champions in the post-war years.

Martin Scott is one of the leading authorities on the Foxhound to-day. He was bred to foxhunting: his father, the late Major Bill Scott was a great friend of Sir Peter Farquhar, and supported his views on modern hound breeding. Bill Scott had a remarkably varied hunting career: he was Master of the United (1927-8), of the Portman pre-war (1928-32), the North Cotswold (1932-47), the West Waterford (1947-49) and the Portman with Sir Peter (1949-52) and the Old Berks (1957-65). Martin Scott was Master and huntsman of the Tiverton (1969-77) and of the VWH (1977-83). He has continued to breed the VWH hounds with notable success, producing some highly influential sires; he is a frequent judge, and has written on Foxhound breeding for a number of publications, including Hunting *magazine, and* Horse and Hound.

Martin Scott MFH (RIGHT) judging at Peterborough in 1977 with Colin Nash MFH.

I first visited the Peterborough Royal Foxhound show in 1968, and have attended every year since. The overall impression over that time was the dominance of two people who are no longer with us, the 10th Duke of Beaufort and Captain Ronnie Wallace. They vied over the years to win the championship here and they did not like being beaten as those who have judged here in those days will know.

The hounds I have been responsible for have also shown here at times, and with some degree of success, but these hounds have never won the much-coveted championship. However, they have sired some of the champions! The great excuse that everyone uses, that they are bred for work, is part of the reason; the other reason is that they are just not good enough, but hunting is what they do best and those who accept Peterborough as the right standard are happy to enjoy the show.

Of course part of the fun is criticising the judges, and as a judge I have had my fair share of abuse from my friends over the years, but if we are take the whole thing too seriously then we need to take care. However, the judges do their utmost to get it right, not only because of the ribbing they may get, fair or not, but because they want to be asked again.

Fortunately I have been asked again, so I cannot have made too many howlers. What is fascinating is that when judging at Peterborough, and being inside the ring, once the eye is in, every single fault is magnified, and while the good showman will try to hide these faults by moving his charges at the critical moment before it shows them, an experienced judge will look over his shoulder when perhaps they are not expecting to be seen, to check up on the hidden fault.

For reasons described earlier – the evolution of the modern type – I believe the Foxhound has improved throughout the land, which has resulted in the standard at Peterborough getting better each year. Of course the standard of judging had to be seen to be consistent, and a small number of influential people made sure that good judges were selected to act as senior judges at Peterborough, bringing on new judges, and reporting back on them.

Readers who care to look at the list of the judges since the war (Appendix 2) will see a recurring theme, where a young judge has been brought on by an old senior one, and then become a senior judge, and if successful that judge has been asked back again. Today with Masterships being shorter, the list of the senior judges has somewhat reduced, and I hope a new fashion is not being brought about.

ANALYSING THE CHAMPIONS

It is worth looking at a list of the champion hounds at Peterborough over the years to help indicate the changes in Foxhound breeding. Of course, the last half of the last century was dominated by two packs, the Duke of Beaufort's and the Heythrop, and after Captain Wallace's move to Exmoor, that kennel to a lesser extent.

In looking over the list of champion since the war, the influence of the larger kennel is to be expected, and it should be so, for if they cannot produce the best hounds regularly, then it does not give the rest much of a chance. The Peterborough champions since the war have come mainly from the three packs, the Duke of Beaufort's with a total of thirty-three (nineteen doghounds and fourteen bitches) the Heythrop twenty-five (fifteen doghounds and ten bitches) and the Exmoor thirteen (seven doghounds and six bitches).

The remainder have been four bitches from the Middleton, three bitches from the Puckeridge, The Portman with three (two doghounds and one bitch) and the South Shropshire with two doghounds and one bitch). Then with two champions to their credit we have the Cotswold with two doghounds, their neighbours the North Cotswold with two bitches, their neighbours the Warwickshire with two doghounds.

The South and West Wilts had two champions one from each sex, as do the Wheatland, while the Pytchley had two bitch champions just after the war. There are eleven packs with the proud record of just one champion, namely the Quorn, Meynell, Crawley and Horsham, Cottesmore, Kilkenny, Tipperary, West Kent, Eridge, North Staffs, Braes of Derwent and the Four Burrow.

THREE MOST INFLUENTIAL SIRES

How did they turn out, which of them were characters, what were they really like? The three most influential champion doghounds must be Heythrop Craftsman 1962, Duke of Beaufort's Palmer 1959 and Portman Wizard 1955.

Others who I would regard as important would be Quorn Raglan ('47), Heythrop Harper ('53), Duke of Beaufort's Crowner ('69), Heythrop Draycott ('77) and Exmoor Fortescue ('77), the brothers Freestone and Friar ('81) and the latter's son Exmoor Dancer ('84), Cotswold Grappler ('85), Exmoor Daresbury ('87) and Heythrop Glazier ('90).

It would be premature to mention any of the younger ones. However, by mentioning these champion hounds, we are omitting a whole host of great stallion hounds and brood bitches that have played their part, and have been bred back to for their good working abilities.

I have included Quorn Raglan ('47) in my list for although I am too young to have known him, his name comes in all Limerick hounds bred by the late Lord Daresbury via their Selfish ('52), and is also widespread in the Belvoir kennel. Quorn Raglan ('47) is a grandson of Pytchley Safeguard ('35) and so brings Welsh blood lines into the Belvoir kennel.

Two brothers from Badminton Rector and Remus ('47) were champions in 1950 and '51; this feat has only been repeated by brothers once since then, while there have been two sets of brother and sisters who became champions.

Portman Latimer ('51) by North Cotswold Landlord ('44), who I was brought up with, was an early champion who although good in his work was not as tough or as hard as his half brother Portman Freeman ('51) who was preferred for his working abilities and therefore used with more success.

Heythrop Harper ('53) more importantly brings in the top line to the Welsh blood of Brecon Paragon 1923, and so does the Duke of Beaufort's Palmer ('59), both coming through Portman sires. Palmer ('59) lived and hunted well into old age, and was known for his great hunting abilities and his longevity which he passed on to many of his daughters. Harper's direct descendants are Heythrop Draycott ('77) and Exmoor Fortescue ('77), both by Meynell Growler ('74).

His direct descendant is Cotswold Grappler ('85) who was champion in 1987, had a beautiful and deep melodious voice, and was also a great jumper; he enjoyed jumping fences just to see what was the other side, and his brothers all turned out well, which is so valuable. His grandson Heythrop Busby ('96) was champion in 1999 and his son Duke of Beaufort's Bailey ('03) was champion in 2004.

Cotswold Grocer ('86) punctured the ball of his foot in his early days which must have held him back, but he and his brother became successful stallion hounds. Tim Unwin introduced the Fell blood of Blencathra Glider ('76) into his Cotswold kennel, and this introduction via Cotswold Glencoyne ('84) produced two champions, Heythrop Glazier ('90) and Wheatland Glider ('87).

This was a great triumph for this two-day-a-week pack from Shropshire, but it did not surprise breeding pundits, because the two main players involved, Mrs Kennedy and then John Foster, have carefully line-bred these hounds for many years. Rosebud was an excellent worker and was freely bred from, her produce was never as pretty as she was but they were just as good in their work. Her sire was Puckeridge Roxburg ('88) bred by John Foster's very old friend Captain Charles Barclay. They went through the war together for five years, and later Captain Barclay married John's sister.

The Puckeridge hounds have been famous for their noses; they have to be, hunting on the cold ploughs of East Anglia. They had produced a champion before the war named Wizard ('28) who ended up in the National History Museum in Madison Square Gardens for all to see. Since the war they have provided three bitch champions Poetry ('51), Pigeon ('81) who produced some excellent progeny still in the pack today, and Devious ('87) who could not produce a good looking one, but has produced some excellent nosed hounds proving that hunting attributes are more important than looks. Heythrop Glazier ('90) has been an outstanding Foxhound, and is now in the pedigree of three-quarters of the Heythrop pack.

It was a brave move made by Mrs Willes when she used Cotswold Glencoyne ('84), by the outstanding Fell hound Blencathra Glider ('76) who not only proved a top-class stallion in the Fells but in modern hounds too. Glazier has been a kind-hearted hound, who only liked hunting and would bay impatiently at the meet until hounds moved off, this trait has been inherited by some of his offspring. He died too young, maybe he burnt himself out in his enthusiasm for his hunting, for he never missed a day's hunting.

His grandson, via the dam, was Heythrop Sandford ('97) champion in 1998 who has never been any problem, has a good voice and is quick on his feet as well as mentally and his aim has always been to please. If Sandford's aim was to please then Heythrop Busby ('96) might be the reverse, in the kennel and in the show ring he is an awkward contrary sort. He could be compared with a difficult child who badly needs motivating, for he sort of shrugs his shoulders at anything, but when he is out hunting he settles in well and hunts away in the middle of the pack and is a steady line hunter.

Duke of Beaufort's Crowner ('69), doghound champion 1971.

Duke of Beaufort's Crumpet ('69), bitch champion 1971.

Duke of Beaufort's Palmer ('83), doghound champion 1985.

Puckeridge Devious ('87), bitch champion 1989.

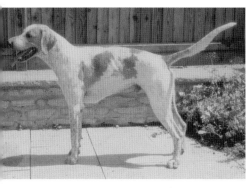

Duke of Beaufort's Palmer ('02), doghound champion 2003 – the 50th Peterborough championship achieved from the Badminton kennel.

Exmoor Daresbury ('87) champion doghound, 1990.

Heythrop Brigand ('54) sired a number of champions including Duke of Beaufort's Brimstone ('58), Craftsman ('62) and Falcon ('60). Falcon was given to Colin Nash at the Old Berks. Colin found him a completely trustworthy hound, and if he saw him forging on ahead he knew he would be right. Heythrop Craftsman ('62) the champion in 1967 had already sired a champion in Heythrop Cardinal ('64) who also became Supreme champion at the last show at the old showground. However, he was not good enough in his work to be used at Heythrop, once again proving that champions have to be good in the field to be used.

However he was an exception to the rule for Craftsman sired a whole host of top class working hounds including Lupin ('67) the champion bitch the following year, and her brother Lurcher ('67) a good strong sort who followed suit the next year. Heythrop Clamour ('69) kept up the tradition, and the following year a brother and sister were champion, both by Craftsman namely the Duke of Beaufort's Crowner and Crumpet ('69). Crowner was a large powerful doghound, and many in the crowd that year preferred his kennel-mate the blue mottle Warden ('68), bred on very similar lines, full of quality and class.

GUPWELL SHOWS 14 CHAMPIONS

However, Crowner was of the doghound mould, a strong tough looking sort yet beautifully balanced with a real masculine head. Of all the fourteen champions Brian Gupwell showed, he picked out Crowner as the best for his work. He was also a great character: he would put the fear of God into the postman when they were walking out, his hackles would go up and he would bay at him! He also put more than the fear of God into many of the Badminton foxes! Other champions with this male line back to Heythrop Craftsman ('62) come via Berkeley David ('81) who sired Exmoor Daresbury ('87) who sired Greatwood ('93) and Redskin ('92) and his sister Raindrop ('92) who were from a wonderful litter.

Tony Collins showed a number of champions at the Heythrop. One of the best hunters he had was Rockwood ('80), but sadly he was infertile which was a disaster, for the Heythrop R line was one of the best at Chipping Norton. However, Draycott ('77) was one of the best. Heythrop Pixton ('75) was Tony Collins's first doghound champion, and in his early days was a bit full of himself as he may have had a bitch too early. However, Pixton had that little extra ingredient 'Fox Sense'.

An example of this came when the mixed pack were having a day in the Saturday country and had run into the unfashionable Bourton Wood. Hounds could do little but Pixton kept on indicating that there was a fox in front. Tony trusted him enough to persevere, and it paid off for the fox jumped up almost at the time when he thought he should give up. Pixton's knowledge and Tony's trust paid off and it resulted in an excellent hunt out to Hinchwick and back and ended in the back of Moreton-in-the-Marsh.

The Four Burrow hounds are well known for their hunting abilities from distant Cornwall and having been in the hands of the Williams family for three generations they were justifiably proud of their hounds. It was during the Mastership of Percival Williams and his son John that they won the bitch championship with Pasty ('54). Her portrait by Lionel Edwards looks down on

Heythrop Glazier ('90) champion doghound, 1993.

Duke of Beaufort's Marlin ('95) champion doghound 1996.

Heythrop Sandford ('97) champion doghound 1998.

South Shropshire Clever ('97), champion bitch 1997.

John at his desk today. Pasty was so good that the family named a superb filly after her who made a name for herself on the flat. This championship did have something rare, in that it may be the only champion shown by an amateur huntsman, namely John.

Over the years Peterborough has had its share of upsets and excitements. One of them happened to John and the hounds that morning on the way to the show, for he left most of the hounds they were showing in Uppingham on the way to the showground. The trailer door opened at the traffic lights, and the hounds escaped to explore the delights of that town.

Fortunately traffic was not as mad as it is today, and they recoverd the hounds, to win the two-couples class, as well as having a second and a third, and finally they won the champion bitch class with Pasty. She was one of a litter of six, out of a good, well above average bitch who had two litters, one of which was outstanding, a daughter named Cactus being about the best bitch John ever hunted, absolutely steady to the hunted fox.

WEST KENT TRIUMPH

The first time I ever judged at Peterborough was in 1973, and I shall never forget the roar which went up when West Kent Payment ('72) won the championship, for the West Kent were a two-day-a-week pack. Payment was a great worker and her breeding became highly influential in the West Kent kennel; her line was used thereafter by their long time huntsman Stan Luckhurst, who said that all the pack, at the amalgamation in 1999, went back to Payment.

One of the two litters she had, experienced a hazardous, start to life. Three of the whelps were born in the kennel whelping pens, but then Payment absconded and was lost for a while. With the help of her puppy walker, Maureen Hale, the bitch was found in a hole in woods about three-quarters of a mile away. They had to dig her and a further seven whelps out of the hole. All survived and became a great litter, used extensively in breeding, West Kent Agent ('77) being one of them. Payment disappeared one day when hunting near Brands Hatch never to be seen again, despite extensive searching, but her name lives on.

Portman Wizard ('55) was champion in 1958, and his influence on the modern Foxhound has been enormous. He had a brother called Winston who was not so good looking, but was a brilliant hunter. However, Wizard was hunted and used by Captain Wallace at the Heythrop with great success, siring their champion Blackcock ('59). Blackcock was a great character who was loaned to other packs. The late Duke of Beaufort was tickled pink with Blackcock one day, after hunting in Lower Woods, when this doghound went back to a drain they had bolted a fox from, to make sure there were no more there. Blackcock was sent to the Kilkenny where his 'Fox Sense' was greatly valued by the late Victor McCalmont.

Exmoor Hackler ('78) whose male line goes back to Wizard sired the first champion brothers in thirty years, namely Exmoor Friar ('81) in 1982 and Freestone ('81) in 1984. These two quality brothers were used extensively; Friar sired Exmoor's champion Dancer ('84) who was grandsire of South Shropshire's Sinbad ('95). Freestone ('81) was used at Berkeley with success and the Duke of Beaufort's Marlin ('95) was by the well used Mostyn ('92), a great-grandson of Freestone. Friar and Freestone were very good doghounds, 'you just knew they were there', according to Captain Wallace.

Duke of Beaufort Ranger ('90) was the biggest character of their recent champions according to Captain Ian Farquhar, for two reasons: he never lied, and when he was sure, he got on with it, and told the world so with his great voice, having the courage of his conviction and not looking over his shoulder.

He recalls hunting round the lakes at Dauntsey when a fox came out in front of him with Ranger close behind, and Ranger hunted down the track shouting his head off and it did not take long for the rest of the pack to join him, so certain was Ranger in his own conviction that he was right. He has passed on this confidence to his children, who are not frightened to use their inherited good voices, 1999's champion bitch Patience ('98) being a granddaughter of Ranger ('90).

OPPOSITE: Duke of Beaufort's doghounds, 2005 by John King

PALMER '03

GARLIC

Gulley
Beaufort 65

ROMBADIER

Johnny
Beaufort.

BAILEY '04

Johnny
Beaufort '05

151

The doghound championship for the last three years, including 2005, has been won by the Duke of Beaufort's hounds, which is a record in itself. Bred carefully by Captain Farquhar, two of whom were walked by the same people, the Barkwith's who live down in Sodbury Vale below Horton Hill.

Captain Wallace rated Desert ('72) as one of the finest bitches he bred, Desert, equalled only by Exmoor Millstream ('94). Of course Exmoor Pixie ('86) was a great person who ended her days with Biddy Trouton, and has a challenge cup named after her at Exmoor. Captain Wallace's last championship win was with Exmoor Emperor ('97) in 2001. He brings in the special male line back to Tiverton Actor 1922, which he treasured as it allowed him to ring the changes, as he called it, varying male line to those of the sire and the dam.

NORTH COTSWOLD INFLUENCE

In recent years the North Cotswold have only kept bitches and over the last few years Nigel Peel has bred a quality pack. His champions have been Daytime in 2004, Grapefruit ('95) in 1996 and Bowwave ('95) in 1997. Grapefruit is one of the best in the field, and has terrific 'fox sense'; she hunts three days without any problem.

However, she was quite hard-headed to start with, and a great deal of patience was needed with her, but once she was settled she would never tell a lie, and her children are just like her. They will always be close to the action, and if there is any mayhem they may be close to it too! She has a high pitched voice which carries really well, and she loves life.

At the meet she will grin at her Master, while Bowwave will start to bay if they stay any longer than ten minutes. Bowwave is more biddable, but she is a wonder on the roads and tracks; she has a deep voice, and is most accurate turning with the fox, and never over runs the line. Neither of these bitches are jealous in their fifth season, and they both have children that have entered well.

Three of South Shropshire's champions at Peterborough were: Charlock ('91) who was so good that she has had four litters; Sinbad ('95) who is a smashing big doghound, acccording to former South Shropshire Master and huntsman, Andrew Cook, who can't fault him and says he is a good fox finder; and according to Andrew their bitch champion Clever ('97) is rather like her sire VWH Guinness ('92), a fast racy bitch who hunts well, but is independent by nature.

The hounds I have mentioned, are only a few of the champions, but their huntsmen have honestly said, that if they are not good enough in their work, they are not bred from. They all have certain characteristics which they will pass on to their offspring, and over the years I would think that the standard in the field and in the show-ring has greatly improved to cope with changing conditions. Patience is required, so that trust can be built up, to allow the hounds to do what they do best, and that is to hunt the fox, which I am certain will continue for many years to come.

11. MEMORIES, MEMORIES...

BRIAN FANSHAWE

(Former Joint Master and huntsman of the Warwickshire, Co. Galway, North Cotswold and Cottesmore)

I first went to Peterborough Royal Foxhound Show in 1953 when the Show was held in the middle of the town. I was proudly attired in my first trilby hat until I received an imperial rocket for not wearing a bowler! I am glad to say Peterborough standards are still upheld.

At that time my parents were the Masters of the North Cotswold and won a prize with a broken coated dog hound called Sailor ('52) by Beaufort Larkspur ('47) ex-Lady Curre's Saucy ('47). Saucy was a pure white Curre bitch and she made a life long impression on me of the value of the best Welsh out-crosses.

My next involvement with Peterborough was when I showed the Warwickshire hounds in 1965. The Warwickshire had not shown since about 1910 when they did not win either Championship and Lord Willoughby de Broke vowed he would never show again! We won the best unentered dog hound special prize with Banker ('65), but Banker was one of the very few hounds that I have bred that showed absolutely no interest in hunting the fox. We probably

Captain Brian Fanshawe (RIGHT), former Joint Master and huntsman of four packs, presenting the cup to Antony Sandeman MFH after Crawley and Horsham Measure ('02) won the bitch championship in 2005.

made him big-headed by exhibiting him as our pride and glory to all and sundry who came to the kennels. Hopefully it taught me never to spoil an unentered dog hound or to show any entered hound that is not first class in the field.

In 1969 I went to Galway and was allowed the pick of a large entry of first season Warwickshire dog hounds. I took several with me but omitted Palmer ('68) who won the championship in 1970. I was not at the show but the following night we were staying with Evan and Gill Williams, then Masters of the Tipperary. Evan congratulated me on achieving the ambition of every hound breeder. I had no idea what he was talking about until he eventually said that I had bred a Peterborough champion. I did however take Palmer's litter sister Pancake and I retained her female line for the rest of my career.

Charlie Bishop, my Joint Master in Galway, and I brought three or four couple of Galway Blazer hounds to Peterborough in 1971 in the back of Charlie's smart new Volvo car. We got a great welcome, but regretfully the hounds picked up a bug en route and did not show well and we only picked up one minor rosette.

I continued to show both the North Cotswold and Cottesmore hounds during my Masterships with intermittent success, mostly with hounds bred from Carlow Stylish ('63). During both Masterships I was using Welsh out-crosses and then I introduced an American cross bred line. I tried to see that the best of these were displayed at Peterborough for others to see, which should be a raison d'etre for showing beyond winning prizes. In reality though, hound shows are not much fun if you don't have any winners.

It has been a great privilege and honour to have judged the Show four times. In the years that I have been going to Peterborough, I don't expect that the standard of the champion hounds has changed a great deal, but the overall quality of hounds throughout the classes has improved out of all proportion. The reason is mostly due to the generosity of the Masters of the leading packs, particularly the Beaufort and Heythrop, in allowing others to use their stallion hounds. The MFHA did a great service to hound breeding shortly before the Second World War when they banned the sale of hounds to other packs, thus removing any fiscal value of stallion hounds.

EDMUND VESTEY

(Former Joint Master and huntsman of the Puckeridge and the Thurlow, and currently of the Thurlow)

Coming from a family with no deep roots in hunting, on becoming a Master of a pack that had not shown at any hound show for many year, I knew little about Peterborough or any other hound show. But we took some of our Red and White Friesians, as they were then, to the first year at the new Showground at Alwalton, and as a break from floundering around in the mud in the cattle section, I went to have a look at what went on in the hound ring, and was hooked.

Not long after, I had a visit in my office in London from a certain Mr Roy Bird. He was struggling to find a sponsor for the Hunter Breeding classes. Did I think our company, J.H. Dewhurst, could be persuaded to take that on? I asked him if he really thought it would be appropriate for a firm of butchers to do that? We looked at each other, we both burst out laughing, we found another solution, and that was the beginning of a friendship that has lasted to this day.

Thanks to Simon Clarke's persuasion, I found myself judging the doghounds with him at the Centenary Show in 1978 when HRH the Prince of Wales was President. As so often, the battle for the championship came down to a tussle between the Duke of Beaufort's and the Heythrop. Captain Clarke seemed to favour the Heythrop dog, while I rather liked the Duke's Monmouth. Finally I asked the Captain if we could really make champion a dog with feet like that, little realising the furore we were about to cause by awarding the championship, I think for the first time, to a dog with such strong Welsh influence in his pedigree. I am glad to say the Heythrop dog became champion the following year.

Twenty years ago I was lucky enough to have the chance to start a new pack of Foxhounds with gifts from a number of kind friends from all over England, but particularly from the late Captain 'Pup' Arkwright of the North Warwickshire who were being forced to disband by new motorways. They came in all shapes and sizes, and it was a wonderful thrill within about ten years to produce out of this mixed bag two young hounds who won their classes. The excitement among the staff and the puppy walkers who were present, was lovely to see, with the feeling that to win a prize at Peterborough, the holy of holies, had really put us on the map.

Peterborough is wonderful, with the marvellous staff in the office, the stewards and everyone behind the scenes under the eagle eye of Mr Roy Bird who has fulfilled his role as Secretary so brilliantly for forty years. Now he is retiring, and it is splendid that he is being succeeded by Mr Andrew Mercer who has organised the 2005 Peterborough Festival of Hunting with such enthusiasm and skill. But let us always remember that without the generosity of the Fitzwilliam family, none of it would have happened.

Whatever the political future may hold for hunting, let us never forget that the ancestry of some of the lovely hounds that come to Peterborough each summer can be traced back seventy-five or eighty generations, or in human terms to about the time of Christ. We cannot let them go. Let us rejoice in the love they give us, the sport and the fun and enjoyment they give us. We *must* maintain the bloodlines of these quite remarkable creatures. We simply cannot condemn them to oblivion.

SIMON CLARKE

(Former Joint Master and huntsman of the South Dorset, Cottesmore, Duke of Buccleuch's, South and West Wilts., and New Forest)

I first attended Peterborough in 1962, and I suspect the quality of entrants had improved throughout the 1950s. The Duke of Beaufort led the way, but Sir Peter Farquhar's Portman had tremendous influence, especially at Badminton. Captain Wallace won his first championship in 1955, and continued with many more, using his Brigand ('54) and Badminton and Portman sires on bitches from the strong Heythrop F lines.

Heythrop Clematis ('60) was champion bitch in 1961 when Bob Field-Marshal and Brian Bell were judging; there was much mocking that she was not a hound but a whippet! Perhaps too much substance had been forfeited in favour of speed? Anyway, Ronnie Wallace introduced more lumber, especially extolling the virtues of his Lurcher ('67) a very heavy dog. Meanwhile the Duke of Beaufort continued to keep up the size of his hounds.

Colonel John Chamberlayne, Secretary of the MFHA, started publishing in the Foxhound Kennel Stud Book the photos of champions from 1959, and the results from 1961.

The show owes a huge debt of gratitude to the Fitzwilliam family. Tom Fitzwilliam sold the Agricultural Society land at a very advantageous price, and was a charming Chairman for many years. Many heroes of the Chase were serving on the Hound Show Committee when I was asked to join in the 1970s. These included Bob Hoare, Charlie Barclay, Tony Murray-Smith, Tony Warre, John Yarborough, and Neil Foster. It remains the custom to have two or three members of the Agricultural Society on the committee, and among these have been Joe Odam, Ted Saunders, and David Reynolds. They have contributed hugely, especially Joe Odam who was President in 2004.

Lady Fitzwilliam took over as Chairman when her husband died, and presided, like him, with wit and wisdom over the affairs of the show. We are incredibly fortunate that Sir Philip Naylor-Leyland continues the Milton connection, and is Chairman, a task he undertakes with great attention to detail, and much hard work. It is splendid that his son Tom became a Steward in 2005.

LORD KIMBALL

(Former Joint Master and huntsman of the Fitzwilliam, and the Cottesmore)

After the war, Lord Brassey was ring steward at Peterborough Royal Hound Show on the old showground on the Eastfield Road.

As always, the standard of turn-out at Peterborough was immaculate. Masters, their wives in their hats, and Hunt Servants in their new season's clothing and Lord Brassey continued the Royal Horse Guards tradition of wearing highly polished brown shoes with a blue suit. The wearing of hats at Peterborough was a tradition not broken until late 1995.

Lord Brassey asked me to join him as Assistant Ring Steward in 1995 when I was Joint Master of the Fitzwilliam. He did the morning, and I did the afternoon, and when he decided to give up, I asked Mr Dermot Kelly, Master of the Meynell to help me. I did the morning, and was able to enjoy the afternoon. The key to much that was achieved at Peterborough owes a lot to Albert Buckle, former huntsman of the Whaddon Chase, who since 1947 looked after the Hunt Servants in the Collecting Ring, and at the same time kept a watchful eye on the Ring Stewards.

It was a great honour to be asked to President of the Show in 1979, after twenty-eight years as Ring Steward, and I was succeeded by Mr Kelly and Mr Vestey.

The competition over the years when I was Ring Steward was intense, particularly between the Duke of Beaufort's and the Heythrop – Master versus Ronnie. I was always accused of winking at Master before going over to the microphone to make the announcement of who had won the class.

On another occasion on one of those very wet, cold mornings, I was concerned that Percy Durno, huntsman of the Heythrop, was trying to catch my eye in the middle of the judging. I asked him what was the trouble, to which he replied: 'Could you please get a message to Lord Ashton that he must put his pullover on when it's as cold as this' – the duties of a Ring Steward are, indeed, legion.

Many Masters wanted to substitute hounds at the last moment. I was always grateful to Roy Bird and his office to whom I always referred this tricky problem. They never let us down.

My lasting impression of the show for over fifty years was the welcome given to a new winner – you get more cheers if you come from Ireland or Scotland than for some of the less fashionable packs in England.

TIM UNWIN
(former Joint Master and huntsman of the Cotswold and Cotswold Vale Farmers)

To a young Master or huntsman 'Peterborough' has always meant two things: they will see some of the best hounds in the land and be able to talk hunting (and other chat) with their peers and elders. Add to this the calendar will tell them that Hunting is only weeks away. The early morning drive through the countryside to the Show will have shown that the harvest has started.

My own memories of the 60s and 70s would recall that a glance round the spectators, all in their usual places, would reveal a large number of very distinguished landowners, who between them owned a large portion of the Kingdom – and often their pack of hounds. A battle of the Gods indeed. A furrowed brow here; a lifting of the eyebrows there; all would be immediately translated by us lesser mortals .

For those who have acted as judges who will forget their first time in the ring, and who was their pillar of strength as senior judge? Mine was the totally relaxed and charming Earl of Halifax.

I had by now been bringing the Cotswold Hounds to the show when I had the good fortune to have Roland Sheppard to show them. This culminated with winning the Dog Hound Championship in consecutive years; Grappler ('85) (in 1987) and Grocer ('86) (in 1988). Grappler was widely used. He had a lovely voice; was a great jumper and helped promote a little substance where it was lacking. He had a strong back, good hocks and was well balanced. Top line Brecon Pargon ('23). Today his grandson Heythrop Busby ('96) (champion in 1999) has also been very widely used.

The dam of Grappler was Clematis ('81) traced back through Old Berks Plaintive ('64) – a present from Colin Nash – and through North Warwickshire Rainy ('38) to Sir W.W. Wynn's early 1900s. As Grappler was mostly white with a little pale blue badger pie, I thought I would pull Bill Lander's leg about this colour – their hounds being entirely tan. He hunted these hounds for many years.

Quick as a flash he replied 'may be you didn't leave him in the oven long enough!'

Pobably of more significance to hound breeders was a journey the same bitch Clematis made to Keswick and was mated to Blencathra Glider ('76), hunted in those days by the great Johnnie Richardson. This produced Glencoyne and Glenrock '84, who achieved a remarkable double as sires of the Champion Dog Hound and Reserve in 1999; Wheatland Glider ('87) (by Glencoyne) and Wheatland Gaffer ('90) (by Glenrock). John Foster was pretty pleased! Pay back time for letting me use his Grappler ('78). Two years later Glencoyne sired another Champion in Heythrop Glazier ('90). This dog was also very widely used. It must be the first time that an outcross (second generation) has sired a Champion (twice) at Peterborough.

Glencoyne seemed to 'nick' with every pack that used him – and there were dozens, *possibly* because, curiously, he also had his male line to Brecon Paragon ('23). Most packs would have this blood in their Kennel. The qualities of the Fell Hound are easiest to assess in their own Country. Athletic they must be and carry no 'baggage'. Good shoulders, especially to come down hill. Good hocks and backs to take them up. Good voice for spreading the news. Good noses on the rock screes and in sheep foil. Sidney Bailey, Huntsman of the VWH for many years, entered three litters by Glencoyne in1988. He once said to me 'They're no trouble. Don't take much feeding. They live on fresh air and foxes!'

The third Champion (in 2001) which I bred was the bitch Captive ('00), whose female line is that of Percy Candour ('39), who was presented to the Cotswold Hunt by the Duke of Northumberland in 1946 when hounds were scarce.

Judging is the focal point of showing. In the 60s and 70s there was a pool of over twenty-five Senior Judges. That figure has declined. Yet the standard of hounds showing has probably improved. Kennel 'types' have been diluted. Now with fewer doghounds being kept the danger is obvious. So again I went 'out' – this time to Brian Fanshawe's acquistion from that great hound breeder in America, Ben Hardaway, to Midland (USA) Hardaway ('89). His son Cotswold Harker ('96) came third in the Stallion Hound class in 1998. Some of his progeny are now back in Ireland where it all started in 1814, when the Duke of Leeds presented a friend from Maryland with Mountain and Muse, who were mated there. Thus the famous 'July' Hound had its beginning in America.

In 1979 Willie Poole was my co-judge for the doghound classes. News preceded him to the show that he had been particularly well entertained on the previous evening in good company, to the extent that he was still in his dinner attire before breakfast. Nevertheless he arrived punctually, well groomed and smartly dressed as usual. I recall one or two grunts of approval from him before he said words to the effect 'Not feeling too special – you carry on'.

After the morning session, someone said to me 'Do you realise you have not given the Beaufort a first prize?' I went over to the gents cloakroom where there was quite a distinguished 'line-up' including Master, who said to his neighbour with some feeling: 'In all my fifty-five years at Peterborough, that was the worst judging I have seen!'

In the afternoon Sir Rupert Buchanan-Jardine and Anthony Hart awarded him first prize in the Brood bitch class: so that was better. In his eightieth year, Master had not lost his competitive edge!

What would those giants of the past have made of our present predicament? I think Master would have sought an audience with the Queen. Dream on.

The 2005 Peterborough Festival of Hunting has been a real buzz. Winners in all rings received longer and louder applause than ever and by more people. Congratulations to Sir Philip Naylor-Leyland and his committee.

ALASTAIR JACKSON

(Former Joint Master and huntsman of the West Percy, South Dorset, Grafton, and Cattistock, current Director of the MFHA)

I first judged in 1975 with Bob Field-Marsham who was of course the perfect senior judge for a young man making his debut at Peterborough. He asked me my opinion on all the major decisions before agreeing or otherwise. When we came to the Championship, it was the usual two green coated packs.

He asked my opinion and I said I thought it was the Heythrop. 'Quite right' he said, 'but let me give you some advice. Avoid Master for the next couple of hours. He's sometimes not very kind to junior Judges when things haven't gone his way!' I took his advice, but had to go to the gents, where I found the Duke in the next stall.

'What did you think of the hounds?' he said.

'Very good indeed, Master' I replied.

'Pity you didn't like mine more' he said with a shake and turned on his heel. I think I got away lightly! The Champion that year was Heythrop Hedgerow ('71). For all the subsequent years that Rosie Wallace came to Peterborough she wore a straw hat with fruits and leaves on it and called it her lucky hedgerow hat.

I next judged in 1980 as senior Judge to Captain John Foster with the dog hounds. I felt rather awkward as he was

Alastair Jackson, former Joint Master and huntsman, and hound breeder, current Director of the MFHA.

a very long serving Master and much older than me. We made Exmoor Fortescue ('77) Champion and in years to come his son, Exmoor Farley ('80), was the dog which made my Cattistock pack and improved their shoulders out of all recognition.

In 1987 I judged the bitches with Robin Gundry and we were lucky enough to have a quite outstanding bitch in Exmoor Pixie ('86) to make Champion. In years to come Ronnie said she was one of the best looking hounds he ever hunted.

In 1994 I judged the bitches with Nigel Peel and it was fun to find an outstanding outsider in Wheatland Rosebud ('92) to make Champion.

In 2000 I judged the bitches with William Wakeham, and we found ourselves faced with a quite outstanding unentered hound in Heythrop Chorus. Although it is allowed within the Rules, it has been very rare indeed for an unentered hound to be Champion at Peterborough. William was very nervous of making such a controversial decision and so I walked over to Simon Clarke and asked if the Peterborough Committee would disapprove of us making an unentered hound Champion. 'Of course not' he said, 'get on with it!' Luckily it was the right decision as she remained an outstanding looking hound and came back a year or two later to win the brood bitch class.

For very many years several of us amateur huntsmen stayed with Betty Cross at Whissenthorpe, where the parties were legendary. One year Newton Rycroft decided to send his famous stallion hound, Medyg ('69), to be shown in the appropriate class. As Betty's son Peter was a Joint Master of the New Forest, the single hound and his huntsman, a young man called Richard Perry, came to stay at Whissenthorpe.

When the port was going round well after midnight, Martin Letts and others decided it would be a good idea to have a closer look at Medyg before he made his appearance at the Show. Medyg was asleep in the stables and Richard Perry in the Groom's cottage when they were summoned to the dining room. Richard put on a white coat and bowler hat and came to the house where the table was pushed back and Medyg showed his paces up and down the dining room in front of a bevy of amateur Huntsmen.

Eventually, when a mask had been taken off the wall to test Medyg's reaction, he and his huntsman were allowed back to bed. The following day at the show Medyg gave a rather lack-lustre performance when he was asked to show his wonderful movement. Sir Newton shook his head sadly and said that he could not understand why his treasured hound did not show himself better.

Woolly hounds were not the norm at Peterborough in the early '70s and Medyg was not placed, but there may have been other reasons and, thank goodness, Sir Newton never found out about the escapades the previous night.

DERMOT KELLY

(Former Joint Master and huntsman of the Meynell and S. Staffs)

Showing hounds at Peterborough, or for that matter elsewhere, is a serious game, but it is an amusing summer game, which *shows the standard of hound to be reached for* and is no substitute for foxhunting. Some people say that it is

Dermot Kelly (RIGHT), as Steward at Peterborough 1979, with Sir Rupert Buchanan-Jardine MFH (CENTRE) and Anthony Hart, MFHA Secretary, judging hounds, shown by huntsman Ted Rafton.

undesirable to show hounds, in that it encourages Masters to breed for a prize-winner whether it is a good hunter or not.

Any owner of a prize-winning hound that is not good in its work and who encourages its use, is doing a grave disservice to foxhunting. Equally, any MFH who uses a stallion hound knowing that is not top-class in its work needs his head examining.

Luckily for breeders of Foxhounds, most of the main and consistent prize-winning packs at Peterborough are also high up among the leading packs famous for their sport, and the number of foxes they account for.

Perhaps this tells its own tale, for if a hound is good in its conformation, it should be able to hunt more efficiently, and with less effort, and thus with this economy of effort be able to devote more of its time to developing 'fox-sense', which is the most vital characteristic of a top-class hound.

Of course, there are exceptions to this rule: of individual ugly hounds being brilliant in their work, but I have noticed that these hounds, although they may be brilliant themselves, end not to run up at top pace into their fifth or subsequent seasons,and are ultimately less valuable to a huntsman than the brilliant hound with good conformation who has greater longevity.

Another important factor is that ugly hounds will probably pass on many of their worst characteristics to their progeny, and then you have a hard job in eradicating the worst conformation faults in future generations.

Judging at Peterborough can be an awe-inspiring business, with the ring surrounded by all the experts and would-be experts, who no doubt think they know very much more than the judge. They may well be right too! Luckily it is not possible to judge hounds from the ring-side, as you have to be able to stand over them properly in the ring to be effective. And anyway when all is said and done, it is the judge's opinion on the day which counts.

Some Hunt Servants are masters of the showing game. If their hounds have a fault, they are quite rightly all out to conceal it from the judges. The judges can make this more difficult for them, if they insist on the hounds being off the couples straight away when they come into the ring to give their show.

The judges will be able to notice a hound's faults when the hound is relaxing when it is back on the couples. No Hunt Servant can keep his hounds alert, and up to the biscuit all the time, so the judge needs eyes in the back of his head.

The two-couples class is often a difficult one to judge, but often there are three good ones in the entry, and one less good which the expert showman will keep well covered up; again it is much more difficult for him when the hounds are giving their show loose. What an honour it is to judge at any puppy show or hound show, but of course the ultimate honour is to judge at Peterborough. If you thought you knew what you were doing before you started, by the end of the judging you may well be only too aware how little you knew.

It is all taken very seriously, and it has been known for certain MFH's to make their displeasure known if their hounds have been placed incorrectly. It is sometimes wise for the judges to take avoiding action after the judging is over to avoid a confrontation until tempers have cooled!

ALBERT BUCKLE

(Huntsman of the Whaddon Chase for twenty-six years, up to its amalgamation in 1980 with the Bicester and Warden Hill, Albert Buckle served for fifty years as Assistant Steward at Peterborough, retiring at the age of ninety at the 2005 show when he was presented with a decanter [Chapter 12].)

Albert recalled Peterborough memories, in conversation with Michael Clayton:

I think it was Lord Kimball who asked me if I would like to be a steward at Peterborough. The show was in the town then, a much smaller place, but it was all right. I used to show the Whaddon Chase hounds at Peterborough and other shows in the early days – we won a championship at Aldershot – but at that time my Masters weren't really into hound shows, so after some years we gave it a miss.

It meant I had the time to be steward, and I've kept it up ever since. I did it in the morning and Brian Pheasey (former huntsman of the Bicester) did it in the afternoons. I reckon the best judges I saw in the fifty years were the Duke of Beaufort, Sir Peter Farquhar, Major Field-Marsham, and Captain Wallace. They knew exactly what they looking for; they didn't waste any time, but they gave every hound on show a proper close look. Of course, when they weren't judging the Duke and Captain Wallace kept on winning the championships as well. Neither of them liked it when they did lose.

Captain Wallace once judged our Whaddon Chase puppy show. He really liked one of the hounds, and told me I should show it at Peterborough. So I brought it along, and the judges chucked it out straight away. Afterwards I was with the hounds round the back, and the Captain comes up and says: 'We all have to put up with disappointments some times.' And I laughed, and said: 'Well sir, it's a long time since you had any disappointments round here!'

Of course, there's a lot of skill in showing the hounds. Brian Gupwell was about the best I saw, and Anthony Adams, who's just retired from the Heythrop, was very good indeed; his hounds never took their eyes off him.

I won't mention names, but I can think of one huntsman who just stood there as if he was feeding hens. No wonder his hounds didn't show. The huntsmen who know what they are doing use a bit of chopped liver with the biscuit; that makes a big difference, and of course they work hard to make sure their hounds show properly.

I've had a marvellous life in hunting; I was lucky to have a wonderful Master in Mr (Dorian) Williams for all those years. I have managed to keep my health – I play golf three times a week – and I've really enjoyed keeping going to Peterborough in retirement.

It was good to finish up with the big show this year. Mind you, it was a job for the judges: there were so many hounds, they had to go in and out so quickly it was hard to look at them properly. Still, it was a very good show – and I'm sure Peterborough has done a great job over the years in helping to keep standards right up for the Foxhound.

Roy Bird was a marvellous Secretary, very good to work with, and I can't speak highly enough of him.

NIGEL PEEL

(Joint Master and huntsman of the North Cotswold, Chiddingfold, Leconfield and Cowdray, Taunton Vale, Cambridgeshire, and Goathland)

'Young men go to Peterborough.' So said Captain Wallace to me when I failed to parade there in 1971, and so I have been ever since.

When I first took a pack of hounds the giants of foxhunting England were very much alive, and the prizes were fought for with the determination of the English at Agincourt.

Few people of my generation who have judged at Peterborough, will forget the sight of Master, 10th Duke of Beaufort, with his fixed stare and whitened knucles – and woe betide you if the judging went the wrong way!

I remember Captain Wallace, when at the Exmoor, having a rotten time one year. He came into the bar after the judging with a face like thunder. Bobby Corbett, Master of the Eglinton and a great supporter of all things social, produced as if by magic a huge tumber of nut brown whisky which he passed the the great man.

The glass was seized, the Captain's back was turned and, without a word, the Master of the Exmoor hounds stamped off into the distance. We were all slightly stunned, and giggled nervously.

'Ah', said Bobby, blowing out a huge plume of cigar smoke. 'I don't think Captain Wallace thinks I am a very serious Master of Foxhounds'.

I have been lucky enough to have had some lovely hounds that found favour in the judges' eyes. The first major prize I won at Peterborough was with a bitch called Grapefruit, who was awarded the prize for the best single unentered bitch hound in 1995. The following year she went on to be made Champion, the first the North Cotswold had since 1911. Grapefruit, who was full of Carlow blood, descended tail female to Carlow Vera ('23), who won the Championship at Peterborough in 1928. Grapefruit was walked by our senior hound trustee, Charlie Warren, who was in his early eighties when she won the first time.

The Duke of Buccleuch was President that year and, by tradition, the walker of the best unentered hound, dog and bitch, is given a tankard. On hearing the result, Charlie, who had been grumbling about old age, miraculously shed twenty years at least, and vaulted over the ring, speeding like Roger Bannister to the Presidential enclosure to receive the tankard from the Duke. The memory of total happiness, coupled with his wife's holloa, will stay with me forever.

It has become fashionable to decry hound shows. I can never understand why it is always the cry of those who breed supremely ugly hounds that 'we breed for work'. I thought we all did that, and perhaps if those who knock the showing tried harder with their breeding, they would rather enjoy it. Peterborough is a great social gathering, a wonderful nest of gossip, and I hope and pray the show and hunting will go on forever.

12. END OF AN ERA – START OF ANOTHER

More hounds than ever before, an exciting new show, and an enthusiastic attendance of hound lovers from far and wide...this was Peterborough on 20 July 2005.

The Festival of Hunting, referred to in Chapter 1, marked a new era in the history of hound shows at Peterborough. It was a defiant answer to the iniquitous hunting ban which became law in February. The Festival displayed a firm commitment to the core aim of the Peterborough hound shows: preserving the breeds at their best for future generations.

Peterborough Royal Foxhound Show became part of the largest gathering of hounds seen in England. For the first time Peterborough Harrier and Beagle Show was held on the same day; the show was supported by eighteen packs of Beagles, and seven of Harriers. Altogether, more than 1,500 hounds were on show; there were separate displays of Fell Hounds, Whippets, Salukis, Deerhounds, and Lurchers, alongside working hunt terriers, and demonstrations of coursing with Greyhounds.

The Fitzwilliam Hound Enclosure at Alwalton packed with Hunt staff and hounds at Peterborough 2005.

Hundreds of hound enthusiasts also enjoyed an exhibition from Melton Mowbray Hunting Museum, an inter-hunt team relay competition, and an array of specialist trade-stands.

It was a breezy, sunny day, ideal for hound showing. Spectators strolled on the lawns outside the Hound Enclosure, thoroughly appreciating the displays.

Andrew Mercer, chief executive of the East England Show, and Secretary-designate of Peterborough Royal Foxhound Show Society, said afterwards: 'The Festival of Hunting was certainly well received, and has provided an entertaining and positive boost to the enthusiasm and commitment of hunting folk amidst challenging times.'

No ring was more popular than that devoted to Old English type Foxhounds. For the first time, the Belvoir competed at Peterborough in a mini-show supported by seven other packs of this type. The ring-side was packed with enthusiasts, thoroughly enjoying this unique opportunity to see the traditional type of Foxhound, in the attractive Belvoir tan, brown and white livery, at its best. In Foxhound showing terms it was a historic day, bringing to full circle the ancient feuds and arguments over breeding trends.

Including the Old English, the Royal Foxhound Hound Show achieved an all-time record of forty-one packs competing at this 117th show, compared with twenty-two the previous year. This overwhelming support was one more sign of foxhunting's defiance in the face of the Hunting Act.

The vital element of continuity was stressed by two presentations made in the ring during the show by the chairman, Sir Philip Naylor-Leyland. Roy Bird was about to retire after forty years as the Show Secretary, only the third in that office since the first show in 1878. He had served also as Secretary of Peterborough Agricultural Society since 1957, succeeding as chief executive of East of England Agricultural Society, until retiring from that post in 1992.

Sir Philip warmly praised Roy Bird's 'unerring attention to detail', and his contribution to the success of the 2005 show, working with the East of England's current chief executive, Andrew Mercer, who was succeeding as Secretary of the Royal Foxhound Show.

Roy, an impeccable, spry, figure, always genial, ensured for forty years consistent standards of service for the running of the show, maintenance of its building and its attendant kennels, and the important luncheon tents for vice-presidents and Hunt staffs. He helped deftly and unobtrusively to retain a reassuring atmosphere of calm orderliness. Outside the show world, Roy was a non-Executive Director of Norwich and Peterborough Building Society, being Chairman of Peterborough when it merged with Norwich and later becoming Chairman of the Regional Society.

Roy said: 'As everyone knows I have enjoyed immensely being secretary of the Hound Show, meeting so many people, and particularly working closely with Lord and Lady Fitzwilliam, and now with the present Chairman, Sir Philip Naylor-Leyland, who is determined to uphold the great traditions of the Society and its Show.'

The other presentation was to Albert Buckle, astonishingly fit and upstanding at the age of ninety, and still in his place as assistant steward at the ring entrance after an extraordinary fifty years in that role. Albert was highly successful as huntsman of the Whaddon Chase for twenty-six years, retiring in 1980, and was now retiring from the role at Peterborough which he carried out efficiently and courteously throughout half a century.

Such was the significance of Peterborough 2005, that (with the kind permission of the Editor of *Horse and Hound*) we conclude this history of the greatest Foxhound show in the world, with the latter part of Michael Clayton's report, and the results, published on July 28, 2005:

In the Fitzwilliam Enclosure the ring had never been more packed with scarlet ranks of huntsmen and their hounds, especially in the two-couple classes. It was a marvellous spectacle, and a huge challenge for judges in sorting out winners.

In the doghound section the Duke of Beaufort's won their fifty-first Peterborough championship; in the bitch section the Crawley and Horsham won their second ever Peterborough championship, and their first in the bitch section. Cheers resounded, especially from their coach-load of supporters from Sussex.

It was a riveting show, but Foxhound breeding's growing problem of declining doghound standards in the advent of the ban, due to fewer doghounds being hunted in modern packs, was apparent throughout the morning. It made judging even more difficult for Stephen Lambert, new MFHA chairman, and former Master and huntsman of the Heythrop and Warwickshire, and Jonathan Seed, Joint Master and huntsman of the Avon Vale.

The Thurlow's dog Richard, a grandson of the influential VWH Gardner ('95), showed well and was considered by the judges good enough not only to win the restricted unentered class, but to receive the *Horse and Hound* Cup as best unentered hound. Remarkably, Richard went on to become reserve doghound champion, a triumph for the breeder, Thurlow senior Master Edmund Vestey.

The Duke of Beaufort's won the unentered couples class with sons of Burglar ('99), with the Fitzwilliam second with sons of VWH Descant ('00).

The Bicester with Whaddon Chase were first in the entered couples class with well matched hounds, with the South Dorset making a rare appearance here to take second place. Following their good performance at Harrogate, the Sinnington won a mammoth two couples class, ahead of their northern rival, the Middleton, and the Beaufort were in third place.

A much applauded Peterborough rarity was a victory in the stallion hound class of the Morpeth from Northumberland, with their Gateshead ('03), a grandson of Exmoor Growler, bred by former Master Roddy Bailey. The Bicester's Daystar ('03) was second, and the Beaufort's Bailiff ('03), champion at Builth this year, was third. Hounds from a dozen packs competed for the championship. The Duke of Beaufort's Gamecock ('04), a grandson of VWH Gardner ('95), emerged the victor, but at the risk of being churlish, he was considered by some at the ringside to be one of the least handsome champions Badminton has produced in its long history of dominance at Peterborough.

The highly experienced Martin Scott, former VWH Master and huntsman, and Mark Hankinson, noted animal artist and Joint Master and huntsman of the Wilton, judged an even larger bitch section, thankfully far more endowed with quality.

Thurlow Richard's litter sister Radiant confirmed the pack's success by winning the restricted unentered class, with the Quorn, an infrequent showing pack, in second place with a nice grand-daughter of Middleton Burglar ('98).

The Heythrop this year have a lovely unentered litter by their distinguished sire, Samuel ('02), and his daughter Study – recent winner of their puppy show – was deservedly awarded the *Horse and Hound* Cup for best unentered hound. Because Stephen Lambert is their Hunt chairman the Heythrop could not show their doghounds, and were among Peterborough regulars having an unusually lean time in the classes for older bitches.

The Beaufort captured the unentered couples prize against considerable competition, with the Fitzwilliam second, and this 'home team' of Peterborough evoked rapture from supporters when it won the entered couples class with a delightful couple of good movers by Heythrop Buckshot ('98). The Cattistock, still knocking at the door, were second with their older Hockey and Hoopla.

Climax of the show's spectacle was inevitably the bitch two-couple class. The judges were sometimes lost to sight among the massed ranks of hounds from twenty-one packs competing. With commendable speed of expert decision, this resulted in a great win for the Worcestershire with a fine group by Beaufort Gunshot ('98), with the Beaufort itself in second place ,and the Cotswold third.
Amid such a multitude of lovely hounds, any pack winning a rosette could value it perhaps more than at any bitch section in memory.

Although a working animal, a hound in the show ring may win by sheer presence, and the Crawley and Horsham's lemon and white Measure ('02), by Heythrop Busby, quickly caught the eye in the brood bitch class.

She was bitch champion at the South of England show two years ago, and has since worn remarkably well. She won the brood bitch class, with Bicester with

Peterborough's champion bitch, 2005, Crawley and Horsham Measure ('02).

Whaddon Chase Dovecot ('02) second, and the North Cotswold bitch Gracious ('01) third.

Then the roof was raised, and a few eyebrows too, when Measure beat an exceedingly strong field to win the championship, with the Beaufort's Gadabout ('04) reserve, and a number of other younger talented bitches rejected in favour of the comely matron from the south. Antony Sandeman, Crawley and Horsham Joint Master and hound breeder for ten years, was justifiably proud: his pack last won a Peterborough championship when their doghound Brandon ('80) was victorious in 1983.

OLD ENGLISH

Tim Unwin, ex-Cotswold Joint Master and huntsman, and Robin Gundry, formerly in that role with the South Dorset and the Wynnstay, had the interesting task of judging the Old English hounds.

There was much ring-side enthusiasm for these hounds, from the Belvoir, Brocklesby, Hurworth, Limerick, Percy, Warwickshire, Sir Watkin Williams-Wynn's and York and Ainsty South. None deserved the 'Shorthorn' nickname derisively given by their critics in the last century. Old English, with fewer lines to choose from, have evolved into a lighter type, and have excellent records of consistent sport.

'Now those doghounds really look like doghounds', said an admiring Martin Letts, of College Valley cross-Fell fame. Sir Watkin Williams-Wynn's won the unentered doghound class, and the Hurworth took the couples class. Second were the Limerick, brought over from Ireland by their English huntsman Will Bryer, formerly whipper-in to the Cottesmore. The Earl of Yarborough's marvellous English pack from Lincolnshire, the Brocklesby, won the stallion hound class with their strongly masculine Ladbrook ('99), and he captured the championship with Hurworth Prefix ('04) reserve.

There were cheers from local supporters for the Belvoir winning the unentered bitch class, and the Duke of Northumberland's family pack, the Percy, won the entered couples class in their debut here. Limerick Purple (02'), by a sire from their 'parent' pack, Belvoir Prancer ('99), was best brood bitch, and the championship went to Sir Watkin Williams-Wynn's eye-catching Primrose ('01) by Belvoir Poacher ('98), with the Percy Spendthrift ('03) as reserve,making more Foxhound history. Many at Peterborough hoped to see the Old English every year, reminding us of the depth of achievement in Foxhound breeding.

PETERBOROUGH ROYAL FOXHOUND SHOW RESULTS:

Wednesday, 20 July 2005:
DOGHOUNDS: Judges – Stephen Lambert and Major Jonathan Seed MFH (Avon Vale).
unentered, restricted – 1, Thurlow Richard (by Grocer '02 out of Rosemary '02); 2, Fitzwilliam Pirate (Cottesmore Pilot '02) – S. Shropshire Cashmere ('00); 3, Bicester with Whaddon Chase Captain (Cotswold Captain '02 – Fashion '02).
unentered couples – 1, Duke of Beaufort's Fotman (Burglar '99 – Foxtrot '99) and Gainsborough (Palmer '02 – Garlic '00); 2, Fitzwilliam Denmark and Dexter (VWH Descant

'00 – Bubble '01); 3, Meynell and South Staffs Draycott and Driver (Cattistock Daresbury '99 – Crumpet '02). *Horse and Hound* Cup, best unentered. – Thurlow Richard.

couples – 1, Bicester WC Bramham '03 (Heythrop Broker '98 – Garlic '00); 2, South Dorset Captain '02 (Planet '99 – Candid '98) and Dalesman '04 (VWH Dolphin '00 – Lattice '01); 3, Meynell SS Ludlow '04 (Beaufort Gaffer '00 – Torrington Farmers' Lupin '01) and Malvern '04 (Heythrop Braggart '99 – Magic '97).

two couples – 1, Sinnington Beacon and Brusher '04 (Berkeley Mangrove '00 – Bramble '00), Marquis and Monarch '03 (Morpeth Grappler '99 – Maxine '00); 2, Middleton Builder and Burglar '04 (Beaufort Burglar '99 – Gravity '00), Grappler '03 (Admiral '01 – Gravity '00), Ruler '04 (Beaufort Burglar '99 – Rescue '00); 3, Beaufort Bombardier '04 (Boycott '02 – Garlic '00), Brahma '04 (Sandown '00 – Brazen '00), Gamecock '04 (Whipsnade '01 – Gannet '00), Paragon '04 (Foxham '99 – Parsnip '01).

stallion hounds – 1, Morpeth Gateshead '03 (Gambler '98 – Gracious '99); 2, Bicester WC Daystar '03 (Miller '99 – Dainty '97); 3, Beaufort Bailiff '03 (Heythrop Busby '96 – Patience '98).

champion doghound – Beaufort Gamecock '04; reserve, Thurlow Richard.

BITCHES: Judges – Martin Scott and Mark Hankinson MFH (Wilton).

unentered restricted – 1, Thurlow Radiant (Grocer '02 – Rosemary '02); 2, Quorn Bonnet (Grocer '03 – Burnet '01); 3, Cattistock Charming (Cotswold Hackler '00 – Chatter '00).

unentered couples – 1, Beaufort Fortune and Fountain (Burglar '99 – Foxtrot '99); 2, Heythrop Stencil and Study (Samuel '02 – Goldfinch '01); 3, Worcestershire Jumble (Exmoor Jusice '02 – Grammar '02) and Ribbon (VWH Rival '02 – Barmaid '00).

Horse & Hound **Cup, best unentered** – Heythrop Study; reserve, Beaufort Fountain.

couples – 1, Fitzwilliam Breezy (Heythrop Buckshot '98 – Madam '98) and Budget '03 (Heythrop Buckshot '98 – Gasket '99); 2, Cattistock Hockey and Hoopla '02 (Eggesford Homer '94 – Millicent '97); 3, Bicester WC Mayfly '04 (Saracen '00 – Maple '99) and Mischief '03 (Safeguard '00 – Mistress '99).

two couples – 1, Worcestershire Gretna '02 (Beaufort Gunshot '98 – Buxom '98), Pollen, Popcorn and Portrait '03 (Beaufort Gunshot '98 – Policy '99); 2, Beaufort Bravery '04 (Sandown '00 – Brazen '00), Cocktail '02 (Middleton Burglar '98 – Cosy '98), Gadabout '04 (Whipsnade '01 – Garnet '00), Garter '04 (Sandown '00 – Galaxy '01); 3, Cotswold Policy '04 (Heythrop Postman '01 – Captive '00), Sally, Sanity and Savoury '03 (Saracen '00 – Candid '00).

brood bitches – 1, Crawley and Horsham Measure '02 (Heythrop Busby '96 – Mayfly '99); 2, Bicester WC Dovecot '02 (Zetland Searcher '95 – Docket '98); 3, North Cotswold Gracious '01 (Heythrop Busby '96 – Grapeshot '98).

champion bitch – Crawley and Horsham Measure '02; res., Beaufort Gadabout '04.

OLD ENGLISH: Judges – Tim Unwin, Robin Gundry.

DOGHOUNDS:

unentered – 1, Sir Watkin Williams-Wynn's Parson (Paterson '01 – Countess '02; 2, Hurworth Grimston (Grafter '01 – Ramble '00); 3, Brocklesby Ludlow (Linkboy '00 – Lettuce '99).

couples – 1, Hurworth Prefix and Prussia '04 (Belvoir Preston '99 – Rattle '00); 2, Limerick Tenant and Tester '03 (Scholar '96 – Tempo '98); 3, York and Ainsty South Lancer and Latimer '04 (Brocklesby Ladbrook '99 – Token '01).

stallion hounds – 1, Brocklesby Ladbrook '99 (Renegade '94 – Lustrious '94); 2, York and AS Colonel '01 (Brocklesby Coaster '97 – Truthful '97); 3, Limerick Tester '03.

champion OE doghound – Brocklesby Ladbrook '99; reserve Hurworth Prefix '04.

BITCHES:

Unentered – 1, Belvoir Rapid (Poacher '98-Rapture '00); 2, Sir W.W. Wynn's Paradise (Paterson '01 – Countess '02); 3, Brockleby Lucky (Linkboy '00 – Lettuce '99).

couples – 1, Percy Spendthrift '03 (Ploughman '00 – Springtime '97) and Worthy '03 (Ploughman '00 – Holdeness Woburn '99); 2, Sir W.W. Wynn's Primrose '01 (Belvoir Poacher '98 – Sector '95) amd Starling '03 (Saddler '00 – Pastime '99); 3, Hurworth Precious and Profit '04 (Belvoir Preston '99 – Rattle '00).

brood bitches – 1, Limerick Purple '02 (Belvoir Prancer '99 – Lupin '95); 2, York and AS Curlew '01 (Ruler '93 – Cinder '94); 3, Hurworth Ramble '00 (Rally '95 – Belvoir Shady '97).

champion OE bitch – Sir W.W. Wynn's Primrose '01; reserve, Percy Spendthrift '03.

THE FUTURE

Leading officials and Vice-Presidents of Peterborough Royal Foxhound Show were among guests at a dinner celebrating the centenary of the Harrier and Beagle show, held on the showground the night before the 2005 Festival of Hunting. They heard a stirring speech condemning the hunting ban, and the government's record on countryside issues, from the President, the Hon. Nicholas Soames MP.

Mr Soames said hunting people 'would not easily or quietly give up their rights,' and urged that the issue continue to be fought until the Bill was amended or repealed.

Whatever the political future holds for foxhunting as a sport, the immensely enthusiastic support for the 2005 Peterborough Royal Foxhound Show appeared to offer much hope and encouragement for those who care deeply about the future of these uniquely beautiful hounds, bred and selected so carefully for hundreds of years.

The great show remains a wonderful setting in which to admire and enjoy the best that Foxhound breeding can offer. After the 2005 show everyone associated with Peterborough Royal Foxhound Show hoped fervently that the heritage of this marvellous working breed may be preserved at its best in the twenty-first century – to provide the sweet cry of hounds as a challenge for future generations to follow across our countryside

The 2005 Committee under the Chairmanship of Sir Philip Naylor-Leyland, Bt., M.F.H. (Fitzwilliam) and Vice-Chairmanship of Mr Edmund Vestey D.L., M.F.H. (Thurlow) comprised the Earl of Yarborough, M.F.H. (Brocklesby), Capt. I.W. Farquhar, L.V.O., M.F.H. (Beaufort), Mr David Reynolds, M.F.H. (Woodland Pytchley), the Lord Annaly, Capt. B.E. Fanshawe, Mr Simon Clarke, Mr Joe Odam J.P., D.L., Mr C.E.W. Saunders, D.L., and Mr C.M.F. Scott.

The Ring Stewards were:

Dog Hounds: The Lord Annaly, Mr T.P. Naylor-Leyland (Assistant), *Bitch Hounds:* Mr. A.W.R. Dangar, *Old English:* Mr R.C. Smith-Ryland and Sir Edward Lycett Green, Bt.

APPENDICES

1. PETERBOROUGH ROYAL FOXHOUND SHOW –
LIST OF CHAMPIONS – up to 2005

Doghound champion first; bitch champion second.

Doghounds			**Bitches**	
2005	Duke of Beaufort's	Gamecock 04;	Crawley & Horsham	Measure 02.
2004	Duke of Beaufort's	Bailey 03;	North Cotswold	Daytime 01.
2003	Duke of Beaufort's	Palmer 02;	Heythrop	Poplin 01.
2002	Duke of Beaufort's	Whipsnade 01;	Duke of Beaufort's	Galaxy 01.
2001	Exmoor	Emperor 97;	Cotswold	Captive 00.
2000	Duke of Beaufort's	Foxham 99;	Heythrop	Chorus 00.
1999	Heythrop	Busby 96;	Duke of Beaufort's	Patience 98.
1998	Heythrop	Sandford 97;	South Shropshire	Clever 97.
1997	South Shropshire	Sinbad 95;	North Cotswold	Bowwave 95.
1996	Duke of Beaufort's	Marlin 95;	North Cotswold	Grapefruit 95.
1995	Exmoor	Redskin 92;	Duke of Beaufort's	Peewit 94.
1994	Exmoor	Greatwood 93;	Wheatland	Rosebud 92.
1993	Heythrop	Glazier 90;	Exmoor	Raindrop 92.
1992	Duke of Beaufort's	Ranger 90;	South Shropshire	Charlock 91.
1991	Wheatland	Glider 87;	Exmoor	Gladness 90.
1990	Exmoor	Daresbury 87;	Exmoor	Ripple 89.
1989	South Shropshire	Crockett 87;	Puckeridge	Devious 87.
1988	Cotswold	Grocer 86;	Exmoor	Singsong 85.
1987	Cotswold	Grappler 85;	Exmoor	Pixie 86.
1986	Exmoor	Dancer 84;	Heythrop	Rosary 83.
1985	Duke of Beaufort's	Palmer 83;	Duke of Beaufort's	Wagtail 84.
1984	Exmoor	Freestone 81;	Puckeridge	Pigeon 81.
1983	Crawley & Horsham	Brandon 80;	Exmoor	Durable 82.
1982	Exmoor	Friar 81;	Duke of Beaufort's	Whimsey
1981	Heythrop	Rockwood 80;	Duke of Beaufort's	Ticket 78.
1980	Exmoor	Fortescue 77;	Heythrop	Berry 78.
1979	Heythrop	Draycott 77;	Cottesmore	Baffle 78.
1978	Duke of Beaufort's	Monmouth 77;	Kilkenny	Famous 77.
1977	Heythrop	Pixton 75;	Duke of Beaufort's	Candid 76.
1976	Duke of Beaufort's	Culprit 75;	Heythrop	Flattery 75.
1975	Duke of Beaufort's	Foreman 74;	Heythrop	Hedgerow 71.
1974	Warwickshire	Grafton 73;	Heythrop	Desert 72.
1973	Duke of Beaufort's	Pontiff 70;	West Kent	Payment 72.
1972	Duke of Beaufort's	Gimcrack 70;	Duke of Beaufort's	Gravel 71.

Doghounds			**Bitches**		
1971	Duke of Beaufort's	Crowner 69	Duke of Beaufort's	Crumpet 69	
1970	Warwickshire	Partner 68	Heythrop	Clamour 69	
1969	Heythrop	Lurcher 67	Heythrop	Dowry 68	
1968	Duke of Beaufort's	Beadle 66	Heythrop	Lupin 67	
1967	Heythrop	Craftsman 62	Duke of Beaufort's	Budget 66	
1966	Heythrop	Clincher	Tipperary	Grizzle 64	
1965	Heythrop	Brewer 63	Duke of Beaufort's	Posy 63	
	Supreme Champion doghound was Heythrop Cardinal 64				
1964	Heythrop	Cardinal	Eridge	Freedom 60	
1963	Duke of Beaufort's	Bugler 62	Middleton & Middleton E	Frosty 61	
1962	Heythrop	Falcon 60	Heythrop	Rocket 61	
1961	Heythrop	Blackcock 59	Heythrop	Clematis 59	
1960	Duke of Beaufort's	Palmer 59	Duke of Beaufort's	Woeful 60	
1959	Duke of Beaufort's	Brimstone 58	Duke of Beaufort's	Baroness 58	
1958	Portman	Wizard 55	Duke of Beaufort's	Doormat 57	
1957	Heythrop	Spanker 56	South & West Wilts	Picnic 55 1	
1956	Duke of Beaufort's	Dresden 53	Four Burrow	Pasty 54	
1955	Heythrop	Harper 53	Portman	Planet 54	
1954	Duke of Beaufort's	Distaff 52	Braes of Derwent	Lenient 49	
1953	Portman	Latimer 51	Duke of Beaufort's	Gravel 51	
1952	Duke of Beaufort's	Ringbolt 50	North Staffordshire	Passion 50	
1951	Duke of Beaufort's	Rector 47	Puckeridge	Poetry 51	
1950	Duke of Beaufort's	Remus 47	Middleton	Rakish 48	
1949	Meynell	Porter 48	Pytchley	Pebble 48	
1948	South & West Wilts	Porlock 46	Pytchley	Crusty 47	
1947	Quorn	Raglan 47	Middleton	Ripple 44	
1946	Duke of Beaufort's	Landsman 45	Middleton	Ripple 44	
No Shows 1940-1945					
1938	Middleton	Villager 35	Rufford	Affable 33	
1938	Braes of Derwent	Comrade 31	Puckeridge	Columbine 37	
1936	Duke of Beaufort's	Pelican 35	Middleton	Ruin 34	
1935	Duke of Beaufort's	Chaser 30	HH	Rarotu 33	
1934	Duke of Beaufort's	Fencer 32	Duke of Beaufort's	Pamela 32	
1933	Cleveland	Ranger 31	Rufford	Hebe 30	
1932	Duke of Beaufort's	Autocrat 32	Duke of Beaufort's	Peerless 31	
1931	Oakley	Goldsmith 31	Oakley	Housemaid 29	
1930	Cheshire	Galway 28	Portman	Wakeful 27	
1929	Oakley	Hospodor 28	Cheshire	System 27	
1928	Puckeridge	Wizard 28	Carlow	Vera 23	
1927	Duke of Beaufort's	Wildboy 23	VWH (Bathurst)	Salient 25	

Doghounds			Bitches		
1926	Quorn	Cruiser 26	Quorn	Woeful 21	
1925	Duke of Beaufort's	Rustic 23	Cleveland	Tempest 23	
1924	S. Staffs	Denmark 22	N. Warwichshire	Rally 20	
1923	N. Warwickshire	Lifeguard 22	N. Warwickshire	Rally 20	
1922	Cattistock	David 20	Hurworth	Famous 20	
1921	Fernie	Cnqueror 17	N. Warwickshire	Rally 20	
1920	Linlithgow & Stirling	Raider 17	Duke of Beaufort's	Rumour 19	

No Shows 1915-1919

1914	Fitzwilliam (Milton)	Wiseman 11	Duke of Beaufort's	Caroline 13	
1913	Linlithgow & Stirlingshire	Factor 10	Southdown	Cheerful 13	
1912	Oakley	Byron 11	Cattistock	Surety 11	
1910	Fitzwilliam (Milton)	Rector 06	Fitzwilliam (Milton)	Frantic 07	
1909	Warwickshire	Trickster 08	Cattistock	Perfect 07	
1908	Fitzwilliam (Milton)	Donovan 05	N. Cotswold	Pilgrim 05	
1907	Hertfordshire	Sampler 05	Croome	Santly 05	
1906	Warwickshire	Wizard 05	Fitzwilliam (Milton)	Sanguine 04	
1905	Fitzwilliam (Milton)	Harper 03	VWH (Bathurst)	Damsel 02	
1904	Warwickshire	Traveller 03	Atherstone	Hester 03	
1903	VWH (Bathurst)	Stentor 03	Mr H.M. Wroughton's	Rapture 99	
1902	Atherstone	Challenger 97	Holderness	Sanguine 02	
1901	Warwickshire	Pedlar 01	Mr. Fernie's	Worthy 00	
1900	Pytchley	Potentate 96	N. Cheshire	Rantipole 96	
1899	Pytchley	Marquis 99	Duke of Beaufort's	Rapture 99	
1898	Mr Austin Mackenzie's	Raglan 98	Warwickshire	Typical 97	
1897	Warwickshire	Tancred 95	Oakley	Dahlia 93	
1896	Warwickshire	Tancred 95	Oakley	Dahlia 93	
1895	Oakley	Dandy 93	Warwickshire	Seamstress 94	
1894	Craven	Vagabond 93	Warwickshire	Waitress 91	
1893	Pytchley	Forager 93	Warwickshire	Royalty 90	
1892	Warwickshire	Hermit 89	S. Cheshire	Rogueish 91	
1891	Oakley	Dancer 88	Warwickshire	Hero 89	
1890	Quorn	Dreamer 87	Warwickshire	Royalty 90	
1889	Warwickshire	Stentor 85	Warwickshire	Factious 85	

1884-1888 – Cup for best doghound or bitch.

1888	Quorn	Warrior 84 (dog)
1887	Warwickshire	Trueman 87 (dog)
1886	Oakley	Graceful 82 (bitch)
1885	Oakley	Rhymer 82 (dog)
1884	Oakley	Feudal 82 (dog)

1878-1883 – No champion cups awarded for single hounds.

2. PETERBOROUGH ROYAL FOXHOUND SHOW SOCIETY – JUDGES – 1959-2005

	Dog Hounds	**Bitch Hounds**
1959	Captain R.E. Wallace, M.F.H.	Lord Irwin, M.F.H.
	G.A.Cowen Esq., M.F.H.	Major R. Peel, M.F.H.
1960	Major R. Hoare, M.F.H.	Sir Peter Farquhar
	J. M.White Esq., M.F.H.	Captain Evan Williams, M.F.H.
1961	Major G.A. Gundry, M.F.H.	Major R.E. Field-Marsham
	Lt. Col. R.W.Palmer	Captain B.W. Bell, M.F.H.
1962	Major A.R. Buchanan-Jardine, M.F.H.	Captain C.G.E. Barclay, M.F.H.
	John Williams Esq., M.F.H.	G.A. Cowen Esq., M.F.H.
1963	Colonel R.F.P. Eames, M.F.H.	Duke of Beaufort, M.F.H.
	Sir R.N.Rycroft, M.F.H.	R.M.C. Jeffreys Esq., M.F.H.
1964	Major V. McCalmont, M.F.H.	Captain Evan Williams, M.F.H.
	A.H.B. Hart Esq., M.F.H.	Lt. Col. G.A. Murray-Smith,
1965	Duke of Northumberland, M.F.H.	Lord Margadale, M.F.H.
	Sir W. Williams-Wynn, Bt., M.F.H.	Sir Peter Farquhar
1966	Major R.Hoare, M.F.H.	Earl of Halifax, M.F.H.
	D.L.P. Kelly Esq., M.F.H.	Major J.J. Mann, M.F.H.
1967	Major A.R. Buchanan-Jardine, M.F.H.	Captain R.E. Wallace, M.F.H.
	Captain S.T. Clarke, M.F.H.	Captain P.F. Arkwright, M.F.H.
1968	H.K. Goschen Esq., M.F.H.	Colonel N.P. Foster, M.F.H.
	J.B. Hosegood Esq., M.F.H.	G.B. Fairbairn Esq., M.F.H.
1969	Captain C.G.E. Barclay, M.F.H.	Major R.E. Field-Marsham
	Major A.M. MacEwan, M.F.H.	A.S. Martyn Esq., M.F.H.
1970	Major G.A. Gundry, M.F.H.	Sir R.N. Rycroft, M.F.H.
	Captain J.D.A. Keith, M.F.H.	J.M. Letts Esq., M.F.H.
1971	D.L.P. Kelly Esq., M.F.H.	Major V. McCalmont, M.F.H.
	Lord Glenarthur, M.F.H.	R.J.G. Berkeley Esq., M.F.H.
1972	Lt. Col. G.A. Murray-Smith, M.F.H.	Captain S.T. Clarke, M.F.H.
	C.L. Chafer Esq., M.F.H.	G.G.A. Gregson Esq., M.F.H.
1973	Sir Rupert Buchanan-Jardine, Bt., M.F.H.	Captain R.E. Wallace, M.F.H.
	Lord Westbury, M.F.H.	C.M.F. Scott Esq., M.F.H.
1974	Duke of Beaufort, M.F.H.	Earl of Halifax, M.F.H.
	J. Williams Esq., M.F.H.	T.H. Unwin Esq., M.F.H.
1975	Captain C.G.E. Barclay, M.F.H.	Major R.E. Field-Marsham
	J.B. Hosegood Esq., M.F.H.	A.I. Jackson Esq., M.F.H.

Dog Hounds		Bitch Hounds
1976	Major V. McCalmont, M.F.H. W.P. Nunneley Esq., M.F.H.	J.M. Letts Esq., M.F.H. Captain B.E. Fanshawe, M.F.H.
1977	C.M.F. Scott Esq., M.F.H. C.W. Nash Esq., M.F.H.	R.J.G. Berkeley Esq., M.F.H. A.S. Martyn Esq., M.F.H.
1978	Captain S.T. Clarke, M.F.H. E.H. Vestey Esq., M.F.H.	Captain R.E. Wallace, M.F.H. Captain I.W. Farquhar, M.F.H.
1979	T.A. Unwin Esq., M.F.H. R.W.F. Poole Esq., M.F.H.	Sir Rupert Buchanan-Jardine, Bt., M.F.H. A.H.B. Hart Esq.
1980	A.I. Jackson Esq., M.F.H. Captain J.E. Foster, M.F.H.	Captain C.G.E. Barclay, M.F.H. Col. The Hon. R.N. Crossley, M.F.H.
1981	J.M. Letts Esq., M.F.H. N.C. Stirling Esq., M.F.H.	Major V. McCalmont, M.F.H. A.L. Austin Esq., M.F.H.
1982	Captain I.W. Farquhar, M.F.H. R.G. Cursham Esq., M.F.H.	Captain B.E. Fanshawe, M.F.H. S.U. Lambert Esq., M.F.H.
1983	C.W. Nash Esq., M.F.H. A.H.B. Hart Esq.	C.M.F. Scott Esq., M.F.H. M.A.J. Southwell Esq., M.F.H.
1984	Sir Rupert Buchanan-Jardine, Bt., M.F.H. J.B. Daly Esq., M.F.H.	Captain R.E. Wallace, M.F.H. N.M.L. Ewart Esq., M.F.H.
1985	A.S. Martyn Esq., M.F.H. W.P. Nunneley Esq., M.F.H.	Captain S.T. Clarke, M.F.H. E.P. Lycett Green Esq., M.F.H.
1986	R.J.G. Berkeley Esq., M.F.H. M.R. Porter Esq., M.F.H.	T.H. Unwin Esq., M.F.H. N.D.B. Peel Esq.,M.F.H.
1987	E.H. Vestey Esq., M.F.H. N.C. Stirling Esq., M.F.H.	A.I. Jackson Esq., M.F.H. R.G. Gundry Esq., M.F.H.
1988	Captain C.G.E. Barclay, M.F.H. D.J.S. Herring Esq., M.F.H.	J.M. Letts Esq., M.F.H. E. Foster Esq., M.F.H.
1989	Captain B.E. Fanshawe, M.F.H. M.J. Barclay Esq., M.F.H.	Major V. McCalmont, M.F.H. Major A.G. Stewart, M.F.H.
1990	Captain I.W. Farquhar, M.F.H. S.P. Roberts Esq., M.F.H.	A.H.B. Hart Esq. L.A. Wallace Esq., M.F.H.
1991	R.J.G. Berkeley Esq. N.M.L. Ewart Esq.	Sir Rupert Buchanan-Jardine, Bt., M.F.H. S.A.H. Hart Esq., M.F.H.
1992	C.M.F. Scott Esq. Major R.I. Bailey M.F.H.	Captain R.E. Wallace M.F.H. Captain J.E. Foster J.P. M.F.H.
1993	T.H. Unwin Esq., M.F.H. M.R. Porter Esq., M.F.H.	Captain S.T. Clarke, M.F.H. D.J. Palmer Esq., M.F.H.

Dog Hounds		Bitch Hounds
1994	R.G. Gundry Esq., M.F.H. A.W.R. Dangar Esq., M.F.H.	A.I. Jackson Esq. N.D.B. Peel Esq., M.F.H.
1995	Sir Rupert Buchanan-Jardine, Bt., M.C., M.F.H. Sir Philip Naylor-Leyland, Bt., M.F.H.	J.M. Letts Esq., M.F.H. F. Houghton-Brown Esq., M.F.H.
1996	Captain B.E. Fanshawe, M.F.H. M.A. Hedley Esq., M.F.H.	E.H. Vestey Esq., M.F.H., D.L., I.R. McKie Esq., M.F.H.
1997	A.H.B. Hart Esq., M.J. Barclay Esq., M.F.H.	Captain I.W. Farquhar, M.F.H. E.G. Knowles Esq., M.F.H.
1998	Captain R.E. Wallace, M.F.H. H.B.J. Busby Esq., M.F.H.	S.A.H. Hart Esq., M.F.H. J.P.G. Andrews Esq., M.F.H.
1999	Captain S.T. Clarke J.E.M. Vestey Eq., M.F.H.	C.M.F. Scott Esq. The Lord Daresbury, M.F.H.
2000	N.D.B. Peel Esq., M.F.H. R.W. Sumner Esq., M.F.H.	A.I. Jackson Esq. W.F. Wakeham Esq., M.F.H.
2001	D.J.Palmer Esq., M.F.H. C.Martin Wood Esq., M.F.H.	J.M. Letts Esq., M.F.H. A.C. Cook Esq., M.F.H.
2002	E.H. Vestey Esq., M.F.H., D.L., Hon J.E. Greenall, M.F.H.	F. Houghton-Brown Esq., M.F.H. M.R. Hill Esq., M.F.H.
2003	Captain B.E. Fanshawe Captain R.J. Inglesant, M.F.H.	I.R. McKie Esq., M.F.H. M.J. Barclay Esq., M.F.H.
2004	A.W.R. Dangar Esq. Major T.R. Easby, M.F.H.	Captain I.W. Farquhar, M.F.H. J.W. Lockwood Esq., M.F.H.
2005	S.U. Lambert Esq. Major C.J. Seed, M.F.H.	C.M. F. Scott Esq. M.K.K. Hankinson, M.F.H.

3. PRESIDENTS 1878-2006

1878 The Earl Fitzwilliam, K.G.
1879 The Earl Fitzwilliam, K.G.
1880 The Earl Fitzwilliam, K.G.
1881 The Earl Fitzwilliam, K.G.
1882 The Earl Spencer, K.G.
1883 The Earl Zetland, M.F.H.
1884 The Earl Ferrars, M.F.H.
1885 The Earl of March, M.F.H.
1886 Lord Willoughby De Broke, M.F.H.
1887 Earl of Yarborough, M.F.H.
1888 G. Lane Fox, Esq., M.F.H.
1889 Col. Anstruther Thomson
1890 A. Brassey, Esq., M.F.H.
1891 The Marquis of Huntly
1892 R. Chandos-Pole, Esq., M.F.H.
1893 The Earl of Lonsdale
1894 T. Parrington, Esq.
1895 H.R.H. The Prince of Wales
1896 Sir W. Williams-Wynn, Bart., M.F.H.
1897 Lord Middleton, M.F.H.
1898 G.C.W. Fitzwilliam, Esq., M.F.H.
1899 The Earl Bathurst, M.F.H.
1900 The Duke of Beaufort, M.F.H.
1901 The Duke of Leeds, M.F.H.
1902 The Duke of Sutherland, M.F.H.
1903 Lord Ribblesdale
1904 Lord Annaly, M.F.H.
1905 The Earl Manvers, M.F.H.
1906 Viscount Portman, M.F.H.
1907 A. Wilson, Esq.
1908 W.H.A. Wharton, Esq., M.F.H.
1909 The Earl Fitzwilliam, M.F.H.
1910 Lord Willoughby De Broke, M.F.H.
1911 The Marquis of Zetland
1912 Lord Leconfield, M.F.H.
1913 Lord Ribblesdale, M.F.H.
1914 Sir W. Williams-Wynn, Bart., M.F.H.
1915-19 No Shows held owing to War
1920 The Duke of Beaufort, M.F.H.
1921 Lord Willoughby De Broke, M.F.H.
1922 Lt. Col. David Davies, M.F.H.
1923 H.R.H. The Prince of Wales

1924 John C. Straker, Esq., M.F.H.
1925 The Duke of Northumberland, M.F.H.
1926 Sir F. Villiers Forster, Bart., M.F.H.
1927 Lt. Col. Sir Dennis F. Boles, Bart., M.F.H.
1928 The Earl Bathurst, M.F.H.
1929 Edward E. Barclay, Esq., M.F.H.
1930 Douglas Crossman, Esq., M.F.H.
1931 Captain Esme Arkwright, M.F.H.
1932 H.R.H. The Duke of York
1933 The Duke of Beaufort, M.F.H.
1934 The Earl of Lindsay, M.F.H.
1935 Lewis Priestman, Esq., M.F.H.
1936 Captain F.B. Atkinson, M.F.H.
1937 The Duke of Buccleuch, M.F.H.
1938 H.R.H. The Duke of Gloucester, K.G.
1939 The Earl Fitzwilliam, M.F.H.
1940-45 No Shows held owing to War
1946 Captain T.W. Fitzwilliam, M.F.H.
1947 Lord Poltimore, M.F.H.
1948 Lt. Col. Sir Harold Nutting, Bart.
1949 Lord Knutsford
1950 Colonel J.G. Lowther, M.F.H.
1951 Lord Irwin, M.F.H.
1952 Colonel R. Milvain, M.F.H.
1953 Lt. Col. Sir Peter Farquhar, Bart., M.F.H.
1954 Major Maurice E. Barclay, M.F.H.
1955 G. Evans, Esq.
1956 Major J.G. Morrison, M.F.H.
1957 The Duke of Northumberland, M.F.H.
1958 The Earl of Feversham, M.F.H.
1959 The Earl of Yarborough, M.F.H.
1960 Sir G. Meyrick Bt. (died March 1960)
       Captain G.E. Belville
1961 Lt. Col. Sir Watkin Williams-Wynn,
       Bart., M.F.H.
1962 The Duke of Beaufort, K.G., M.F.H.
1963 The Marquess of Exeter, M.F.H.
1964 Colonel Sir Ralph S. Clarke, M.F.H.
1965 The Duke of Beaufort, K.G., M.F.H.
1966 The Earl Fitzwilliam, M.F.H.
1967 Sir Alfred L. Goodson, Bart., M.F.H.
1968 G. Percival Williams, Esq.

1969 The Right Hon. The Earl of Halifax,
1970 The Right Hon. The Lord Ashton of Hyde
1971 Captain R.E. Wallace, M.F.H.
1972 The Lord Daresbury, M.F.H.
1973 The Earl of Dalkeith, M.F.H.
1974 M.F. Berry, Esq., M.F.H.
1975 H.R.H. The Princess Anne
1976 Sir Rupert Buchanan-Jardine, Bart., M.F.H.
1977 The Countess of Feversham, M.F.H.
1978 H.R.H. The Prince of Wales, K.G., K.T., P.C., G.C.B.
1979 M.R. Kimball, Esq.
1980 Lt. Col. G.A. Murray-Smith, M.F.H.
1981 Captain C.G.E. Barclay, M.F.H.
1982 R.J.G. Berkeley, Esq., M.F.H.
1983 H.K. Goschen, Esq., M.F.H.
1984 Major G.A. Gundry, M.F.H.
1985 Mrs. U. Murray-Smith
1986 The Duke of Northumberland, K.G., G.C.V.O., P.C., T.D., F.R.S., M.F.H.
1987 Lt. Col. Sir Henry Tate, Bart.
1988 The Earl of Yarborough, M.F.H.
1989 Lady Crossman

1990 His Grace The Duke of Beaufort, M.F.H.
1991 His Grace The Duke of Beaufort, M.F.H.
1992 Sir Watkin Williams-Wynn, Bart., M.F.H.
1993 E.H. Vestey, Esq., D.L., M.F.H.
1994 Major J.A. Warre, M.C.
1995 His Grace The Duke of Buccleuch and Queensberry, K.T., V.R.D., J.P., M.F.H.
1996 Lt. Col. Sir John Miller, G.C.V.O., D.S.O., M.C.
1997 The Late The Hon. Lady Hastings, D.L., M.Phil., M.F.H.
     Deputy President Sir Stephen Hastings, M.C., M.F.H.
1998 Sir Ralph Carr-Ellison, T.D., E.D.
1999 The Baroness Mallalieu, Q.C.
2000 Sir Philip Naylor-Leyland, Bart, M.F.H.
2001 A.H.B. Hart, Esq.
2002 The Late A.H.B. Hart, Esq.
     Deputy President Mrs. A.H.B. Hart
2003 S.T. Clarke, Esq.
2004 J. Odam, Esq., J.P., D.L.
2005 Captain B.E. Fanshawe
2006 Roy W. Bird, Esq., M.B.E.

4. VICE-PRESIDENTS 2005

Honorary Life Vice-President Mrs J.B. Hannum (U.S.A.)

The Duke of Beaufort, M.F.H.
The Duke of Buccleuch and Queensberry, M.F.H.
The Earl of Yarborough, M.F.H.
The Lord Daresbury, M.F.H.
The Hon. G.P.P. Bowyer, M.F.H.
Lt. Col. The Hon. R.N. Crossley, M.F.H.
The Hon. J.E. Greenall, M.F.H.
Sir Philip Naylor-Leyland, Bt., M.F.H.
T. Adams, Esq., M.F.H.
J. Aldous, Esq., M.F.H.
I. Anderson, Esq., M.F.H
N.J. Ashcroft, Esq., M.F.H.
C.J. Austin, Esq., M.F.H.
M.J.R. Bannister, Esq., M.F.H.
N.W.A Bannister, Esq., M.F.H.
T. Bannister Esq., M.F.H.
H.J.M. Berkeley, Esq., M.F.H.
W. Bishop, Esq., M.F.H
P.P. Backman-Howard, Esq., M.F.H.
M.H. Bletsoe Brown, Esq., M.F.H.
G. Boon, Esq., M.F.H.
W.P. Borrett, Esq., M.F.H.
F. Houhgton Brown, Esq., M.F.H.
J.K. Buckle, Esq., M F.H.
S.M.G. Butler, Esq., M.F.H.
D.A. Chapman, Esq., M.F.H.
J. Christofferson, Esq., M.F.H.
S.E. Clark, Esq., M.F.H.
M.G. Carke, Esq., M.F.H.
F.S.P. Claxton, Esq., M.F.H.
R.G. Cooper, Esq., M.F.H.
J. Cowen, Esq., M.F.H.
K. Creamer, Esq., M.F.H.
M. Davies, Esq., M.F.H.
R.M. Dungworth, Esq., M.F.H.
Major T.R.J. Easy, M.F.H.
Captain I.W. Farquhar, M.F.H.
M.J. Felton, Esq., M.F.H.
C.F.O. Ferry, Esq., M.F.H.
S.C. Fordham, Esq., M.F.H.
E. Foster, Esq., M.F.H.
C. Frampton, Esq., M.F.H.
R.H.F. Fuller, Esq., M.F.H.
M. Garner, Esq., M.F.H.

R. George, Esq., M.F.H.
J.J Gordon, Esq., M.F.H.
C.G. Gundry, Esq., M.F.H.
E.R. Hanbury, Esq., M.F.H.
Major R.F. Hanbury, M.F.H.
M.K.K. Hankinson, Esq., M.F.H.
J.C. Harris, Esq., M.F.H.
H.D.R. Harrison-Allen, Esq., M.F.H
J. Henderson, Esq., M.F.H.
M.R. Hill, Esq., M.F.H.
C. Hodgson, Esq., M.F.H.
R. Hough, Esq., M.F.H.
F. Houghton-Brown, Esq., M.F.H.
C. Hueber, Esq., M.F.H.
M. Hutchinson, Esq., MF.H.
J. lbbott, Esq., M.F.H.
Capt. R.J. Inglesant, M.F.H.
R.A. Innes, Esq., M.F.H.
D. Jones, Esq., M.F.H.
E.W. Jobling-Purser, Esq., M.F.H
L. Kirkby, Esq., M.F.H.
S. Knight, Esq., M.F.H.
M. Lampton, Esq., M.F.H.
J. Martin Letts, Esq., M.F.H.
D. Lewis, Esq., M.F.H.
J.W. Lockwood, Esq., M.F.H.
P.H. Lyster, Esq., M.F.H.
G.T. Lyon Smith, Esq,. M.F.H.
D.R. Manning, Esq., M.F.H.
P. Martin, Esq., M.F.H.
I.R. McKie, Esq., M.F.H.
N. Millard, Esq., M.F.H.
C.R. Millington, Esq., M.F.H.
G.H. Morlock, Esq., M.F.H.
A.C. Morton, Esq., M.F.H.
L.W.J.K. Neale, Esq., M.F.H.
A. Osborne, Esq., M.F.H.
D.J. Palmer, Esq., M.F.H.
C.L. Parker, Esq., M.F.H.
LA. Pearse, Esq., M.F.H.
N.D.B. Peel, Esq., M.F.H.
D. Potter, Esq., M.F.H.
D.L.J. Redvers, Esq., M.F.H
D. Reynolds, Esq., M.F.H.
C.W. Richmond-Watson, Esq., M.FH.
A.P. Sandeman, Esq., M.F.H.
Major C.J. Seed, M.F.H.

R.C. Selwyn Sharpe, Esq., M.F.H.
A.G. Sim, Esq., M.F.H.
R.J. Smith, Esq., M.F.H.
R. Smith, Esq., M.F.H.
C.W. Smyth-Osbourne, Esq., M.F.H
C.H. Sporborg, Esq., M.F.H.
R. Standing, Esq., M.F.H,
R.W. Sumner, Esq., M.F.H.
J. Thomas, Esq., M.F.H.
R. Thomas, Esq., M.F.H.
R.S. Thompson, Esq., M.F.H.
C.J. Thorogood, Esq., M.F.H.
J.C. Timm, Esq., M.F.H,
E. Upton, Esq., M.F.H.
E.H. Vestey, Esq., M.F.H.
J.E.M. Vestey, Esq., M.F.H.
R.J.H. Vestey, Esq., M.F.H
T.R.G. Vestey, Esq., M.F.H.
A. Waugh, Esq., M.F.H
M. Westwood, Esq., M.F.H.
G. Worsley, Esq., M.F.H.
The Duke of Northumberland
The Earl Bathurst
The Lord Annaly
The Lord Denham
The Lord Kimball
The Lord Mancroft
Major Sir Rupert Buchanan-Jardine, Bt.
Sir John Barlow, Bt.
Sir David Black, Bt.
Sir Watkin Williams-Wynn, Bt.
Sir Ralph Carr-Ellison
Sir Michael Connell
Lt. Col. Sir John Miller
P.J. Adkins, Esq.
D.D. Aldridge, Esq.
Major C.B. Amery
I.M. Anderson, Esq.
R. Ando, Esq.
E.W.E. Andrewes, Esq.
J.M.G. Andrews, Esq.
D.H. Arkell, Esq.
R.T. Asplin, Esq.
C.R. Atkinson, Esq.
R.I. Bailey, Esq.
M.J. Barclay, Esq.
Major T.P.E. Barclay

J.C. Barton, Esq.
R.J.G. Berkeley, Esq.
E.A.T. Bonnor Maurice, Esq.
Captain L. Bonhick
R. Bowers, Esq.
H.F. Bowley, Esq.
R. Brierley, Esq.
B.R. Burton, Esq.
H. Busby, Esq.
C.N. Butters, Esq.
R.I. Cambray, Esq.
J.W.G. Cameron, Esq.
A.R. Campbell, Esq.
P. Campbeil, Esq.
R.A. Campbell, Esq
A.R.P. Carden, Esq.
G.W.N.H. Clark, Esq.
S.T. Clarke, Esq.
T.R. Clarke, Eaq.
M. Clayton, Esq.
A.S. Clowes, Esq.
B. Coles, Esq.
H. Colgrave, Esq.
A.D. Collie, Esq.
Major E.F. Comerford
A.C. Cook, Esq.
P.E. Cowen, Esq.
A.W.R. Dangar, Esq.
L. Dungworth, Esq.
M. Elliot, Esq.
A.R.L. Escombe, Esq.
Captain B.E. Fanshawe
B.G. Fillery, Esq.
P. Fitzwilliams, Esq.
R.J. Fleming, Esq.
Captain J.E. Foster
Lt. Col. N.J. Foster
G. Fowles, Esq.
T. Fulton, Esq.
G.C. Nicholas Lane Fox, Esq.
J.D. Fretwell, Esq.
W.J.M. Gee, Esq.
M.C. Gibson, Esq.
The Rev. S.H.M. Godfrey
A.H.B. Grattan-Bellew, Esq.
J.S. Greenwood, Esq.
T. Gwyn-Jones, Esq.
I.A. Hale, Esq.
Capt. H.C.P. Hamilton Major
H.R. Hampson
P. Harland, Esq.
I. Harris, Esq.,
S.A. Hart, Esq.
J.D. Harvey, Esq.
T. Haworth, Esq.

I.S. Haynes, Esq.
P. Hayward-Scowcroft, Esq.
J. Heler, Esq.
M.J.T. Higgs, Esq.,
M.H.J. Holt, Esq.
Rex Hudson, Esq.
Major D. Ide-Smith
M. Inness, Esq.
A. Jackson, Esq.
C.E.J. Jerram, Esq.
M.D.M. Knight, Esq.
E.G.T. Knowles, Esq.
S. Lambert, Esq.
O.C. Langdale, Esq.
J. Lawes, Esq.
D.G. Lee, Esq.
J.R.M. Layland, Esq.
C.G.M. Lloyd-Baker, Esq.
A. Lockwood, Esq.
J. Lowthian, Esq.
G. Luck, Esq.
N.F.W. Lyde, Esq.
M.R. Lyles, Esq.
R.J. Lyles, Esq.
G.L. Lyster, Esq.
B. Mackaness, Esq
E. Mahony, Esq
C. Mann, Esq
Lt. Col. R.C.J. Martin
Lt. Col. L.W. McNaught
J.A. McNeish, Esq.
J.L. Miller, Esq.
J.R. Millington, Esq.
Dr. C.J. Mitchell
R.A.M. Moore, Esq.
His Honour Judge Morrell
W.H. Morrish, Esq.
J. Mottram, Esq.
T.R.P.S. Norton, Esq.
J. Odam, Esq.
T.A.C. Page, Esq.
Col. J.L. Parkes
T.C. Parkes, Esq.
E. Perry, Esq.
N.G.W. Playne, Esq.
R.A. Pobgee, Esq.
R.W.F. Poole, Esq.
M.R. Porter, Esq.
R.F. Porter, Esq.
N. Reed-Herbert, Esq.
H. Reynolds, Esq
S.P. Roberts, Esq
Captain R. Sale
A.P.D. Sallis, Esq.
W.F. Saunders, Esq.

C.M.F. Scott, Esq.
J.T.D. Shaw, Esq.
A. Skyrme, Esq.
B.R. Abel Smith, Esq.
J.L.T. Smith, Esq.
K.W. Smith-Bingham, Esq.
R.C. Smith-Ryland, Esq.
A.J. Sparrow, Esq.
P.A. Stevens, Esq.
N.C. Stirling, Esq.
D.R. Stoddart, Esq.
P.L.B. Stoddart, Esq.
I. Storer, Esq.
R.J. Strong, Esq.
J. Thomas, Esq.
P.F. Till, Esq.
R.C. Tomkinson, Esq.
T.M. Trollope-Bellew, Esq.
Dr. B.G. Trower-Greenwood
W. Turcon, Esq.
R. Tyacke, Esq.
T.H. Unwin, Esq.
N.J.W. Wakley, Esq.
D.L. Wallace, Esq.
Col. V.G. Wallace
P. Walwyn, Esq.
R.F.H. Ward, Esq.
C. A. Warde-Aldam, Esq.
J.R. Weatherby, Esq.
Lt. Col. C.R.H. Wells
J.H. Whaley, Esq.
J.N. Whaley, Esq.
C.F.P. Whitley, Esq.
P.J.H. Wills, Esq.
L. Wilson, Esq.
N.R.W. Wright, Esq.
T.D. Wright, Esq.
Countess S. Goess-Saurau.
    M.F.H.
Lady Jane Benson, M.F.H.
Lady Victoria Fellowes, M.F.H.
The Hon. Mrs. Townshend,
    M.F.H.
The Hon. Mrs. Westropp,
    M.F.H.
Mrs S.P. Allen, M.F.H.
Mrs L.M. Anderson, M.F.H
Mrs P.M. Anderson, M.F.H
Mrs L. Barlow, M.F.H
Mrs L. J. Bowman, M.F.H.
Miss K. Boyd, M.F.H.
Mrs B.A. Brickell, M.F.H.
Miss F.M.L.A. Busby, M.F.H.
Mrs V. Cresswell, M F.H.
Miss W.G. Evans, M.F.H.

Mrs R. Fenwick, M.F. H.
Mrs C. Foster, M.F.H.
Mrs J. Foster, M.F.H.
Mrs S. George, M.F.H.
Mrs D. Gisling, M.F.H.
Mrs R.D. Green, M.F.H.
Mrs C.J. Grove, M.F.H.
Mrs A,C. Hare, M.F.H.
Mrs J.V.M. Hastier, M.F.H.
Mrs H.M.B. Hillard, M.F.H.
Mrs C. Hopkins, M.F.H.
Mrs S.L. Horner-Harker, M.F.H.
Mrs P.A. Kennedy, M.F.H.
Mrs E.P. Letts, M.F.H.
Mrs J.H. Mains, M.F.H.
Mrs V.J. McKie, M.F.H.
Mrs M.A. Morris, M.F.H.
Mrs H. Oldershaw-Dubey, M.F.H.
Miss E. Pearse, M.F.H.
Mrs N.D.B. Peel, M.F.H.
Miss S. Pinney, M.F.H.
Mrs. J. Piper, M.F.H.
Mrs. D.C. Ramp, M.F.H.
Mrs. A. Ranking, M.F.H.
Mrs. J. Shaw, M.F.H.
Mrs. J. Steward, M.F.H.
Mrs. B. Till, M.F.H.
Mrs. D. Trembath, M.F.H.
Miss K. Turner, M.F.H.
Mrs H.C. Tyler, M.F.H.
Mrs E.A. Verity, M.F.H.
Mrs J.E.M. Vestey, M.F.H.
Mrs S.D.K. Whitely, M.F.H.
Mrs J. Whittington, M.F.H.
Mrs P.J.H. Wills, M.F.H.
Mrs K. Madocks Wright, M.F.H.
Ann Countess of Yarborough
Lady Gillian Alders
Lady Felicity Blithe
Lady Maria Coventry
Lady Caroline Gosling
Lady Celestria Hales
Lady Isabella Naylor-Leyland
The Hon. Mrs J. Cavendish
The Hon. Mrs Gibbs
The Hon. Mrs Whaley
The Hon. Mrs Wills
Lady Barlow
Lady Crossman

Lady Proby
Lady De Ramsey
Miss J. Aldridge
Mrs M. Amatt
Mrs K.E.G. Amery
Mrs L. Anderson
Mrs P.F. Arkwright
Mrs K.A. Barclay
Miss L.E. Bates
Mrs V.M. Blackeney
Mrs S. Brankin-Frisby
Mrs J.A.M. Brookhouse
Mrs J.G.P. Buxton
Mrs J.W.G. Cameron
Mrs J.H.E. Chichester
Mrs S.T. Clarke
Mrs C.A. Compton
Mrs T. Cooke
Mrs I.S. Craven
Mrs J. Curtis
Mrs H.D.J. Daly
Mrs J.E. Debenham
Mrs R.G.B. Dewar
Miss T. Dillon
Mrs L. Dungworth
Mrs A.R.L. Escombe
Mrs P.J. Farquhar
Miss E.A. Gadesden
Mrs D.J. Garwood
Mrs P.M. Gibson
Mrs E. Goffe
Mrs L.A. Hale
Mrs M.J.Hales
Mrs S. Hamilton-Shaw
Mrs A.G. Hawkins
Mrs D. Hellyer
Mrs A. Henson
Mrs D.A. Hewitt
Mrs C.N. Higgon
Mrs J.M. Hignett
Mrs B. Hoare
Mrs M.A. Holt
Mrs J.E. Hopkins
Miss J.A. Hoskins
Mrs H.J. Houghton
Mrs A.M.K. Hudson
Mrs C. Humphrey
Mrs A. Jackson
Mrs J.M. Jagger
Mrs J.M. Kennedy

Mrs P.N. Leigh
Mrs G.L. Lyster
Mrs J. Marriott
Mrs D. McDougall
Mrs C. McKenzie
Mrs. S.C. Morrish
Mrs C.W. Nash
Mrs J.A. Nelson
Mrs C.V. Nesbitt
Mrs P.F. Nicholson
Mrs A. Oates
Mrs R.M. Parker
Mrs S.M. Payne
Mrs R.S. Perkins
Mrs R.W.F. Poole
Mrs A.J. Ralli
Mrs J.A. Renwick
Mrs G.F. Robertson
Mrs D.C. Samworth
Mrs C.M. Sanderson
Mrs R. Schicht
Mrs B.M. Scott
Mrs K.E. Abel Smith
Mrs A. Smyth-Osbourne
Miss J. Stafford
Mrs S. Stafford
Mrs R.Standing
Mrs R. Stobart
Mrs P. Strawson
Mrs P. Strudwick
Mrs P. Sykes
Miss S.J. Taylor
Mrs J.M. Tice
Mrs D.M. Trollope-Bellew
Mrs B.E.C. Trouton
Mrs D.S. Tuke
Mrs C.M. Vanderstegen-Drake
Mrs P.E.R. Vaux
Mrs E.H. Vestey
Mrs C. Villar
Mrs D.R.F. Wallace
Mrs E.L. Wallace
Miss D.D. Watters
Mrs J.R. Watters
Mrs K.M. White
Mrs M.M. Willett
Mrs D. F. Wood
Miss J.U. Wood

5. SUBMISSION TO THE BURNS COMMITTEE

Lord Burns's Committee of Inquiry into Hunting, was set up by the Labour government. The Committee took evidence widely, and reported in June 2000. Below is the submission made by Sir Philip Naylor-Leyland, Chairman, on behalf of the committee of Peterborough Royal Foxhound Show Society, on 11 February 2000.

Peterborough Royal Foxhound Show Society was founded in 1878, and has subsequently held 111 shows. It is the most renowned Hound Show in the world. In Britain there are four other regional Shows recognised by the MFHA – at Harrogate, Ardingly, Builth Wells and Honiton. In addition there are other, smaller, hound shows, particularly in the Lake District and Wales.

The purpose of Peterborough Show is to judge, under competitive conditions, the best of the working Foxhounds in Britain for their conformation and activity. The Show has considerable influence over the selection of stallion hounds and dams (the bitches) that will produce the working Foxhounds of the future. Foxhound breeders assemble at Peterborough to assess the virtues of the range of stallion hounds being exhibited, and to gauge the standard of quality to which breeders themselves should aim.

The Judges chosen are the foremost contemporary experts on the Foxhound.

The Show is open to the 15,000 hounds registered in the Foxhound Kennel Stud Book (FKSB). Pedigrees of most of the hounds in the FKSB can be traced back to 1800, since which time the Foxhound has undergone a process of continuous improvement to cope with the conditions of today. The genetic material in the FKSB represents the dedicated efforts of British Foxhound breeders over more than 200 years. To the credit of breeders, the Foxhound has been bred continuously for 'work' and not merely for 'show'.

The Society has 389 Vice-Presidents, some of whom are fourth generation Masters of Hounds. They bring with them to the Show their friends, and an increasing number of Foxhound breeders from abroad. The total attendance is in the region of 1,200, and will include Hunt members and supporters, as well as puppy walkers, who vie for the prizes awarded to the 'walker' of the winners of the classes, for the young hounds.

The number of Hunts exhibiting at Peterborough varies between 20 and 25 packs. Over 250 hounds will be shown on the day. Some 20 specialist Trade Stand exhibitors, mostly supplying hunting equipment, attend the Show. The Show also brings trade to the local economy, particularly hotels and others providing accommodation and catering.

CONCLUSIONS

Without foxhunting in Britain the following would result:

1. The majority of the 15,000 registered Foxhounds in Great Britain, having no longer a working purpose, would be put down.
2. Peterborough Royal Foxhound Show and its Society would cease to exist.
3. Part of our national heritage, represented through the breeding of a supreme working dog over centuries, would be irretrievably lost.
4. The Peterborough Royal Foxhound Show is to hound breeders what the Derby is to Thoroughbred racehorse breeders.

Sir Philip Naylor-Leyland, Bt., MFH
Chairman and Committee
Peterborough Royal Foxhound Show Society
11th February, 2000

6. FOXHOUND CONFORMATION

Judges in a Foxhound show of hounds registered in the Foxhound Kennel Stud Book, look for the following key points of conformation:

Height: not more than 26 inches to the point of the shoulder.

Colour: neither the colour of the hound's coat nor its eyes is of any importance and is not considered.

Stern: the hound's stern, its tail, should ideally be straight, although a slightly curved stern is sometimes overlooked if the rest of the conformation is good.

Head: the hound's mouth must not be under-shot, or over-shot which means that neither its lower or upper jaw should protrude noticeably. Some like a doghound to have a wider jowled, noticeably masculine head, but this is a personal preference.

Neck: a longer neck is preferable to a short one.

Shoulders: a key area of conformation. They should slope back into the body rather than be noticeably upright. A good length of humerus bone is highly desirable. Looking down from above the shoulder blades should not appear to be set widely apart. A certain amount of breast bone should be visible in front when looking at a hound in profile, but it should not be 'bosomy'.

Elbows: elbows that stick out are bad; even worse is a 'tied in' elbow, restricting the hound's movement and its speed across country. A long elbow 'slash' is desirable, giving the foreleg plenty of room for extension in a long stride which covers the ground. Young hounds are sometimes more 'out at the elbow' but this fault rectifies with maturity, and allowance made for this.

Foreleg: should be strong and reasonably straight. The knee should not 'knuckle over'; it is preferable if it is slightly back. As in a horse, the pastern is better if it slopes back, rather than be straight in line with the knee. It should be a shock absorber, helping durability.

Foot: A fault the judge looks for is a 'toe down'; one toe-nail is seen to be much lower than the others, a sign of a foot fault likely to cause lameness, and a fault which can be communicated in breeding. The hound's feet should neither be too fleshy, nor too tight.

Chest: Neither a wide 'bosom', nor so narrow that both legs seem 'to be coming out of the same hole'. The chest should be proportionate with the rest of the hound's conformation.

Back: either a straight back, or a slightly arched back known as a 'wheel back' are acceptable. The backbone should not stick up in a knobbly fashion, but be set between two lines of muscle. A weak, narrow back, with a pronounced dip below the spine to the ribs is known as a 'roach back' which is a fault.

Body: some spring in the ribs is essential, but depth through the heart is vital to provide room for the hound's 'engine'. Under-line of the body can 'run up' towards the hind legs, but accentuation of this means the hound is too narrow gutted.

Loins: Should be broad and strong, with tops of quarters, the pin bones, set well apart. Plenty of muscle on buttocks and second thighs. Should not have a 'chopped off' appearance at the back.

Hind legs: Should tend towards straightness, neither cow-hocked nor sickle-hocked as in bad horse conformation. Hocks should be set low and not way back behind the hound's body.

BIBLIOGRAPHY

Books I have consulted include the following:

Baily's Hunting Companion (Baily's, 1994)

Baily's Hunting Directory (Baily's)

British Hunts and Huntsmen, J.N.P. Watson, Vols I, II and III, (Batsford,1982 1986)

English Foxhunting, Raymond Carr (Weidenfeld and Nicolson, 1976)

Famous Foxhunters, Daphne Moore (Saiga Publishing, 1978)

Fields Elysian, Simon Blow (J.M. Dent, 1983)

Foxhunting, Sir Charles Frederick and others (Lonsdale Library, Seeley Service, 1930s)

Foxhunting from Shire to Shire, Cuthbert Bradley (George Routledge, 1912)

Foxhunting in the Twentieth Century, William Scarth Dixon (Hurst and Blackett, 1925)

Foxhunting, 10th Duke of Beaufort (David and Charles 1980)

Foxhunting, A. Henry Higginson (Collins 1948)

Foxiana, Isaac Bell (Country Life, 1929)

Good Sport with Famous Packs 1885–1910, Cuthbert Bradley (George Routledge, 1910)

History of the Althorpe and Pytchley Hunt, Guy Paget (1937)

History of the Puckeridge, Michael Berry (Country Life, 1950)

Hounds of the World, Sir John Buchanan-Jardine (Grayling Books, 1937)

Huntsmen of our Time, Kenneth Ligertwood (Pelham Books, 1968)

Huntsman's Log Book, Isaac Bell (Eyre and Spottiswoode, 1947)

John Leech and the Victorian Scene, Simon Houfe (Antique Collectors Club, 1984)

Jorrocks's England, Anthony Steel (Methuen, 1932)

Leicestershire and the Quorn Hunt, Colin D.B. Ellis (Edgar Backus, 1951)

Ronnie Wallace, A Manual of Foxhunting, R.E. Wallace, edited Michael Clayton (Swan Hill Press, 2003)

Ronnie Wallace, the Authorised Version, Robin Rhoderick-Jones (Quiller Press, 1992)

Rycroft on Hounds, Hunting and Country, Sir Newton Rycroft, edited James F. Scharnberg (2001, The Derrydale Press)

The Book of the Foxhound, Daphne Moore (1964, J.A. Allen)

Memoirs The Duke of Beaufort, (Country Life, 1981)

The History of Foxhunting, Roger Longrigg (Macmillan, 1975)

The History of Hunting, Patrick Chalmers (Seely Service, 1936)

The Yellow Earl, Douglas Sutherland (The Molendinar Press, 1980)

Thoughts on Hunting, Peter Beckford (1781, re-published J.A. Allen 1981)

Tom Firr of The Quorn, Roy Heron (Nimrod Book Services, 1984)

Index